MARIO CUOMO

BY WILLIAM O'SHAUGHNESSY

MARIO CUOMO
Remembrances of a Remarkable Man

VOX POPULI
The O'Shaughnessy Files

MORE RIFFS, RANTS AND RAVES

IT ALL COMES BACK TO ME NOW
Character Portraits from the Golden Apple

AirWAVES
A Collection of Radio Editorials from the Golden Apple

WITH STEVE WARLEY and JOSEPH REILLY

SERVING THEIR COMMUNITIES
A History of the New York State Broadcasters Association

MARIO CUOMO

Remembrances of a Remarkable Man

WILLIAM O'SHAUGHNESSY

WHITNEY MEDIA
PUBLISHING GROUP

New Rochelle, New York 2017

Library of Congress Control Number: 2016936481

Printed in the United States of America

19 18 17   5 4 3 2 1

First edition

For a failed baseball player
with too many vowels in his name

CONTENTS

Photographs follow pages 132 and 228

FOREWORD

I'm grateful to Mario Cuomo for many things and for his countless expressions of friendship during the thirty-eight years I was privileged to know him. Among his many beneficences were the Introductions he wrote for my four previous anthologies for Fordham University Press. As I've so often acknowledged, I am not at all deserving of his blessing, imprimatur, or generous friendship, especially when it comes to anything associated with scholarship, writing, or the mother tongue, the English language.

Two years after the governor left us we remember him as a deeply religious figure of insight, creativity, passion, and moral courage. As a lawyer, scholar, author, and governor of dazzlingly facile mind, he taught us how to think, how to write, how to feel, how to argue, and how to love.

This book, then, is meant only to resemble something of a letter to a friend I loved and admired. Call it a love letter if you will. And on this very subject, I was flattered beyond words to have received the following wholly undeserved piece, which was originally intended as a Foreword to a future book on which I'm presently working and which is destined to be yet another anthology of interviews, editorials, musings, eulogies, and commentaries, my fifth such effort for Fordham University Press.

But this one is about Mario Cuomo, who has now departed for what Malcolm Wilson, the great Fordham orator (who also served as governor), once called "another and, we are sure, a better world." And I'm reminded that Mario spoke at several book parties that launched the publication of my earlier anthologies at the Maccioni family's iconic New York restaurant Le Cirque. At each star-studded event, several hundred showed up, including some real writers: Gay Talese, Peter Maas, Ken Auletta, Barbara Taylor Bradford, Richard Johnson, Phil Reisman, Emily Smith, Walter Cronkite, Cindy Adams, and Dan Rather. They came not to hear me but to be with Mario Cuomo—except at the gathering for my most recent book, at which his wonderful and luminous daughter Maria Cuomo Cole filled in for her ailing dad. No one was disappointed as the graceful Maria read a lovely tribute to my poor literary work penned by her illustrious father.

And well before the publication of that next anthology I expect we'll have yet another lovely evening at Le Cirque provided by the Maccionis to mark the release of this memoir about Mario Cuomo, which my editors felt should take precedence over the planned anthology of interviews and commentaries. My only regret, of course, is that Mario himself won't be physically present for either one.

Please understand again that I imagine this book only as a memoir of a remarkable friendship, not as a formal biography. Nor is it intended as a political book. The following Foreword was actually written by Mario M. Cuomo himself for my "next book." As you can see, I've "borrowed" it for this "love letter" as yet another expression of that extraordinary friendship I treasure. It was his last gift to me. I'm only sorry my writing, memory, and scholarship were not worthy of his friendship. Or of the great man himself.

BROTHER BILL

Bill O'Shaughnessy's previous books were so good, I couldn't put them down.

His personal commentaries, written with casually elegant language, make you wish the whole country was hearing and reading his work. Actually, the whole world can now savor his genius thanks to the Internet and WVOX.com. He is a journalist, commentator, connoisseur, a strong political presence, and a forceful advocate of great causes.

During his remarkable fifty-year run as the permittee of WVOX and WVIP, O'Shaughnessy has used his great Gaelic gift of words, a sharp mind, deep conviction, and the capacity for powerful advocacy to inspire the fainthearted, guide the eager, and charm almost everyone he meets. As a broadcaster and author, he has written and spoken simple truths and powerful political arguments with a good heart.

As an interviewer, Bill O'Shaughnessy is a magic miner of fascinating nuggets coaxed from a host of extraordinarily interesting people, some of them celebrities and others previously undiscovered neighborhood gems. O'Shaughnessy is among a select few who create magic with their words. He always brings us a rich flow of genuine American opinions and sentiment.

Few people have as rich a talent for "writing for the ear"— Charles Kuralt and Charles Osgood, certainly. Also the late, legendary Paul Harvey. And Bill O'Shaughnessy.

He can't describe a scene as well as Jimmy Breslin. He's not as "easy" a writer as Pete Hamill. But when he's on his game, Brother Bill is better than anyone on the air or in print.

We didn't always agree politically. But O'Shaughnessy has never lost his instinct for the underdog. He is a constant reminder of a Republican Party that was much better for this country.

He's also an elegant, entertaining, and spellbinding speaker. He might have taken all these gifts and made himself a great political leader or a very rich captain of history. Instead, fifty years ago, he

devoted himself to what then was a small and struggling radio station, and ever since then, thanks to his brilliance and dedication,
he's created what has become his much-praised WVOX/Worldwide
and the highly successful and innovative WVIP, where many different and emerging new voices are heard in the land.

Somebody said to me about his previous four books, "That's
quite a body of good work O'Shaughnessy has put together, all
while we were dazzled by his high style and glittering persona." I
guess that's right. But it is not the body of work; it's the *soul* of the
work that I have always been more attracted to.

And that's what O'Shaughnessy does. He doesn't deliver homilies about it. Maybe he doesn't even know it fully. But he is a lover.
He loves people. He loves understanding them. He loves not just
the big shots, but he loves all the little people too. And you can see
it, you can read it, you can *feel* it, and you can hear it on the radio.

The man is a lover. He uses one word few people in our society
use regularly (unless they are in the apparel business!): *sweet*. The
highest compliment he can give you is not to tell you this guy is
bright, successful, dazzling in his language or ability, but that he's
sweet, or that she's sweet, or that it's sweet. Well, that, in the end, is
what I like about him. He understands life, he understands love, and
he knows how to portray it.

And always—if you push the discussion with him—you find, not
far from the surface, a profound yearning to use his own great gift
of life to find more sweetness in the world or perhaps even to create some himself. I know him. And he will find a way, or he will
spend the rest of his life trying.

So it's all here: O'Shaughnessy the businessman, reporter, broadcaster, commentator, friend of politicians of all stripes, religious
leaders of all stripes—and even an occasional politician "in stripes"!

So I've given you no new knowledge of Bill in this Foreword to his new book. But custom requires that I repeat the obvious, if only to remind ourselves why we are so pleased he was persuaded to put together another work.

One of his great passions is the First Amendment, that nearly sacred guarantee of our unique American freedom of speech and expression, which is being challenged at the moment by government agents seeking to make themselves the dictators of public tastes and attitudes. And Bill O'Shaughnessy is one of the few respected authorities on the subject who have spoken out against these powerful and dangerous political forces, even at the risk of reprisal.

His speech "Obsequious Acquiescence" has been widely read and admired by some of the best legal minds in America, including the estimable Floyd Abrams, the distinguished national First Amendment expert. Indeed, for his lifetime of work on free speech issues, Bill was called "The Conscience of the Broadcasting Industry" by the prestigious Media Institute think tank in Washington.

He's also a philanthropist and humanitarian. And the down and out in the broadcasting profession have been the beneficiaries of his dynamic and creative fundraising efforts for the Broadcasters Foundation of America, which he presently serves as chairman of its Guardian Fund to assist the less fortunate in what Brother Bill calls his "tribe."

In *The Screwtape Letters* the great C. S. Lewis wrote that what the Devil wants is for a man to finish his life having to say he spent his life not doing either what is *right* or what he *enjoyed*. For the many years I've known him, Bill O'Shaughnessy has spent most of his time doing things he ought to have been doing and enjoying them immensely.

I have myself been blessed with a glittering array of loyal friends from every phase of my already long life, people willing to weigh my many inadequacies less diligently than they assess what they find commendable. None of these friends has tried harder than Bill O'Shaughnessy to give me a chance to be useful. He is a man of his words. But I'll never have the words I need to express my gratitude adequately to him.

Everyone in our family calls him "Brother Bill." By any name, he is very special.

Mario M. Cuomo

2014

PREFACE: THIS IS PERSONAL

Mario Matthew Cuomo left us after a magnificent life in his eighty-second year on the very first day of the new year, 2015. The fifty-second governor of New York was much more than the sum of his public papers preserved in the great Archives of the State of New York on Madison Avenue in Albany, or the more than 700 soaring and graceful speeches he gave on matters temporal and spiritual, or his eight books that have been translated into many languages and are part of private and public libraries all over the world. Mario Cuomo was much more than the sum of what he accomplished—he was an example for us to follow, and memories of his beautiful life will inspire and instruct us for many years to come.

He was a child of immigrants who grew up to be governor of what he called "the only state that matters." Mario was glib of tongue, agile of mind, and generous of heart. His admirers, and there were many all over the world, tried to install him in the White House as president of the United States. Failing that, they implored him to accept appointment to the Supreme Court, the highest tribunal in the land, where he could continue his lifelong affair with "Our Lady of the Law." Declining all importunings and flattery, this gifted son of a Queens greengrocer who came to this country from an Italian hill town to dig ditches became instead the great philosopher-statesman of the American nation. As a public man he was also a preacher who made many of us wiser about love.

I will forever remember him because of all the gifts and good fortune bestowed on me, I was privileged to know the sweetness of his friendship for thirty-eight of my seventy-seven years. His favorite word was "sweet"—as in, "You can make a community better, stronger . . . even sweeter . . . than it is." It is a designation and word most men are not comfortable with.

All our colleagues in the public press and every journal, blog, and magazine in the land noted his departure. Most who practice in our tribe "warehouse" these things known as obituaries. They have them preserved in computers and filing cabinets all ready to go, often to coincide with your last breath. So I know I'm late with all this, and far more gifted writers like Mike Lupica, E. J. Dionne, Terry Golway, Bob McManus, Wayne Barrett, Steve Cuozzo, Stephen Schlesinger, Jeffrey Toobin, Ken Kurson, David Shribman, Jeff Shesol, Ken Auletta, Mike Barnicle, Bob Hardt, Paul Grondahl, David Greenberg, Erica Orden, and Hendrik Hertzberg have already written lovely reminiscences that historians and the Cuomo family will collect and treasure. One of his daughters, Maria Cuomo Cole, has already begun to assemble all the graceful tributes to her father.

It must, however, be noted that one prominent journalist has not yet been heard from: the iconic Gay Talese, whose legendary *Esquire* essays "Frank Sinatra Has a Cold" and "The Silent Season of a Hero" about DiMaggio scream for yet a third Talese piece on another quite extraordinary Italian American from Queens whose contributions in the realm of public service were every bit as stellar as those provided by Sinatra in a recording studio and by Joe D. on a baseball diamond. Every time I see Talese around town of an evening or strolling Park Avenue in his fine clothes, I grab him by the pick stitching on his well-cut lapel: "You gotta do Mario!" Talese, a real writer of great gifts, is himself eighty-three, and however trim and fit he may be, his own clock is ticking. He writes now of bridges on Staten Island. Better he should write of one who *built* bridges . . . to our better nature.

As this book went to press I had the good fortune to be seated next to the great writer at a black-tie dinner at 21. He spoke movingly of Mario and how the governor was motivated and inspired by his roots:

Mario didn't run for president because he came from "village'" people . . . like me. We're from the south—Calabria. That's like being from the south in this country. It's different. It's made up of villages. We're village people. We're not "national." We're all from southern Italy, our parents, our grandparents. We like to stay close to home and sleep in our own bed. Sinatra, Lady Gaga, DiMaggio, Tony Bennett, Talese. Mario Cuomo was the best of the village people, the most honorable. He was the Crown Jewel of Italian immigration. You always ask me why I didn't write about him. The truth is I didn't want to hurt him, I admire him so much. You said you make no pretense toward objectivity in your book. And you shouldn't. His father dug sewers. It's amazing what his father did. You guys are Irish. Your people could be cops [and] firemen and the wives could be nannies. You spoke the language. Italians had to dig ditches because we didn't speak the language. It makes Mario all the more amazing.

My colleagues in the public press rushed to their typewriters, computers, and yellow legal pads to note Mario's passing and assess and evaluate his stewardship of the eighty-two years he'd been given. One of the first off the mark with a tribute was Terry Golway. The brilliant Kean University professor, historian, author, and journalist who once served as a columnist and member of the editorial board of the *New York Times* and the *New York Observer* was always a special favorite of the Governor.

Here are some excerpts and lovely highlights from his appreciation:

Mario Cuomo became a political sensation through a medium thought to belong to another era: words. Beautiful, poetic, meaningful words, spoken in a strong, clear voice, with a cadence that turned even a clumsy phrase into a baroque masterpiece.

Embedded in all those beautiful words there was a palpable love of American possibilities. He was an Italian-speaking kid from Queens who become not just an orator but a philosopher whose texts will be read for as long as American political thought matters.

On January 1, 1983, after taking the oath as governor of New York on the first of the 4,380 days he would spend in residence on Eagle Street, Mario Cuomo spoke of "the idea of family, mutuality, the sharing of benefits and burdens for the good of all. No family that favored its strong children or that in the name of even-handedness failed to help its vulnerable ones would be worthy of the name."

Here was this man from Queens, all but saying that powerful people in the body politic were peddling lies. "It has become popular in some quarters," he said, "to argue that the principal function of government is to make instruments of war and to clear obstacles away from the strong. It is said the rest will happen automatically. The cream will rise to the top. Survival of the fittest may be a good working description of the process of evolution, but a government of humans should elevate itself to a higher order, one which tries to fill the cruel gaps left by chance, and by a wisdom we don't fully understand."

He came to the podium, waved, and then excused himself from "the poetry and temptation to deal in nice but vague rhetoric, the usual preliminaries."

Instead, he offered a polite but passionate assault on Ronald Reagan's America, his shining city on a hill: "A shining city is perhaps all the president sees from the portico of the White House and the veranda of his ranch, where everyone seems to be doing well," Cuomo said. "But there's another part to the shining city, where some people can't pay their mortgages, and most young people can't afford one; where students can't afford the education they need, and middle-class parents watch the dreams they hold for their children evaporate. . . . There is despair, Mr. President, in the faces you don't see, in the places you don't visit in your shining city. In fact, Mr. President, this nation is more a 'Tale of Two Cities' than a 'Shining City on a Hill.'"

Cuomo continued with phrase upon devastating phrase, pleading with the American people to see the poor and disenfranchised not as failures and losers, but fellow citizens.

Mario Cuomo's hold on the imagination of his fellow Democrats was all about soaring rhetoric and political poetry. But it was the governor himself who noted that politicians campaign in poetry but govern in prose. His principled stand against capital punishment—which he shared with his predecessor, Hugh Carey—won him accolades as did his nuanced defense of abortion rights, brilliantly argued in a speech at the University of Notre Dame in 1985.

Combined with his wonderful speeches, those two positions earned Cuomo a reputation as the Democratic Party's leading liberal spokesman at a time when liberalism was banished to the political wilderness.

Cuomo published a collection of his speeches, reminding so many of his supporters why they adored him. The volume was called *More Than Words*. It is a suitable epitaph for a politician who used words to inspire, to probe, to critique, and to provoke. Yes, he will be remembered best as an orator, but there was something more about him, something more than the pretty pictures he painted with the English language.

He was unafraid to challenge a comforting narrative with impertinent questions at a time when others preferred to simply go along and get along. That required more than words. That required ideas, courage, and intelligence.

Mario Cuomo had all three.

The reader can see and savor Golway's entire original piece at Politico.com, where his graceful essays now often appear.

I've hesitated until now because I could not summon the strength or find the desire to sit over a legal pad with a pen and then speak words into a microphone in a radio studio that place Mario Cuomo in the past tense. Everything that he was lingers. And will for years.

Even now I'm afraid it was a friendship I taxed too much with impatience, distractions about marital issues, tales of chaos around my hearth and home, much of it of my very own making, irreverence, and even, occasionally, impertinence. I mention impertinence because although we would occasionally "edit" each other's pronouncements and writing, I was constantly aware that I was not worthy to loose the strap of his sandal when use of the English language was at issue, and on many occasions I told him so. Yet undaunted by the prospect of adding anything of value or perspective to a pronouncement of the great man, I would usually attach a handwritten note to a working draft: "*You hold the bat like this, Mr. DiMaggio...*" Very few of my "suggestions" made it into the final transcript. Apply the impertinence to me anyway for even presuming to dare tweak a pronouncement of one of the greatest minds of our time. But now... now I sit alone.

Or am I alone...?

Often late at night or early in the morning when he would be embarked on a lovely riff about one of the great issues of the day that was too good, too wise, too exquisite for my meager brain, I would plead with him to stop, please stop wasting the magnificent product of that bright, fine, beautiful mind on such an unworthy and untutored Irish dunderhead.

As the governor recognized very early on, almost at our first encounter, I'm not exactly a belletrist or writer of fine literary works known for their aesthetic qualities and originality of style and tone as he was. He was more alive to the world of ideas and to the study and lessons of history than most of us could ever hope to be.

At any rate, I cannot add to the official canon of his work or improve on the recitation of his many accomplishments as a mediator, a college professor, an author of eight books including *The Blue Spruce* for children, a Lincoln scholar, a diarist, an attorney in the service of what he called Our Lady of the Law, and then as secretary of state, lieutenant governor, and governor of New York state, and even later as the most esteemed partner of the big, white-shoe Manhattan law firm founded by Wendell Willkie. It is part of the popular lexicon, his public and legal career, and it resides now in the history books of a nation and in those voluminous archives in the state capital in Albany, while his mortal remains rest in St. John's Cemetery in Middle Village, Queens.

As a public orator, he was a man of his words. And in every season, for all his rhetorical gifts and power at the lectern, Mario was always searching for meaning and purpose, always looking toward the light, and never quite sure he had done enough to fulfill the moral obligations inherited from his father, Andrea, or his mother, Immaculata Giordano, or later from the Vincentians of St. John's. As Mario was fond of saying, "Every time I've done something that doesn't feel right, it's ended up not being right. I talk and talk and talk, and I haven't taught people in fifty years what my father taught me by example in one week."

You can see—and feel—the yearning and struggling of a beautiful soul in *The Diaries of Mario M. Cuomo*, published by Random House in 1984:

I've fought a thousand fights but not enough the good fight. I've not—truly enough—kept the faith. I've hurt people by bad example, even my own family.

For whatever combination of genetic, environmental, and educational reasons, I have always found it easier to discern a challenge than to acknowledge success.

I've always preferred privacy. Loneliness has never been the threat to me that the world has been. The more deeply I have become involved in opening myself, revealing myself, discussing myself, the more vulnerable I have felt.

Why, then, am I in politics at all? I take power too seriously to be totally comfortable with it.

Every day, a thousand lost opportunities: every day closer to the end. If only everything we did, we did in light of that, how differently we'd act. We would have so few regrets.

But now I look back on nearly fifty years and I'm pained by the memory of so many hurts, so many mistakes, so many missed opportunities. So much weakness. It's a hard game, but "the game is only lost when we stop trying." So, on with the effort!

So for my part, I can really tell you only small things about the man, for I always thought of him as a teacher, albeit a great one, possessed of that beautiful soul that far outshone all his accomplishments in the public arena.

We spoke often of our souls, our sons, our daughters, and only occasionally did the great issues of the day, fleeting and temporal as they were over the years, intrude on his relentless searching and brilliant musings about matters eternal.

Our friend Joe Reilly told me of an evening at the bar of an Albany pub frequented by "political types." The affable, gregarious—and generous—Reilly was descended upon by some staffers from the Executive Chamber (the governor's office). One of them, after a cocktail or two, said, "Joe, we know you're a friend of O'Shaughnessy, the Westchester radio guy who's a big fan of the Gov. They seem to talk a lot on the phone early in the morning and late at night. What the hell do they talk about?"

Reilly said: "Don't go there; just don't go there. They talk about their sons and daughters and their souls. They're 'out there.'" Reilly then changed the subject. I mention this little vignette as relayed to me by my Irish friend because I want to make sure the reader understands that the governor, if you haven't already figured it out, mercifully spared me any of those complex and difficult issues that came under the heading of "prose"—those very complicated issues a governor has to deal with 24/7.

As I approach the ambiguities, confusion, and uncertainties of old age, I hope I've not succumbed to what Pete Hamill calls "the glib seductions of nostalgia." As I move into those ambiguities, my mind drifts back across many seasons of a unique friendship with a marvelous man who just happened to be a liberal icon of our American nation. It's been noticed, by more than a few of my friends, that I've always looked at the Cuomos, especially Mario, through rose-colored glasses. To which I have to plead, "Guilty." But that admission also puts me squarely in the same boat as the very first woman Chief Judge of the New York State Court of Appeals, Judith Kaye, who, when asked if she had any "objectivity" about one Mario Cuomo, answered, simply and honestly, "No."

The late Bob Grant, fiery and provocative dean of radio talk show hosts, who was lethal on the subject of Mario, accused me more than once of being a "stooge for Mario Cuomo" (which appellation never prevented the cranky old WOR and WABC star from generously plugging all four of my previous books). Incidentally, importuned by my friend Rick Buckley, who owned WOR, I tried mightily to persuade the governor to appear on Grant's final WOR show, to no avail. "I saved his job once at WMCA," said Mario about the fellow who practically made a career out of bashing him almost daily on the air. But I was never able to get them together. Still I liked Grant, cranky and acerbic though he was.

My feelings and great affection for Mario Cuomo, you should thus be advised, also place me in the very same pew with the late Jack Newfield and the crime writer Nick Pileggi. My mind drifts back to a late-night conversation at the Executive Mansion in Albany. William Kennedy, the novelist and Albany historian, was there too. And when the subject of Mario Matthew Cuomo came up, Pileggi (or it may have been Newfield) said, "Hell . . . we've all gone over the edge on this guy . . . from objectivity to admiration and awe a long time ago." So I figure if tough, no-nonsense, unsentimental journalists like Newfield and Pileggi were not immune to Mario's charms . . . well, the hell with it. I'm sorry . . . I loved the man. And

I'm not alone. A few months ago, in a public conversation with *Vanity Fair*'s Michael Shnayerson up on the stage at the New York Public Library, the writer Ken Auletta of *New Yorker* fame almost teared up at the mention of Mario's name. MMC has that effect. Still. The great Chris Matthews, without whom MSNBC would surely resemble a bowling alley, once urged caution upon young people who would idolize politicians. "Imperfection grows." But also, I'm persuaded, do decency and goodness and thoughtfulness.

As I write this, we have just marked the first anniversary of the great man's passing. I hope I've done justice to the memory of a great man. I'll let scholars and perhaps other journalists, commentators, and broadcasters aim for impartiality. I'll take a pass because I loved the man. I realize full well that subjectivity has a field day in all my recollections of Mario Cuomo. And I'm quite aware that objectivity is akin to the coin of the realm in the Republic of Letters. And as I don't aspire to standing or high estate in that rarified realm, I'll not tolerate any criticism of my friend in these pages.

With these reminiscences, I'm not trying to make him an icon or, God forbid, a martyr of a long-ago age, or even a hero of a distant myth. It was especially clear to me that Mario tried to observe and adhere to in his personal life those lofty lessons about which he spoke so often. He often shared with friends the torment he encountered almost every morning when he would stride into the state capitol charged up to begin his day's work. "Should I stop and chat with the elderly man who sells newspapers or the blind shoeshine man and listen to their problems and complaints . . . or should I breeze by and hurry upstairs to the governor's office where I can try to save thousands with a few phone calls and the sweep of my pen . . . ?" But in the next breath he would recall Mother Teresa's counsel as relayed to him by John F. Kennedy Jr.: "You save them one . . . by one . . . by one." Thus in this book I've attempted to show that Mario was a man who tried to live the lessons he preached.

He was, in every telling and by every account, a very *real* flesh-and-blood retail politician as well as a statesman and philosopher. And like Nelson Rockefeller, when Mario Cuomo walked into a room . . . you knew he was there.

MARIO CUOMO

I

Whence He Came

Dying is something you have to do all by yourself. There are no cohorts, no accomplices. It's a solo act. Except . . . except perhaps in the case of one particular, very special Italian, who, when he left us, was actually accompanied by several mythical sandlot ballplayers who had achieved great notoriety in the semi-pro leagues on the worn and dusty diamonds of Queens so many years ago. It can now be told that among those who departed with Mario Matthew Cuomo on January 1, 2015, as he slid across home plate for the last time, were the near-legendary ballplayers Glendy LaDuke, Matt Dente, Connie Cutts, and the incomparable Lava "Always Hot" Libretti, all of whom, according to the old men of the neighborhood, answered to the name *Mario M. Cuomo*, who was constrained by "official" league bylaws that allowed him to play on exactly one team at any given time.

And there was one more he took with him across the plate. The famed philosopher A. J. Parkinson, author of so many wise and pithy sayings and thoughtful observations, also retired from our dull, confused lives when Mario Cuomo departed on that New Year's Day as night fell over the great city he never really wanted to leave.

The failed baseball player, it should be known, left a desk drawer filled with A. J. Parkinson's wisdom that he had been collecting for years. We spoke often of these things and of the colorful characters who populated his old neighborhood. One marvelous name stays: a distinguished gentleman named Mr. "Cat-Killer" Cardone, who was most assuredly *not* the son of Immaculata Giordano and Andrea Cuomo. But I think he really existed in the old neighborhood.

Before the governor's father, Andrea, became a greengrocer at that fabled grocery store in South Jamaica, Queens, he was a laborer with a strong back who dug ditches with pick and shovel for storm sewers (they called them "trenches" in those days) in New Jersey. Mario described his father in moving terms: "I watched a small man with thick calluses on both hands work fifteen and sixteen hours a day. I saw him once literally bleed from the bottom of his feet, a man who came here uneducated, alone, unable to speak the language, who taught me all I needed to know about faith and hard work by the simple eloquence of his example." How then, one wonders, could the man from Tramonti have such a graceful son, so nimble of mind and gifted of tongue, who became an impresario, in fact, of the English language?

As I think of Mario's father, Andrea, my mind drifts back to a spring day in 1995. It was the first of May, and Mario had come to the Immaculate Conception Church in Jamaica, Queens, to speak for his ninety-three-year-old mother, Immaculata Giordano, who had come to this country from Tramonti, just outside Naples in the Provincia di Salerno, and who had just gone to another and, we are sure, a better world earlier in the week.

For a woman who had arrived in this country with just an address of a husband who had come before her, there were ten priests of the holy Roman Church. One of the priests was president of St. John's University. But the main celebrant was an old Irish priest who talked of the promise of Saint Paul: "Eye has not seen, ear has not heard, and neither has it entered into the mind of man what God has prepared for those who love Him."

And then the youngest son of Immaculata Cuomo went up on the altar to explain his mother. He had spoken with power and grace and eloquence on many subjects all over the world. But this was for the one he called "Momma," and you leaned forward to hear him say:

I tried to write a speech. I wasn't able to. I mean, what do you say? Momma was so strong, so dignified, so intuitive. She used to regret her lack of education. Maybe it's better she didn't know cybernetics from a salami slicing machine—or megabytes instead of the struggle for survival. She was better with her intuition than you were with your education and intelligence. She knew only this— that no one could have assembled all this magnificence and all this complication if it wasn't going to come out all right in the end. She knew this, and you could not have a mother like this without being awestruck by her strength. She was not of a world where Porsches are parked next to BMWs. I have written and spoken about Momma and Poppa. Many of the stories are in the public domain. I think of Poppa, who wrote sermons in the sand at the beach with his hands. We remember the charity of their souls and the largeness of their hearts. I only want to quote from the Book of Proverbs: "Her value is far beyond pearls. Her husband, entrusting his heart to her, has an unfailing prize. She brings him good all the days of her life. She rises while it is still night and distributes food to her household. She has strength and sturdy are her arms. She reaches out her hands to the poor and extends her arms to the needy. She is clothed with strength and dignity, and she laughs at the days to come. She opens her mouth in wisdom and on her tongue is kindly counsel. Her children rise up and praise her at the city gates."

[3]

The governor finished his simple tribute with, "So, laugh for us, Momma. The years are behind you—and try to make a little room for us."

Mario Cuomo then sat down. And when they blessed the body of his mother and finally bid her to rest, he went straight back to work at his office at the Willkie Farr & Gallagher law firm.

Outside the church, the talk was of her dignity and sense of humor. I had discovered something of this when I encountered Immaculata Cuomo in a Bob's Big Boy restaurant on the New Jersey Turnpike several years before. She was on her way to Washington for the wedding of her grandson Andrew to a daughter of Robert Kennedy. As I came upon Mrs. Cuomo, I inquired, "Excuse me, but are you *Rose Kennedy*?" Without missing a beat, this marvelous old woman said, "Now stop that, Bill O'Shaughnessy. You know very well who I am. And I know who I am."

In 1996 Simon & Schuster published an updated version of Mario's *Reason to Believe*. It contains a lovely chapter called "Something Real to Believe In." Here's a stunning excerpt:

In an easier world we would all have the time we need to study history, with its syndromes, fads, cycles, and implicit suggestions as to how to do things better the next time.

But even then, if we did not probe a little deeper in our exploration, we would still be overlooking something—perhaps the most compelling truth of all. Accumulating deep below, drifting up between the cracks, insinuating itself into our consciousness, is a sense that there's something missing. The political answers seem too shallow, too shortsighted, too harsh. There must be something deeper, grander, stronger—even sweeter perhaps—that can help us deal with our problems by making us better than we are . . . instead of meaner. All around us is the feeling that we will not progress if all we manage is the superficial manipulation of our day-to-day inconveniences. Surely we will not be able to achieve the better society we hope for by deliberately increasing our fragmentation, disintegration, alienation, and hostility.

We feel this hunger for larger answers as a vague ache of uncertainty and dissatisfaction. We play around with words that hint at it—"values," "character," occasionally even "morality." We see it in the yearning for something to fill the vacuum that has disconcerted us increasingly over the last fifty years: no great hero or heroine, no uplifting cause, no reassuring orthodoxy or stimulating new rationale.

Give me something real to live by, to live for, something bigger than myself alone. Because for all my personal fears, for all the energy I put into the struggle for my own survival and that of my family—I know in the end that I am not enough for me.

Momma knew that truth. She knew it without polls, which, after all, mostly just measure confusion. She knew it with a wisdom more subtle than computers or macroeconomic modeling and more perceptive than even the most exquisite of our political punditry. And she taught it indelibly—by the quiet magnificent example of her own life and the occasional stunning power of her simple words. One day in the late 1930s, she was giving scraps of food from our little grocery store to a Gypsy woman and her children, when one of our Italian customers—a laborer, callused and bent by the pick, the shovel, and the wheelbarrow—asked her in angry tones, "Why do you give that to them free when we have to pay?" Momma's answer came in her rough, uneven Italian, but it was this: "Because she's hungry and she's doing all she can do for herself. Because she's like me. That's why I give her bread to eat. Why do you question that?"

At the moment, however, rather than facing the implications of our intertwining fates, we are turning our gaze to conjurers eager to persuade us that our obligations in the world end at our own front door.

It is a simple truth our hearts already know: we cannot reach the levels of strength and civility we should with one-third of our people striding up the mountain with perfect confidence, one-third desperate in the ditches by the side of the trail, and the third in between wondering whether they'll slip down into the ditch themselves.

We can create a nation stronger, wiser, and sweeter than it has ever been. But it can only be done together. Momma understood that. So should we.

Mario Cuomo also understood the power of working with people for a common good instead of against them in order to make a point or win a concession—it was his "something real to believe in."

Of course, his other big "something real to believe in" was his spectacular wife, a woman named Matilda Nancy Raffa, who, truth be known, has almost as big a following internationally as he did. Through sixty of his eighty-two years, she was by his side—or rather, he by hers. She is to this day widely heralded on the continent and especially in Italy for her work as head of the Mentoring USA organization, which assists teenagers.

Mario once famously accused Matilda of being "the single most effective instrument" of his success. This remarkable woman travels abroad like a visiting head of state. During one such visit, the governor called a friend and said, "I understand some guy she met in Lake Como is greatly taken with Matilda. He's a singer . . . named Luciano Pavarotti . . . a very good one, I'm told . . . I don't know if I have to worry . . . ."

"Well, can you sing, can you even carry a tune?" the friend asked.

"No, but I can take him out on the *basketball* court."

"Well, then I think you should worry only a little . . . ."

———————————

Mario M. Cuomo came into our lives at exactly the right time. Jack Kennedy's brains were blown out in Dallas in 1963, and Bobby Kennedy died on a greasy kitchen floor in Los Angeles in 1968. Martin Luther King Jr. was shot through the face on the balcony of the Lorraine Motel in Memphis in the same year.

During this bleak time, in 1965, Sir Winston Spencer Churchill also went to what Malcolm Wilson, the great Fordham orator, would describe as "another and, we are sure, a *better* world." (Mario used to say, "In a debate Malcolm would beat you up in English . . . and finish you off in *Latin!*")

In a desolate period devoid of anyone of standing, stature, or staying power in the body politic, and lacking the presence of any individual at all resembling a hero in the public arena, one winter afternoon I encountered one Mr. James Breslin Sr., famous reporter and writer (and lifelong pal of Mario's), at Costello's Bar on the East Side near Grand Central and cheek-by-jowl with St. Agnes Church (where suburban Catholics loaded with guilt go during the week when they are too lazy to make their way down to the Franciscans at St. Francis of Assisi on 31st Street). Jimmy Breslin looked across the table through the smoke and haze and, with the smell of stale beer in his nostrils, said, "Who's to write about these days?" He had once called Churchill "the last great statue of the English language." It was 1977, and we were still reeling from the fallout of Spiro Agnew, Richard Nixon, and Watergate.

And now my mind drifts back to the arrival of a largely unknown New York secretary of state who came by the WVOX radio station in Westchester for an interview. I had read of the man in offbeat, bohemian journals like the *Village Voice* where Jack Newfield, Wayne Barrett, Pete Hamill, and Ken Auletta often wrote of a certain especially gifted politician from the outer borough called Queens, a man who spoke in graceful sentences and elegant paragraphs.

Mistaking him for John Santucci, the district attorney from Queens, I'm afraid I kept him waiting for at least twenty minutes (something he always kidded me about and never let me forget). During that interview I asked him about his resolute and principled stand on capital punishment. "Did your God tell you to be against this?" He looked across the microphone, our eyes met and locked, and Mario Cuomo said softly, "Look, even a Republican who doesn't wear socks can understand this: Vengeance doesn't work. It just doesn't work . . . ."

As soon as the New York secretary of state left our radio studio, I raced to the phone and called some local Westchester Democrat warlords of the day—Samuel George Fredman, William F. Luddy, Max Berking, William "Kirby" Scollon, and M. Paul Redd—and asked, "Who *is* this guy . . . I mean, who the hell *is* he?"

One could say that Mario Cuomo was truly a son of the Roman Church, with the mind of a Jesuit and the heart of a Franciscan. He often quoted Jesuits and was conveyed to his final rest from a Jesuit church. But he *loved* the Franciscans. "How the hell can you beat the Franciscans? Three Hail Marys for a homicide! They forgive us gently and generously. *You* could be a Franciscan," I once heard him say to a woman I once knew. And he spoke often of his admiration for "a tired Franciscan who, even after fifty years, pulls himself up into the pulpit each morning to preach the Good News to a few people in near-empty pews in a cold, drafty church."

As a youngster, Mario Matthew Cuomo was an altar boy during the week in his parish church, and on Saturday he was a *shabbos goy* at the local synagogue, doing the menial work that is forbidden to Orthodox Jews on the Sabbath. He listened and learned in both places and grew up to apply the ancient teachings of both religions.

I saw this one night as he sat on the banquette of table number 2 at Sirio Maccioni's Le Cirque restaurant in the Bloomberg building on 58th Street, trying to console a mother who had lost her only son in a terrible accident at the age of twenty-two. "I choose to believe [in an afterlife] because the alternative is so bleak . . . and hopeless."

For all his attractive and appealing public persona, Mario was really a very introspective and spiritual individual. Once when he was trying to explain the inconsistencies on display among those Catholic laymen and bishops who oppose abortion but are nowhere to be found on state-sanctioned vengeful killings known as capital punishment, a friend retorted, "Damn, Mario, you should have been a cardinal." It was the only time I ever saw him at a loss for words, as he actually considered it, but for a moment.

It really wasn't too many years ago that the governor of New York was actually *persona non grata* at certain Manhattan Catholic schools and institutions. Let's just say his presence was not "encouraged," according to the dictates of an obscure and now long-forgotten archdiocesan auxiliary bishop. I'm sorry to say, an Irishman. Yet Mario always acknowledged the legitimacy of the anti-abortion and pro-life advocates. At Notre Dame he said, "I accept the Church's teaching on abortion . . . . I believe in all cases we should try to teach a respect for life. And I believe that despite *Roe v. Wade* we can, in practical ways."

As his son and heir Andrew Cuomo said some years later, "My father had a lot of 'tension' with the Church. And the earlier generation of Catholic politicians had still more tension because the Church was trying to tell people, 'You should govern as a Catholic.' And my father and many other Catholic elected officials were saying at the time, 'No, I live my life as a Catholic. I *govern* according to the Constitution, the laws, and the oath.'"

These days, Andrew is starting to sound more and more like his father. He told a reporter, "I believe my father is not gone and that his spirit is with us." And in his 2016 State of the State address, Mario Cuomo's son said, "Every time we walk by a homeless person, most of us can't even bear to look, we can't bear to make eye contact. We pretend we don't see them. Why? Because we don't want them to see us—because it diminishes us . . . to walk past a brother or sister, sitting on a sidewalk and doing nothing. Every time we walk by a homeless person we leave a piece of our soul on that curb."

I once inquired of a bishop, now a cardinal of the Roman Church, why the hierarchy, or certain members thereof, were, shall we say, "uneasy" with, or in some cases downright hostile to, Mario. Was it his powers of articulation, his rhetoric, his way with words? This great churchman thought for a moment and said, "No, it's not his rhetoric they fear, or his glibness. It's his *goodness.*"

But times change. And in 2010 Timothy Cardinal Dolan wrote a beautiful column warmly embracing Mario's statement to the *Wall Street Journal* that the scandal-ridden Church was *not* its flawed predator-priests or the bishops, cardinals, vicars, deans, and metropolitans far removed from the poor and cloaked in their scarlet finery and trappings of gilt and satin and gold. "*Christ* is the Church," reminded the failed baseball player from Queens. "*Christ!*"

To the *Wall Street Journal* editor:

Like all Peggy Noonan's pieces, "The Catholic Church's Catastrophe" is beautifully written and intelligent.

I hope she will give some thought to writing another on how Catholics are able to "cling to their faith" notwithstanding the many serious sins of the church's priests and popes over the church's 2,000-year history.

As Peggy reminds us, Christ told Peter he would be the rock on which Christ would build his church. But he also pointed out to Peter that despite his bestowal of that unique responsibility, Peter would—on his first night of service—commit three serious sins by denying Christ three times.

It has always seemed to me Christ was letting Peter and all the rest of Christendom know that for all the years to come, the church would be charged with the mission of spreading Christ's word, but its members would be vulnerable human beings who may sin seven times a day.

In fact, Christ is our religion, not the church, and that's why Catholics are behaving rationally, as well as loyally, when they continue to believe.

Mario Cuomo

New York

Indeed, Mario was over the moon to hear Pope Francis describe the kind of priests he envisioned and hoped for: "I want shepherds with the smell of sheep . . . and a father's smile. In the sea of words in today's world . . . you must act as the whistle of the shepherd whose sheep recognize him perfectly and let themselves be moved by him."

A few months before Mario departed, the current archbishop of New York, who wrote in that 2010 column, "Thank God for Mario

Cuomo," was told that the governor was fading. As he stood in the sunlight outside St. Pius X Church in Scarsdale, New York, the affable Timothy Cardinal Dolan, always full of bonhomie, stopped in his tracks, the color draining from his face as he leaned heavily on his crosier, the ornate bishop's crooked staff, and removed his miter: "Oh, my God. I'll have to call Matilda. I'll go and see him."

"THE LECTURE OF MY LIFE": MARIO CUOMO AT THE 92ND STREET Y

On January 25, 2010, a cold, rainy night, Mario took the stage at the 92nd Street Y in Manhattan to deliver "The Lecture of My Life," which succinctly encapsulated who he was and how he came to be. This is what he told an overflow crowd of prominent New Yorkers that night.

Throughout my youth I was only *mildly interested* in politics.

The things I came to believe in most deeply I learned from the sweaty example of my immigrant parents' struggle to build a life for themselves and their children; the nuns at St. Monica's Church in Jamaica, Queens; the priests at St. John's University; the great rabbis I met during the Second Vatican Council—and from the enlightened vision and profound wisdom of an extraordinary man, Pierre Teilhard de Chardin, a French paleontologist who participated in the discovery of "Peking Man" and who understood evolution. A soldier who knew the inexplicable evil of the battlefield. A scholar who studied the ages. A philosopher, a Catholic theologian, and a teacher.

He reoriented our theology, rewrote its language, and linked it, inseparably, with science. His wonderful books *The Phenomenon of Man* and *The Divine Milieu*, dedicated to "those who love the world," made negativism a sin.

Teilhard glorified the world and everything in it. He taught us to love and respect ourselves as the pinnacle of God's creation to this point in evolution.

He taught us how the whole universe—even the pain and imperfection we see—is sacred. He taught us in powerful, cogent, and persuasive prose, and in soaring poetry.

He envisioned a viable and vibrant human future: "We are all foot soldiers in the struggle to unify the human spirit despite all the disruptions of conflict, war, and natural calamities."

"Faith," he said, "is not a call to escape the world, but to embrace it."

Creation is not an elaborate testing ground with nothing but moral obstacles to surmount, but an invitation to join in the work of *restoration*; a voice urging us to be involved in actively *working to improve the world we were born to—by our individual and collective efforts* making it kinder, safer, and more loving.

. . .

Without books or history, without saints or sermons, without instruction or revelation, *two things* about our place in the world should occur to us as human beings.

The first is that the greatest gift we have been given is *our existence, our life*.

The second is that since we all share the same principal needs and desires, our intelligence naturally inclines us to treat one another with respect and dignity.

The Hebrews, who gave us probably the first of our monotheistic religions, made these ideas the foundation of their beliefs. *Tzedakah* is the principle that we should treat one another as brother and sister, children of the same great source of Life. And *Tikkun Olam* is the principle that instructs us to join together in repairing the world.

Rabbi Hillel pointed out that these two radiantly logical principles together make up the whole law. "All the rest," he said, "is commentary."

Jesus agreed it was also the whole law for Christians. "The whole law is that you should love one another as you love yourself for the love of truth and the truth is, God made the world but did not complete it; you are to be collaborators in creation."

Teilhard confirmed for me the intelligence and efficacy of the words of both Hillel and Jesus.

. . .

From all these sources: my struggling immigrant parents and neighbors, the nuns and priests and rabbis, Hillel and Jesus and Teilhard, Our Lady of the Law—with whom I fell profoundly and irretrievably in love—and my own other life experiences—by the mid-seventies I felt I had all the simple, basic values I needed to build a life for myself and my family.

I have learned the vanity of trying to know and to define fully the infinite and the eternal.

But I have also learned that in the end even if my intelligence is too limited for me to *know absolutely the truth of things,* I can nevertheless choose to believe—and call it "faith" if I must—if that promises me meaningfulness.

I can respond to the ancient summons of *Tzedakah* and *Tikkun Olam*, knowing my own religion's faith rests solidly on those same two pillars.

I'd rather be committed to those propositions than not.

I'd rather believe, because it's better than the anguish of fearing futility.

And better than the bitterness of despair.

And because it brings meaning to our most modest and clumsy efforts.

2

Public Service

Most of the tributes, appellations, and encomiums bestowed on and written of Mario Cuomo since his passing (and how I hate that phrase) reminded a sad nation of his stunning rhetorical gifts and his mastery of matters political. How he rose from the back of Andrea Cuomo's grocery store in Queens, New York, to become chief executive of a state that Franklin Roosevelt, Grover Cleveland, Charles Evans Hughes, John Jay, Theodore Roosevelt, Hugh Leo Carey, Thomas E. Dewey, Herbert Lehman, Averell Harriman, Alfred E. Smith, and our dazzling Westchester neighbor Nelson Aldrich Rockefeller had also governed.

The essence of his public service, I think, can be found in these words from his first inaugural address, in 1983. He never forgot his origins, but he also never lost sight of his predecessors, nor of the state's expectations of him:

> We are the sons and daughters of giants, and because we were born to their greatness, we are required to achieve.
>
> So good people of the Empire State I ask all of you, whatever your political beliefs, whatever you think of me, to help me keep the moving and awesome oath I just swore before you and before God.

Pray that we all see New York for the Family that it is.

That I might be the State's good servant. And God's too.

And, finally, Pop, wherever you are—and I think I know—for all the *ceremonia*, and the big house, and the pomp and circumstance, please don't let me forget?

I can't depart these reminiscences without recalling a phone call I received early one morning in cottage 92 at the Lyford Cay Club in the Bahamas. My wife exclaimed, "It's 8 dollars a minute!" "He's paying for it," I reminded her.

This long-distance phone call concerned the Supreme Court. Not accepting my excuse that this topic was "well above my pay grade," Mario said, "C'mon, O'Shaughnessy, you have an opinion about damn near everything."

I also sensed, and it was later confirmed, that Matilda and Andrew were pressing him to say yes to President Bill Clinton, who was trying to determine via George Stephanopoulos if Mario would accept an appointment to the nation's highest court.

Now, I could easily see this Italian from Queens with the powerful intellect mixing it up with those previous lords of the law like John Marshall, Oliver Wendell Holmes Jr., Charles Evans Hughes, Louis D. Brandeis, Benjamin Cardozo, Thurgood Marshall, and William O. Douglas. As an elegant writer, Mario would have penned graceful opinions—whether in the majority or among the dissenters—that would have surely placed him among those great stylists Justices Holmes, Brandeis, and Robert H. Jackson. And it would have been reward enough just to see him engage with the late Mr. Justice Antonin Scalia, whom he called "Nino" and greatly admired but didn't always agree with.

But I pressed on with my objection, arguing that some wise-guy reporter would one day do a story on the construction and composition of the High Court that would include the line "Justice Cuomo . . . appointed by William Jefferson Clinton," of whom I was not, as Mario Cuomo knew, exactly a fan. I also pointed out that if he wrote a majority opinion, the *Times* would give it maybe three short paragraphs ("If you're lucky")—and only about one graph if he penned the minority finding.

More important, Mr. Justice Cuomo would be precluded from freely speaking his mind on all those great issues of the day, those not before the Court and even some on the docket.

The governor, who seemed to almost exactly intuit where I might be on the Question, then said, "But it's a *great* job, Brother Bill—you don't have to even wear underwear! You're impossible, O'Shaughnessy." Click.

The next day Andrew relayed his rejection to the president via Stephanopoulos.

With Justice Scalia's passing in February 2016, the thought occurs that Heaven and the "celestial bar" just got a lot more interesting with Mario Cuomo and Antonin Scalia competing, in all their radiant brilliance, for the approval of Our Lady of the Law. At the very least there is sure to be an elevation of heavenly jurisprudence when these two gifted Italians from Queens engage in their new realm.

———————————

On the other hand, I did once dispatch a late-night plea to beg Mario to merely "consider" jumping into the presidential sweepstakes. Still, my heart wasn't really in it, as reflected in this WVOX commentary from 1991 entitled "Don't Run, Mario!"

I have a troubled, confused mind about some of the great issues of the day. This will come as no surprise to those who tolerate my ravings here on the radio each morning. It is about the economy, about presidential politics—and about Mario Cuomo. The confusion in my meager brain goes beyond new car sales, housing starts, the GNP, and unemployment figures. It is somewhere out there beyond the reach of the stock market, which is the playground of an elite few.

What ails America, my own personal country, is not the value of the dollar abroad or the possible failure of our banking system. The whole damn mess—the problem—is not something you can reach out and touch. It concerns the spirit and soul of a struggling republic. The newspapers and television commentators focus on charts, graphs, and downward spirals or the pronouncements of narrow, limited politicians who don't understand either. The media of the day should forget about Star Wars and smart bombs rained down on desert rats like Saddam Hussein and Gaddafi. These are easy stories to file.

A sense of disconnectedness is the real issue. It is a big, sprawling, awkward word, devoid of romance or glamour. But it is slowly tearing apart the America we love and pray for on this Thanksgiving Day.

How do you get at the spirit of the country? You get there, I think, only with love . . . and by that other peculiar word Cuomo uses that so unsettles the eager, plastic politicians abroad in the land with their red ties and transparent ambition: the word . . . is sweetness.

It is not Cuomo's way with words or his oratory that recommends him, or even the genius of his bright, fine mind. Ultimately, the governor brings to all of this only a decency, an innate goodness, and an ability to feel people's pain. George H.W. Bush, in his cigarette boats and golf carts, will never understand, as nice a man as he is.

"You can make us sweeter than we are," the governor told two thousand broadcasters recently. Some of my colleagues, who will never hear his music, were uneasy hearing this particular word from a big, strong, failed baseball player with too many vowels in his name. Real men don't talk like this—and certainly not governors. Or presidents.

So I don't want Mario Cuomo to run for president. There, I've said it! My mind—read, dwindling purse—does. But my heart is not in this game. Of only this I'm sure: Mario Cuomo is operating on a level far beyond [that of] every other contemporary politician. He doesn't know it yet, but he has even gone beyond being governor of New York. The stuff he is selling and what he is about are not shaking hands at factory gates in Cleveland or playing word games with cartoon-like Sam Donaldson or prickly, brittle, bespectacled George Will.

Cuomo is the only public person who can go inside people, to places where politicians rarely get and few belong. He may yet be the greatest Supreme Court justice . . . or the Thomas More of our century. But he doesn't need *Air Force One* as his vehicle to get there, or the Oval Office as his podium. Cuomo needs only himself, and so does the nation. I care not about the forum, the setting, or the venue. I would even take him from behind that big, ornate desk at the Capitol and strip Cuomo of his robes and mantle and high estate and send him out into the streets with the people in their restlessness, confusion, hurting, pain, and hopelessness.

The place for Cuomo is not in the editorial boardroom of the *New York Times* or jousting with a lightweight like Dan Quayle. As I see it, his ideas will prevail, even if he were to spend the rest of his days standing down at the bar at 21 singing "Danny Boy," like his predecessor Hugh Carey.

This is lousy political and tactical advice with which, in one grand gesture, I hereby once again alienate all the political operatives who are chanting, "Run, Mario, run!" But he doesn't belong with Fortune 500 fat cat executives, dazzling them with economic theory. The governor doesn't need to do one more position paper or show up for one more photo opportunity. He needs only to remember another November night a few years ago, when the heavy, electronic gates at the Governor's Mansion at 138 Eagle Street slid open to let out an old, unmarked Chevrolet. No troopers, no reporters were in the automobile as it headed for a Protestant men's shelter in a rundown, drodsome section of Albany known only to the poor and the homeless. It was a sad, alien place, which might have been reconstructed in the mind of William Kennedy, the great Albany writer.

The governor of New York was behind the wheel with his young son Christopher the only passenger. A father and his son were on a mission this Thanksgiving night to deliver sixty pumpkin pies, which had been run up in the kitchen of Matilda Cuomo.

And on a lonely Albany street, Mario and Christopher Cuomo unloaded all sixty pies, carefully, one after the other. Just as they completed their sweet task, the executive director of the shelter came running out to insist that he be allowed to tell the governor of New York all about the wonderful workings of the shelter. He was especially proud of their efficient procedure for delousing the men before they entered the premises. After the impromptu "tour," an unsettled governor and his young son sped back to the mansion.

This little vignette, which comes drifting back to me on this Thanksgiving Day, tells everything about Cuomo. Anyone else I know would have felt very good about delivering pumpkin pies to the homeless. Some would have had photographers present; others would have merely leaked it to the press. But back on

Eagle Street, the light in the tiny office on the second floor burned late into that cold night. And after his own family had retired, their stomachs filled with the good food of Matilda Cuomo's holiday table, Mario Cuomo sat alone, wondering and churning and struggling about those lost, lonely souls he had encountered earlier on the dark side of our capital city.

There goes our invitation to the White House.

It was about this time that I received several phone calls from a California congresswoman named Nancy Pelosi, who didn't know how to convince Mario to run for the highest office in the land: "Mr. O'Shaughnessy, I realize I'm talking to a Republican, but I understand you know Governor Cuomo. What the hell can I say to him from way out here in San Francisco to get him into this thing? He's wonderful, and he's what we need . . . ."

His personal magnetism and gifted tongue made Mario one of liberalism's most compelling champions. He was our lodestar for large-hearted but practical government that acknowledged budgetary limits and fiscal constraints while still providing shelter for the poor and homeless, work for the idle but willing, care for the elderly infirm, and hope for the hopeless and destitute. "Progressive pragmatism," he famously called it.

Nancy Pelosi wasn't the only distaff admirer of Mario Cuomo abroad in the land. There was another powerful woman in Washington, D.C. Mary McGrory, the flinty, brilliant Washington scribe, was a tough, perceptive dame who was quite immune to the blandishments of Washington solons and panjandrums. But she too was crazy about Mario Cuomo: "The Republicans have nobody like Cuomo, an intellectual with street smarts, a first-generation American who is crazy about words and ideas." McGrory was especially taken by Mario's hopeful and oft-repeated observation that "Democrats would rather have laws written by Saint Francis of Assisi than Charles Darwin."

McGrory's great admiration and enthusiasm for the governor was not unrequited. (She was also keen on John F. Kennedy and Adlai Stevenson.) In an aside to Maureen Dowd, that other shy, modest, retiring woman of letters, Mario once confessed, "I'm not myself when I'm with Mary. She's crazy. She can get anything she wants from me. She is magnificent. Not only is she smart, gracious, nice, she's also human. She's got just enough of the devil in her so you know she's real and beautiful. And if she didn't have a little bit of the Irish in her—and a little bit of Boston too—she'd be just too perfect."

Mario had many deep philosophical talks with McGrory. When the governor told her about his lifelong quest for "sureness" and his oft-repeated story of Paul's dramatic encounter with the Lord on the road to Damascus, he admitted to her, "The Lord has not yet obliged me with a shaft of lightning in the tush as was visited on Saul of Tarsus"—as Mario told it again and again for any and all who inquired about his search for "sureness."

And yet, there was one thing about which Mario was sure: that he made the right decision in declining to run for president, remaining in his elected post as governor of New York.

Mario's service in Albany ended, of course, with the stunning election upset of 1994 when he lost his bid for a fourth term to George Elmer Pataki, an affable and attractive state senator from Peekskill who parlayed Mario's opposition to the death penalty and New York's perennially high taxes into a narrow victory that was interpreted as part of a sweeping national "Republican Revolution." Pataki was also the beneficiary of a brilliant campaign run in the Empire State by a dedicated group of supporters who included Senator Alfonse D'Amato; upstate power lawyer John O'Mara; the pugnacious Zenia Mucha, a bright, tough-as-nails P.R. gal who is now a top exec with the Disney Corporation; feisty state GOP chairman William Powers, a former Marine; and Pataki mentor and law partner William Plunkett. (Plunkett later became a great friend of Mario Cuomo's. Al D'Amato is now a confidant of Mario's son Andrew. Wonders never cease.)

During his third term, Mario was left to his own devices while Andrew was toiling away in Washington as secretary of Housing and Urban Development in Bill Clinton's administration. Andrew, to this day, regrets not doing more to assist in that campaign.

The truth is, we were all surprised. But I do recall an ominous "warning" about Mario's last campaign from a brilliant young man who once worked for the governor. Luciano Siracusano, now a successful Wall Street type, shared his unease in a confidential note:

October 28, 1994

I'm glad he's talking about "love" again. It was good to see that he still believes in what he's doing and in himself. To win, especially in a three-way race, he must energize his base and motivate them to turn out. They need to know that he still believes. The ads are pathetic. Everybody loves to dance around the heat and fire. The Governor must be allowed to breathe fire. His folks should film segments from these next two weeks of rallies and unleash some of the Governor's emotive and cathartic powers on these numbed and frozen hearts. Do it with film, not video, and let the pieces speak for themselves. No slogans. No music. No voice-overs. Just reveal the truth and release some of the ether in his soul. If his political geniuses lack faith in what's possible when the Governor's blood turns to brandy, then they deserve to lose.

3

Mario's "Music"

His favorite song was "Stranger in Paradise" as sung by his friend Tony Bennett, and he loved Johnny Burke's lyrics for "Polka Dots and Moonbeams" ("There were questions in the eyes of other dancers. There were questions, but my heart knew all the answers . . . and perhaps a few things more . . . .").

He was also moved by Ray Noble's "Love Is the Sweetest Thing," later a great instrumental by Artie Shaw.

Love is the sweetest thing.
What else on earth could ever bring
Such happiness to everything
As Love's old story . . . ?

Mario liked two other songs from the Great American Songbook, lovely ballads favored by musicians, torch singers, and that dwindling breed of cabaret performers. One such was Jimmy Van Heusen and Johnny Burke's haunting "It's Always You":

Whenever it's early twilight
I watch till a star breaks through
Funny, it's not a star I see

It's always you.
Wherever you are you're near me.

The gorgeous and plaintive lyrics of these and other romantic songs favored by the governor, come to think of it, are, at first glance, merely romantic. But they would work as well in a religious context.

Maybe Mario was just drawn to the simplicity and sweetness of it all. As I recall, another achingly sensitive song that commended itself to his favorable judgment (and mine) was Rube Bloom and Sammy Gallop's beautiful "Maybe You'll Be There":

Each time I see a crowd of people
Just like a fool I stop and stare
It's really not the proper thing to do
But maybe you'll be there.
I go out walking after midnight
Along the lonely thoroughfare
It's not the time or place to look for you
But maybe you'll be there.

Tony Bennett was a pal, and the great singer idolized the governor. At Mario's seventieth-birthday party, held under a huge white tent in the back yard of Maria and Kenneth Cole's sprawling estate in Westchester, Chris Cuomo emceed the proceedings in his trademark dazzling and witty style as speaker after speaker took to the microphone to praise Mario. Chris said, "Dad, we've had enough Democrats, Hillary Clinton, Chuck Schumer . . . it's time for a Republican. We found only one, your shy friend Bill O'Shaughnessy."

As the applause and laughter subsided, I looked at Mario surrounded by his granddaughters: "Governor, I'm going to *sing* for you, because frankly, I'd rather sing in front of the great Tony Bennett [he was next up at the mike] than even attempt to *talk* in front of you!" Then I said some awkward things to convey my great affection and admiration for Mario.

As I handed the microphone to Tony Bennett, he said, "Thanks for the plug, Bill." And turning to the governor, Bennett said, "I have just one song for you. It's called 'It Had to Be You.'" And then the great crooner sang *a capella* as several hundred of Mario's friends and family wiped away tears.

Mario was also a great admirer of Tony Bennett's painting. The last of our crooners is also a brilliant and accomplished artist. He signs his works by his real name, Benedetto. Tony's painting of the Lincoln Memorial graces the cover of the reissued edition of Mario's *Lincoln on Democracy*, published by Fordham University Press.

Mario returned the favor on January 29, 2007, when he took pen in hand to write a gorgeous foreword to *Tony Bennett in the Studio: A Life of Art and Music*, a stunning coffee table book featuring the paintings and artwork of Anthony Dominick Benedetto a.k.a. Tony Bennett:

Ever since Tony Bennett began drawing chalk pictures on the sidewalks of Astoria, Queens, 75 years ago, he has painted—and sung—he says, "Because I have to. I've got to sing. I've got to paint." I've known Tony Bennett much longer than he has known me. I enjoyed listening to him sing "The Boulevard of Broken Dreams" on a jukebox in 1949. In 1954, I danced with Matilda to the strains of "Stranger in Paradise" on our honeymoon at the Condado Beach Hotel in San Juan. He cannot tolerate discrimination, hypocrisy, or unfairness of any kind. Tony feels the world's pain and does all he can to soothe it, with music, with painting, with advocacy, and always . . . with great love. Once, Tony said to me that sometimes when the sound of a standing ovation is

[29]

ringing in his ears, or he receives another honor for one of his paintings, or he's sitting with Susan quietly enjoying a blissful moment, "I think to myself, 'This is heaven.'" I asked him, "But then, what comes after heaven?" He said, "I can't even imagine; I'm just going to keep going like this for as long as I can."

I can't imagine either what comes after heaven. But I know this: What gives Tony's music the sweetness, the emotion, and the power that make it so moving—and what gives his painting the insight and sensibility that are so apparent—is not his throat, or his eye, or all his hard work. It's his heart. And his soul. Tony is a lover of all that is good and beautiful, and that makes him a great singer, painter, and philosopher. More than that, it makes him a truly beautiful human being. John Keats got it right: "A thing of beauty is a joy forever: Its loveliness increases; it will never pass into nothingness." Never. "The Best Is Yet to Come." That's Tony Bennett.

It seems people just loved to sing for Mario Cuomo. Case in point: his attendance at *my* mother's funeral . . . .

I remember it so well. And because it wasn't something I was exactly looking forward to, I also remember arriving somewhat late for my mother's service in Mount Kisco.

As I pulled up to Saint Francis of Assisi Church I noticed an unmarked (and quite ancient) state police cruiser, and climbing out of the shotgun seat next to the trooper-driver was the governor of New York. "What the hell are you doing here? Your schedule says you're supposed to be in Buffalo today," I said.

"I'll explain later, Brother Bill. You'd better get in there and do what you have to do. We'll talk after the Mass."

Mario, as I recall, sat well in the back of the church, while his trooper stood respectfully by the door. The governor stayed for the entire Mass and had to suffer my poor remarks and my brother Jack's much more graceful eulogy. And later that evening, I picked up the phone for a call from the Executive Mansion. "It was good; you did fine, Brother Bill. But you went too fast. Incidentally, who were those two old gals in the pew just in front of me?"

"Oh, those two dames were some of the characters my mother collected over the years. Actually, they were a couple of her drinking buddies. Why?"

"Well, they were very quiet during the first part of the Mass. Until the sign of peace. And when they saw who was behind them, they started singing much louder. So loud, in fact, I actually took a quick glance toward the back of the church to see if my trooper was still there! I mean, at this point they were really belting it out to the high heavens!"

Although you could not accuse Mario Cuomo of being a "long-hair" or classical-music devotee, he adored the soaring "Ode to Joy," the last glorious movement in Beethoven's ninth and last symphony.

For me at least, Mario's taste in music revealed a lot about his philosophical outlook on life: a longing to make things better than they are.

Mario always said he prayed for "sureness," which he described thusly: "You're on the road to Damascus, and you're suddenly hit by a tremendous bolt of lightning. The Lord then appears in all His . . . or *Her* . . . refinements and says, 'Get back on that horse, Saul. And, incidentally, your name is now *Paul.* Oh, and one other thing: You're a *saint!*'—*That's* sureness: a lightning bolt in the tush!"

He had the reverence, bordering on awe, of a first-generation American for the majestic English language. All the days of his life Mario was constantly searching for meaning, for clarity, or, as he often said, for "sureness." You could hear it in the themes he chose. All the while, in the back of his brilliant, fertile mind was the gentle caution he received early on in Catholic school that we never quite "get it" in this life. The old priests used to insist we are capable of only "glimpses" of enlightenment, happiness, or absolute Truth. Undeterred, Mario never stopped searching.

The governor loved to tell another "biblical" story, which he would recite in the vernacular and tailor for his audience—in my case, the recipient being a stumbling, faltering, weak Roman Catholic who struggles for coherency and meaning in his life and in his broadcasting endeavors. He put it this way for me:

> The Lord was bopping along a dusty street one day with some pals when a wise guy broadcaster . . . a scoffer . . . a journalist . . . came up to Jesus and said: "Hey, Rabbi, fancy running into you. I heard you were pretty good in the temple last night. In fact, they say you literally knocked it right out of the ballpark." And Jesus, accepting the compliment gracefully, said, "Well, yah, I had a pretty good night . . . ."
>
> "'What the hell did you tell them, Rabbi, that so unsettled the elders? Could you sum it up for me in about ten minutes? I'm very busy and I have to be on the air soon."
>
> The Lord said: "Look, I know how busy you are. I'll do it for you in less than a minute: Love your neighbor as you love yourself, for the love of Me; for I am Truth."

Then Mario the philosopher added his own advice: "That's all you need. That's *The Whole Law*. You don't need a guy to come down from the mountain with tablets. That's *everything* . . . ." Or as he said on another occasion, "How simple it seems now. We thought the Sermon on the Mount was a nice allegory and nothing more. What we didn't understand until we got to be a little older was that it was the whole answer, the whole truth. That's the way—the only way—to succeed and to be happy, to learn those rules so basic that a carpenter's son could teach them to an ignorant flock without notes or formulae."

He preached variations on the theme throughout his life. In every interview with us on the radio and with each speech, lecture, or address from the lectern—no matter the subject—he somehow returned, again and again, to *Love Your Neighbor* and *The Whole Law*, tenets that he saw as not only instructions but also as just plain common sense, not to mention the essence and *raison d'être* of all our religions. Time and again he would go back to Galatians 5:14: "For the whole law is summed up in a single commandment, 'You shall love your neighbor as yourself.'" He then brought his audience around to the ancient Hebrew notions of *Tzedakah* and *Tikkun Olam.*

Tzedakah is a central theme of Judaism; at its root it means justice or righteousness. To get there we all have a communal social obligation to take care of one another. We are all brothers and sisters.

Tikkun Olam literally means "repairing or healing the world." We all have a responsibility to transform or, in the words of Father Pierre Teilhard de Chardin, "to *complete* the world." "That's *your* job; that's *our* job," Mario instructed us, "to be God's *partners in Creation, to collaborate in its completion.*"

———————————

On a beautiful summer day in 1993, Governor Cuomo arrived at South Haven Park in Suffolk County to sign an historic piece of legislation protecting 50,000 acres of pine barrens stretching through Brookhaven, Riverhead, and Southampton, while designating yet another 50,000 acres for future development, thus pleasing both Long Island's environmentalists and powerful business interests, who had each spent millions of dollars in what the journalists of the day called the "War of the Woods." It was exactly the sort of sensible compromise that would appeal to Mario, who saw it as a victory for future generations. As he stood in the heat of that July day, the governor delivered himself of these soaring impromptu remarks, another expression of the spiritual themes that coursed through most of his public pronouncements.

And so this is an environmental state. And the Pine Barrens now is its latest, most glorious expression.

This is what the State is the best at. Nobody thinks of us that way because if you're anywhere in the United States and somebody says to you, "New York," the instant Pavlovian response is for your mind to summon up a subway mugging in Manhattan. That's what happens when you say, "New York." Nobody thinks of us as environmentalists. But that's what we are.

And all the Tom Jorlings and Orin Lehmans who built the greatest park system in the United States, all of those deserve special credit for—to use the word again—the *legacy* that this place will leave to all of the generations of children who will not know the people who lived today.

That's what I like best about the issue. I don't know about you, but I've lived now for more than half a century. And I have done a lot of things in a lot of places, and I've had a lot of fun. I've played professional baseball, and I've been a professor, and I've been a lawyer, and I've been a businessman; and I have a great family with the most beautiful woman in the world who decided to be my wife, and five children and grandchildren. I've been governor. I've met kings and princes and presidents.

And I'm still a little confused about life and what it really means, and I know that way down deep we're always looking for something bigger than we are. Something more beautiful. Something we can throw our arms around and wrap our souls around and say, "This is right! This is good! This is something I can believe in with passion.

This is something I can give myself to." Sometimes it's a person, and then they take them away. They shoot them down, and they murder them, and they break your heart. And you give up on people and you look around for causes. And you run out of them. And you get into public life and you're not even allowed to say "morality" or "God" or "religion." They rule all of that out.

And you find this truly barren land and you're looking for something larger than yourself, and then it occurs to you! Niagara Falls! The Adirondacks! The Pine Barrens! The water under Long Island Sound! The rivers! The chestnut tree in the park in South Jamaica, Queens! The environment. Ecology. Preserving it! Saving it! Fighting for it!

I won't save a single fish in a single lake for me to catch with all that we do for the clean water. But somebody . . . somebody will have a fish. Some child ten generations from now who doesn't remember our names or even the place as it used to be will benefit from this.

I found it! Eureka! Something larger than me. Something beautiful. Something better than I am. Something to believe in. Something to give myself to selflessly. Not because I'll be able to build a house and make a dollar. Not because it will make me richer. Not because they'll pin a medal on me, but because it's good. It's right.

And no quarrel. And no dispute and no equivocation with sureness.

I go to bed tonight having signed a bill and made it a law, knowing that I did the right thing.

Thank you for that.

I wonder . . . indeed, I wonder if Mr. Lincoln himself could have done better on his feet in the sunlight on that magical July day in the pine barrens of Long Island. . . .

In 2015 Pope Francis also spoke in very clear, unmistakable terms about protecting and preserving Creation: "A Christian who does not protect Creation, who does not let it grow, is a Christian who does not care about the work of God, that work that was born from the love of God for us. There is a responsibility to nurture the Earth, to nurture Creation, to keep it and make it grow according to its laws. We are the lords of Creation, not its masters." On another occasion, Pope Francis told his listeners, "God will judge you on whether you cared for Earth. It is a grave ethical and moral responsibility. Creation is not a possession which we can rule over, nor is it the property of only a few. Creation is a marvelous gift God has given us so that we will care for it."

Somewhere—and I think I know where—a sweet, good man, another one with too many vowels in his name, is smiling. Mario would have loved and had a deep admiration for the Argentinean Jesuit, Jorge Mario Bergoglio, had he been able to stick around long enough to embrace him.

In almost any situation Mario leaned toward the underdog, the put-upon, the guy under fire. I saw this instinct operating when, in my own tribe, Dan Rather was behind the eight-ball at CBS in 2007 in that Texas Air National Guard–George W. Bush contretemps. Mario worked quietly behind the scenes to assist the embattled anchor-man when the elders at CBS News turned on Dan. And now, when Brian Williams has been hung out to dry by the holier-than-thou NBC-Comcast hierarchy, I have no doubt that Mario Cuomo would have been among those defending and trying to rehabilitate Williams. I'm sure of it. For among his other becoming traits, Mario forgave people their oddities and eccentricities. His acceptance of me among his friends, tenuous at times as it was, is certainly proof of that.

Mario was a great student of the English statesman—and Roman Catholic saint—Thomas More, whose likeness was always on display in the governor's offices. Mario studied More's works of philosophy, including the fictional *Utopia*, long before Pope John Paul II named the beheaded English chancellor and Renaissance humanist scholar "patron saint of political leaders."

He could appreciate a graceful turn of phrase or the use of powerful imagery as crafted by others. He was very admiring, for example, of a passage in President George W. Bush's 2001 inaugural address quoting John Page writing to his friend Thomas Jefferson shortly after the Declaration of Independence was published. Governor Page of Virginia said, "We know the race is not to the swift nor the battle to the strong. Do you not think an angel rides in the whirlwind and directs this storm?"

Mario was also an admirer of the somewhat controversial New York poet and essayist Walt Whitman (Mario was always careful to call him "one of our most popular" poets, as opposed to "one of our greatest"), and Cuomo borrowed from the last—and best—line of Whitman's "A Backward Glance o'er Traveled Roads": "The strongest and sweetest songs remain yet to be sung," which the governor used to stunning effect in one of his State of the State addresses. He also praised—and often quoted—Whitman's poem "Excelsior," which found immodest reflection in New York's state motto.

As his son Andrew often reminds us, Mario was very much enamored of the idea that "New York was a beacon for the nation." He loved the word *excelsior* and used it often in correspondence with friends as encouragement to "rise higher, surpass and go ever upward." To those who would inquire of its meaning, the former law professor would gently but proudly remind you that the Excelsior battle cry, which in 1778 inspired the official seal of his beloved state of New York, was actually "derived from the Latin *Excelsior*, the same root from which we get the English words *excel* and *excellent*." And then he would add: "Both Longfellow and Walt Whitman wrote poems based on *excelsior*, which revealed both men as dreaming and hoping for a happy world that is constantly moving higher, ever upward." Mario heard their music.

And we can't forget to mention that Mario also listened to the counsel and prompting of his "favorite philosopher," the aforementioned A. J. Parkinson.

Late one night the ever-present Parkinson, who often visited his wisdom on Mario by the cold light of early dawn, whispered these haunting lines about God:

I struggled to know, but found
the ultimate truths were unknowable.
I struggled to believe what I could not know,
but found I had not the strength.
Now I hide in ceaseless activity,
clinging to hope, pretending it is belief,
and calling it FAITH.

I've stayed too long on the spiritual as I try so inartfully, awkwardly, and imprecisely to draw the measure of a truly extraordinary man. But I've argued for years, even when he was governor and often to the displeasure and consternation of his political advisors, that he had gone beyond deciding how many Bob's Big Boys to place on the New York State Thruway. I am among those who found Mario to be a much better and more skillful and able governor than he is sometimes given credit for. He always said he suffered from the "Dumb Blonde Argument," which means that he was so gifted and articulate that he couldn't possibly have been a good *manager*. But his handling of the minutiae of governance, the "prose" as he called it, no matter how impressive, was always secondary to the gentle and lasting metaphysical instruction he gave on cosmic issues to a nation looking for some lasting meaning and purpose.

Mario Cuomo valued clarity and did not flee from complexity. Even those who admired the former governor have to acknowledge that, as a result, Mario was disliked, nay despised, by a small, virulent group of rabid haters who never forgave him for his principled stand on capital punishment or his nuanced, misunderstood position on abortion. They could be heard almost daily, in all their full-throated animus and vulgarity, on Bob Grant's daily radio programs and even, to this day, venting on the Internet. A "right to life" zealot named Julie recently took to the Internet to criticize his stand on abortion and requested her followers to "pray for Mario Cuomo." Someone I know sent the good woman a note: "Dear Julie: I pray *to* Mario Cuomo!" And forever and ever let the record show that one Mario M. Cuomo personally hated and loathed abortion because of its "violence and vulgarity," as he told me early one morning.

The governor also had a very "lively" and respectful correspondence with Wellington Mara, patriarch of the New York Giants football team, over the best ways to curb the evil of abortion. Mr. Mara was a strong pro-life advocate. And, in truth, so too was Mario Cuomo. He knew that whatever name you try to put on it, it's still genocide, infanticide, killing, murder . . . death.

Make no mistake: Mario was constantly struggling, questioning, searching for guidance and enlightenment in both his personal and public lives. The stunningly candid words of Mr. Lincoln most certainly apply to the author of *Lincoln on Democracy* and *Why Lincoln Matters*: "I have been driven many times upon my knees by the overwhelming conviction that I had nowhere else to go. My own wisdom and that of all about me seemed insufficient for that day." Cuomo also loved this quotation from the writings of Camus: "In the midst of winter, I found within myself an invincible summer." And he was a great admirer of *The Emperor's Handbook* by the educator David Hicks and his brother Scott, featuring the timeless counsel, writings, and instruction of Marcus Aurelius, the Stoic philosopher and emperor.

Mario was greatly taken with a slim but powerful and touching book, *The Man Who Planted Trees* by Jean Giono, a parable about a shepherd in the foothills of the French Alps who quietly and consistently planted one hundred acorns a day in a desolate valley ravaged by two world wars. Gradually, the sorrowful region is reborn with new life. The seventy-four-page book is a reflection on how much good one person can accomplish in a lifetime and on how to live life with deep meaning. Mario made sure his friends received copies of the lovely little story.

THE FIRST AMENDMENT

Harry Jessell and Donald V. West, great editors of communications journals, and Rob Taishoff, scion of the legendary family of journalists who founded *Broadcasting & Cable* magazine as our sentinel on the Potomac to sound the alarm about government incursions on free speech, are always asking me where Mr. Cuomo came out on censorship. Here's where:

In his book *Reason to Believe*, filled with powerful themes, Mario speaks brilliantly of the important First Amendment but also places the responsibility for the coarsening of our culture squarely on *us*. These comments really resonate with me, a self-proclaimed First Amendment voluptuary—even to this day. He was speaking of *values*:

There is among the American people a growing unease with the harshness, the coarseness, the violence, depravity, and obsessive sexual emphasis of American life.

At the very least, we should make sure that our laws do not tear at the fabric of the values we cherish.

We must resist absolutely the temptation for any brand of more direct government intervention. It would mean giving grandstanding politicians or faceless bureaucrats the power to decide what should be written or produced or seen or heard. In addition to raising grave First Amendment concerns, it would be hopelessly impractical. Who would be wise enough to decide which violence was okay and which was morally destructive? What standards would they use to censor what we see and hear? Would news coverage of war atrocities and vicious real-life crimes be appropriate, but not fictionalized accounts of murder and mayhem? Or would it be the other way around? Would violence inflicted by heroes be treated the same as the violence of villains? Should the main test be the context of the violence or how graphic or realistic it is? What about slapstick cartoon violence, the kind Bugs Bunny and Elmer Fudd inflict upon each other? Too violent? How about opera or professional wrestling? Or Arnold Schwarzenegger or William Shakespeare?

Yes we should, and I do—right here. But no matter how eloquent our arguments, self-policing by business will have only limited effect. Like all business[es], media companies function in a profit-driven free enterprise system. Their main obligation, their fiduciary duty, is to produce profits for their shareholders. Few of them recognize any moral obligation beyond that—even if some politicians insist they should.

The ultimate truth, I think, should make us a lot more uncomfortable. If we agree that government censorship is impermissible and self-policing relatively ineffective, we must also agree that any effort to clean up the airwaves and other media will have to start much closer to home, with us. The executives of movies and TV and music aren't jamming sex and violence and profanity down our throats. The American people are choosing it from an ever-expanding menu. The viewers, not the producers, boost the ratings of the titillating kiss-and-tell TV talk shows in which people announce to an audience of two million strangers sins that people of my generation would have been ashamed to whisper in the privacy of a confessional. The music-buying public, including millions of suburban kids from what we would be quick to call "good" homes, eagerly buy gangsta rap CDs with vulgar and vitriolic lyrics. We the people—we ordinary Americans—buy the tickets for the blockbuster films in which murder, mayhem, car crashes, and explosions occur at the same rapid pace that once characterized the witty banter between Nick and Nora or Tracy and Hepburn. We're the ones with the lust for sex and blood, scandal and perversion. We are the ones caught in this uncomfortable contradiction: the desire for what disgusts us, the disgust for what we desire.

A television network or a Hollywood studio will offer us virtually whatever material [that a] vast number of people will watch. They're businesses designed to make a profit; we can no more expect them to substitute thoughtful documentaries for bloody cops-and-robbers shows than imagine that McDonald's will overlook our appetite for French fries and high-mindedly insist that we accept side orders of spinach instead.

If it's clear that we cannot legislate our way out of the moral miasma of the media, it should be equally clear that the trail upward to a stronger, sweeter culture will not be carved with the tools of government action.

We need to think of ourselves as a family. We need to give our children an example so big and sweet and joyful that they can be brave in the face of degradation and emptiness. We need to envelop them in the warmth of our national ideals, as my parents enveloped me in their love, taught me fairness and a sense of responsibility, and offered their own eloquent examples of hard work, humility, self-sacrifice, and persistence.

SWEETNESS

As Andrew Cuomo is always quick to remind us, "My father was right, on so many things." For example, Andrew recognized and appropriated the power and beauty of Mario's one special word and favorite appellation: *sweetness*. Andrew's recent Christmas card from the governor's mansion had this lovely phrase: "Together we will make New York a stronger, safer and *sweeter* place." Mario would have been pleased.

RE: IMMIGRANTS—AT AMFAR'S "HONORING WITH PRIDE" DINNER, ELLIS ISLAND, NEW YORK

On June 21, 2000, Mario Cuomo spoke movingly about America as a "mosaic" instead of a "melting pot."

The venue was Ellis Island, for many thousands their first view of our country.

Just say "Ellis Island," and for millions of Americans, the nostalgia is immediate and profound. America at its best: open arms, generously sharing a unique abundance; welcoming seekers of freedom, fairness, and opportunity.

And adding new souls to the magnificent mix of tints, accents, colors, and creeds that make up what we *used* to call our "melting pot."

The "melting pot" image suggested that the vast diversity of the immigrant waves would somehow melt down into a unique, new, beautifully bland homogeneity.

The new arrivals would abandon their cultures, their creeds, and their orientation, and morph into some kind of safe nondistinct, prototypical American.

That was an unrealistic expectation, *and* an undesirable one.

It's clear after two hundred years that the strength of this nation is not blandness, but rather it is our diversity—the sparkle of it, the clang and clatter of it, the excitement and the richness of it.

From the beginning, a better image than the melting pot would have been the mosaic.

America, made up of fragments, of different size and shape and color. Each beautiful by itself. But when joined with all the others, and harmonized within the design set forth in the Constitution, they create a greater strength and more scintillating beauty than any homogenized new stereotype ever could.

That has always been our highest aspiration as a people.

But so far, it's still only a dream *un*fulfilled: we are still struggling to arrange the pieces.

I'm reminded of a good man, A. J. Parkinson, who could have written a real keynote for this evening if he were still alive. He was a bright and sensitive soul, learned and wise, and he had suffered great and inexplicable calamities in his own life. In his last pain-wracked days he was weary and worn by the struggle, but these are his last words, which I think tell us all we have to remember:

I still see only one way out:
To keep going forward,
Believing ever more firmly.
May the Lord only
Keep alive within me a
Passionate delight in the
World. And may He
Help me to be, to the very end—
To the *very* end—fully human.

"ENDURING WISDOM IN AN IVORY TOWER":
MARIO CUOMO AND MR. LINCOLN

A wet, stifling summer heat hung over the great city as Mario Cuomo sat in his corner office at the Willkie, Farr & Gallagher law firm high up on the 42nd floor of the Equitable Building on 52nd Street in Manhattan.

It was the summer of 2003. The grand statesman, orator, and conscience of American Democrats was seventy-one. On the office wall hung mementos of his twelve years in Albany when he was governor of the Empire State. Even now, thirteen years later, it is impossible to be around Mario Cuomo without also wishing he had listened to the urging and importunings of the elders of his party to run for president. His young partners at the big international law firm founded by Wendell Willkie also believed the man in the corner office would have been a magnificent justice of the Supreme Court of the United States.

But on that summer day the liberal Democrat sat during his lunch hour talking about the patron saint of Republicans—Abraham Lincoln, who is one of Cuomo's heroes. Cuomo told a visitor:

Abraham Lincoln is at once our most popular president and the most used—and abused—by scholars, historians, and contemporary speakers. Everyone knows of his humble roots, his strength during the terrible War Between the States when he had to deal with a whole range of life-and-death issues like war and slavery and equality. Nine hundred thousand Americans died during those four years. And then there was his martyrdom. But most of all we are attracted to Lincoln because of his wisdom. It is an enduring wisdom that speaks for all the ages, a wisdom that transcends the evolving realities of the day.

He had this magnificent eloquence. Nobody wrote like he did. He was constantly dealing on a very high moral plane during all the days of his life. That eloquence—that wisdom—resounds to this day and speaks to us and instructs us still. No president in our history has ever received the admiration, reverence, or the near-sanctification that Abraham Lincoln has received. More books have been written about him, more articles, more newspaper columns, more movies made, than about any other figure in our history. Why is Lincoln so popular? Is it his upbringing, the way he rose up from a log cabin to the White House—which appeals to me and to most Americans—that somewhere in our bloodline there is the pioneer spirit that we still respond to? Is it the achievement of [his] having kept the nation together after the Civil War? Is it the beginning of the end of slavery that he's responsible for? Is it all of those things, plus an incredible wisdom that emanated from him and the magnificent words he used both orally and in his writings?

To explain, his position on the most profound issues, the equality of all men and women, made the *aspiration* of the Declaration of Independence the *reality* of the Constitution. Because the Constitution, as we all know it, wasn't nearly as lofty in its achievements as the Declaration was in its aspiration. In my new book, our second on Lincoln, we talk about today's problems: Iraq, terrorism, the military tribunal, the problem of poverty in the world and even in the United States of America. After we list the problems we add what we believe Lincoln would say about the problems if he were confronted with them now. Obviously, some of them are of a specific nature that he could have hardly imagined, like cloning or even abortion. Or even Internet communication. So there are a lot of specifics in our daily list of challenges that the great Lincoln wouldn't have been able to imagine. But it's hard for me to imagine any problem at all that the great sweep of his logic and common sense wouldn't have reached in some form. Specifically, he has many views on war and when one should *go* to war. And even specifically on *preemptive* war—like what has now been described by some as the first truly "preemptive" war declaration by the United States of America against Iraq. And the question of globalization and how he felt about international relationships. How he felt about the distribution of assets in this country.

The gap between the wealthiest people in America and everybody else is growing rapidly and in a very divisive and fragmenting way. CEOs are now paid three hundred times what workers are paid. Not long ago it was only ten times what the workers were paid. Here is an astonishing number: four hundred Americans at the very top average $175 million a year! That's $69 *billion* total! The average wage is $42,000 in this country.

How would Lincoln feel about gay marriages? Some representatives of the gay community have recently claimed him as one of their own because he traveled the circuit as a lawyer, and in those days the few hotels and rooming houses they had as you traveled from town to town were often packed, and men often had to double up. What's your guess as to what Lincoln would have said about gay marriages?

We're not going to pretend that he thought specifically about all the problems we're thinking about now. Every politician on every side appears to take for granted that a connection to Lincoln is good for them—whether it was Eisenhower, the Republican; or Reagan, the Republican; or Roosevelt, the Democrat; or Clinton, the Democrat; or Wilson, the Democrat. Everyone has a picture of Lincoln on his wall. Lincoln was called a Republican. But the Republicans of Lincoln's day were more like the Democrats of today. And the Democrats of Lincoln's day were more like the Republicans of today.

As for 9/11 and why Muslim terrorists would attack us . . . Lincoln said a lot about wars and how he never saw a war he would want to get into unless he was absolutely forced to—and how he was against "preemptive" war, how he was against invading another nation on the theory we were afraid they were about to invade us—which is precisely what we did in Iraq. He answered that question very specifically and said he would be against it—and he knew how you should deal with people after you defeat them in a war, how you should try to embrace them and make them friendly, as the best protection against their wanting to go to war against you again.

Abraham Lincoln said an awful lot that would be useful today, whether you're a Republican or a Democrat. He has been called all sorts of things over the ages. He's been called a conservative by people like Jack Kemp and Lou Lehrman. Lincoln scholars have written of him as the great liberal. David Donald, who wrote the book that won all the prizes just a few years ago, said Lincoln was proud to call himself a liberal president. And J. R. Randall, the great Lincoln scholar, wrote a whole book, *Lincoln, the Liberal Statesman*. Those labels don't really fit, neither conservative or liberal. I would say there is no label flexible enough and wide-reaching enough to embrace the magnificent riddle that was Lincoln. He was much more complicated than any label will allow you to be.

The Lincoln who called himself first a Whig and then a Republican imposed upon the people of the United States of America the first income tax. Not only did he impose the first income tax, he did it unconstitutionally. How do you like them apples?

Why does his wisdom survive? Why does the wisdom of the Founding Fathers survive? Why does the wisdom of the Old Testament survive? Why does Confucian wisdom survive? Why does Buddhist wisdom survive? Some things are true, timelessly. And Abraham Lincoln had the ability to think profoundly about the most basic, sweeping, and important moral principles.

There are two great bodies of belief written in our early days. One, the Declaration of Independence. And the second, the Constitution. The Constitution—as Lincoln well knew, because he was a wonderful lawyer—is a set of laws and rules and has the force of law [saying] you must live by it. The Declaration of Independence has no force as law. It was nothing more than a declaration of aspiration by the Founding Fathers. But in it, they said things Lincoln believed were on a higher level of morality than the Constitution. The Constitution did not create an equal society. It created a slave-ridden society and absolutely assured that slavery would stay in place at least for a while. The Declaration of Independence prayed for and committed the country to equality without slavery. Lincoln's beliefs were at the level of the Declaration of Independence, not at the reduced level of the Constitution. That was his aspiration. That was what he talked about, and that's what he prayed for. That's what he fought for, and that's what this country believes in even more than it believes in the Constitution. It believes in what we should have been much sooner and what we can be.

The Declaration talks about self-evident truths. Self-evident means you don't need a tablet and a man in a gown with a beard coming down a mountain to deliver it to you like Moses. Self-evident means you don't need a church, you don't need a book, you don't need a history or a school, you don't even need an ancestor to tell you. You figure it out for yourself that all men are equal. That it is better for us to love one another than not to. We all have the right to proceed as long as we don't hurt anybody else in achieving our own destiny. We have our own version of happiness and belief and trust and love. That's the Declaration of Independence. That's what [Lincoln] believed in. That's the highest level of belief in this country, and that's why we respond to Lincoln, because that's the level at which he spoke to us, timelessly, transcending all the changing realities evolving on a day-to-day basis—day to day, year to year, century to century. *Timeless* wisdom. We understand it. We respect it. That's why we love Lincoln.

Lincoln also had a unique ability to craft arguments of raw power and breathtaking beauty—and to argue with the seamless logic of a great lawyer and the large heart of a great humanitarian. He produced unforgettable words that his mind sharpened into steel and his heart softened into an embrace.

Walking to the elevator, after listening to Mario Cuomo talk about his latest paean to Abraham Lincoln, I thought that practically everything the New York lawyer with too many vowels in his name said about the great Lincoln could easily apply to Cuomo himself.

I almost held the elevator to tell him. But when it arrived on the 42nd floor, I got in and pressed "L." Mario Cuomo went back to continue writing his love letter to a tall, craggy man who died 138 years ago and left us only with a national holiday and some wisdom that endures in gorgeous words.

But as I walked across town to meet Nancy Curry, my mind kept drifting back to Mario Cuomo with the thought that maybe God is not yet quite finished with the former baseball player who grew up behind a grocery store in Queens, and who was to be found this day up in a Manhattan ivory tower trying to apply to the challenges of our age the words and wisdom of a president who came out of a log cabin in Illinois.

I had heard a few of Mario Cuomo's recent stem-winding speeches myself, most recently at Iona College, where the president—a Christian Brother—called him "the greatest thinker of the twentieth century." I'd also heard him at the Bedford Democratic Dinner, where Cuomo recited for a room of well-heeled WASPs the simple instruction of the ancient Hebrews: "You are all children of one God entitled to dignity and respect from one another" (*Tzedakah*) and "Repair the universe" (*Tikkun Olam*).

In the summer of 2003, Mario Cuomo and Lincoln worked the same territory.

4

Mario's Legacy

I first learned of the awful malady that would eventually take him after three and a half years, while I was standing outside a posh hotel. I remember the night. The governor had just given a wonderful speech for our mutual friend Joe Spinelli at the St. Regis in Manhattan. I was sitting in the back of the ballroom, plotting my getaway, when I felt a tap on my shoulder.

"Are you going to walk me out, O'Shaughnessy?"

"I've been doing it for thirty years; let's go," I said as we headed for the elevator.

Outside on 55th Street we were descended on by shy, modest, retiring Ariana Huffington, who was chatting up her latest book. When she finally yielded and we were alone on the sidewalk, the governor, out of earshot of the doormen, said, "That wasn't good enough for Spinelli; I should have done much better for him."

"Look, you could have read from the damn Manhattan phone book. You were terrific. The crowd loved it. Don't give me that stuff. You were wonderful," I assured him.

But as we stood there under the ornate *porte cochere*, I sensed something was bothering the great man beyond his tribute to Spinelli, which he alone found lacking. He then described a condition in which the body creates too much amyloid protein. "It's not curable, but it's manageable. Don't worry," he said as he got into a cab. He never told me—or anyone in his family—that the doctors had told him he had three years.

I think he knew right away the prognosis was not good.

My mind drifts back to an early-morning phone call on October 17, 2011, just a few days after the governor made a surprise appearance at the West Side penthouse of Eric Straus, scion of a great broadcasting family. His mother was Ellen Sulzberger Straus, who, with her husband, R. Peter Straus, ran WMCA back in the 1960s and '70s. A cousin of Punch Sulzberger, publisher of the mighty *New York Times*, Ellen Straus was an attractive, formidable woman who made sure her station was deeply involved in the urban civic issues of the day. She also founded the first on-air "Call for Action" to assist listeners with neighborhood problems. She provided a platform for Barry Gray, "Long John" Nebel, Malachy McCourt, the legendary provocateur and Cuomo nemesis Bob Grant, and an articulate young Italian lawyer from Queens who was starting to make a name for himself in the city.

The occasion that October night was billed as something of a farewell "salute" to our mutual friend Joe Reilly on the occasion of his retirement from the New York State Broadcasters Association after thirty years.

The governor spoke with great affection about Reilly and greeted his successor David Donovan. He then thanked Eric Straus and his wife, Varinda. And as we took the long ride down the elevator from the penthouse, I noticed something in the governor's eyes—a far-away look. As I put him in the waiting car, I wondered, I wondered. . . .

I found out a few days later via a phone call during which I made these notes about our conversation.

"Brother Bill, I tried to reach you over the weekend. I hope I was
OK at the Straus thing. I was really unprepared when you put
me on. The reason I went is because I'm looking back on a
whole lot of situations in my life and I'm trying to 'right' them,
because I don't know how much time I have left. Ellen Straus,
back in the WMCA days, gave me the first opportunity before
a microphone, even before I became secretary of state; and I
wanted to repay that by going not only for our pal Reilly but for
Eric Straus, her son.

"And, Bill, if you know of any other situations where I could play some
catch-up ball and make a few things 'right,' I hope you'll let me
know. I had to leave early and I hope they didn't mind. I had had a
very long day at the office and had to make three very important
phone calls about that ridiculous, complicated [Bernard] Madoff
matter." (He had accepted a difficult assignment as something of an
arbitrator or special master.)

"Governor, you were magnificent, and you don't need me to tell you.
Joe Reilly's friend Lydia had tears in her voice and on her face when
I went back up to the Straus apartment. They were just so damned
grateful for your presence. And you don't need to 'make up' for
anything, with anyone. Sirio Maccioni has a great line he typically
attributes to his own when he says, 'Italians have a saying that if
you wake up in the morning and nothing aches, you're *dead*!'
You're not going anywhere for a good long time. I can't imagine a
world without you and your magnificent heart and your strength.
Nor can anyone else. I spoke with 'The Extravagant One'—your
daughter Maria—and she tells me your heart is strong. So stop
feeling 'few' about things."

"I would feel a lot better if you told me [that] Margaret—my daughter,
'The Doctor'—told you that!"

"You will stick around long enough to see your son and heir with his left hand on a damn Bible and his right held aloft swearing to protect, preserve, and defend the Constitution and all of us. You have led a generous, loving life and inspired millions who aren't finished with you yet. You have lessons yet to teach. The universe is not yet complete. I love you, Mario."

"I know, Brother Bill. Talk to you later."

He knew. . . . Mario knew that God had pulled his file and that he was on the back nine headed for the clubhouse and was fast approaching the end of what he himself called "my already long life."

We spoke often of the "diminishments" we all suffer as we get older. It's a word appropriated from the Jesuit philosopher-paleontologist Pierre Teilhard de Chardin, a perfect word from a brilliant Jesuit. But forget diminishments. Mario Cuomo always said *he* wanted to go out sliding across home plate with an inside-the-park home run!

For me, there were no such aspirations. I always told Mario I aspired only to be the third-base coach, waving him home and yelling, "C'mon, Mario, you can make it!" Phil Donahue, some years ago, had a similar notion. He told an interviewer he wanted one day to be "a herald for Mario Cuomo."

And so as if it were ordained, in the final years of a magnificent life, he battled that rare but nasty, draining condition called amyloidosis, which assaulted and finally smothered his powerful, loving, and generous heart. In the face of it he even tried experimental therapies and untested regimens as his physicians at Columbia-Presbyterian, with the constant, loving encouragement of his daughters and Matilda, helped him fight the relentless and debilitating disease for which there is no cure. But by holding on until his son and heir Andrew Mark was sworn in for a second term as governor of

New York, Mario Cuomo, the failed baseball player with too many vowels in his name, made it, with his last and final breath, safely across home plate as America cheered through tears, with respect and admiration for the greatest public orator of our time.

But he was more than that, a lot more. Like the title of that magnificent collection of his speeches published in 1994 by St. Martin's Press reminds us, Mario was always about "more than words."

The *Boston Globe* once called him "the great philosopher-statesman of the American nation." In early December 2014, exactly one month before he died, the *New York Observer*, in a graceful editorial written by Ken Kurson, called Mario "a national treasure and a living legend of the rarest sort: He commands respect from friend and foe alike." And Kenneth Woodward, a well-known writer on matters religious, said of Mario, "Everything which proceeds from his bright, fine mind glistens with the sweat of moral conviction." I can't do any better than that.

And so I'm absolutely convinced that hundreds of years from today, long after the dust of centuries has fallen over our cities, searchers and strugglers and scholars will discover anew some of his magnificent speeches and soaring pronouncements and realize that during our awful time, and in the midst of all our mistakes and confusion, there was . . . there *was* someone. Those gracefully crafted speeches from his mind and heart will surely last as long as anything conjured up by the great Churchill.

He maneuvered words the way Nelson Riddle arranged notes. And his phrasing, like Sinatra's and the classy Mabel Mercer's, was exquisite and impeccable.

Again was "Ah-*gain*."
Japanese was "Jap-an*eess*."

Opportunity was "Ah-pour-tee*yune*-it-ee."

Governor was "Guh-ver-*nor*."

Here's a beautiful example of Mario's way with words. It was written for one of his daughters forty-eight years ago, in July 1968, when he was thirty-five. He called it "A Picture with a Theme":

Before us sit the green hills, behind and above one another. Some standing on shoulders, pretending at majesty.

All kinds of green; deep and dark, almost black green, traces of the recent gentle rain, the rain's gentlest kiss on the earth's cheek.

Up from behind the dark hills the sun rises with a massive gentility; quietly, inexorably, its blinding brilliance softened by the clouds between; its warmth lying easily over everything; gently erasing, as it comes, the rain drops before it, breathing its soft warm breath upon it all and with an invisible stroke polishing the hills and grass to a high brilliance, making the emerald hills glitter gemlike, bedecking the crown of each of the small lake's numberless ripple waves with a tiny shining diamond.

And the beauty hums its own song—not a siren or a sullen song but a silent, soothing serenade.

Nearly without warning the clouds darken. Slowly at first, then feeding on their own advance, faster. Dark now and ugly. Black clouds, swollen and bloated. Mean brothers of the gentle rain, blowing and roaring their ugly ceremonial song. Then finally spitting out their howling distemper—battering at the quiet defenselessness, churning to distraction the quiet waters—flailing wildly with sheets of hard, stinging water—clubs and knives, roaring, crashing, howling, hating, furious.

And we sit huddled and clasped, backs to the fierce tempest.
Frightened at first, but then remembering that it has come before—
and will again—but always, after a while, it spends itself.
And the sun will return with its song.
Gently and inexorably.
And, if we are here, we will hear it again.

―――――

Even those you might expect to have significant disagreements with Mario Cuomo held him in high regard. I don't know if I do greater injury to the reputation of Richard Nixon—*or* the governor's—by recalling the many thoughtful exchanges they had with each other via handwritten notes and late-night telephone calls over the years. And George H.W. Bush would dispatch notes telling friends, "Make sure Mario Cuomo knows how much I appreciate the reference to a former president in his book."

Famous for his magnificent speeches, the governor was also a masterful letter writer, and he took special delight in crafting persuasive letters of recommendation to colleges and universities. And hundreds of deserving men and women were almost instantly accepted as a result of glowing missives from Mario Cuomo to the presidents and admissions directors at Yale, Harvard, the Kennedy School of Government, MIT, and, of course, St. John's University and Fordham. As he liked to say, "The best exercise for the heart is reaching *down* . . . to help someone *up*."

―――――

BLESSED IS THE PEACEMAKER

Mario's 1974 book, *Forest Hills Diary*, about his efforts as a mediator in that famous contretemps between a group of outraged citizens and the administration of Mayor John V. Lindsay over the city's plan to build 840 units of low-income housing (in a predominantly Jewish neighborhood), helped establish Mario, then a young Brooklyn lawyer, as a brilliant and skillful negotiator. Mario never lost the conciliatory touch, and over the years he was often called upon to act as a special master and court-appointed mediator in federal cases.

The governor also reluctantly played a critical peacemaking role by calming furies and resolving disputes in many difficult situations among his personal friends. Difficult and painful as it was, he always devoted the time, effort, and infinite patience to ameliorate the roiling difficulties and feuds buffeting some of his closest friends in their personal lives.

And he was very good at it. A parish priest or professional family counselor really had nothing on "Father" Cuomo when he would wade gingerly and skillfully into family rivalries amidst all the hurt feelings. And I'm not just referring to the times I sought his wisdom and counsel in my own confusion and chaotic life. In every telling, he was very adept at the mediation game—both professionally and on a deeply personal basis—because everyone trusted him as an honest broker and confidential repository of their feelings and interests.

He also wrote letters of support to all manner of co-op boards and condos and banks for his friends. There were many assistants over the years in the service of the great man, but only three personal and confidential secretaries: Pam Broughton, Mary Tragale, and Mary Porcelli, his dedicated last amanuensis, who remembers one letter to a parole board for a young man who had turned his life around. His father was a maintenance man who never forgot the governor's kindness.

He also kept up a great correspondence over the years with a wide range of friends and acquaintances, mostly in the form of timely handwritten notes of consolation and encouragement when life had turned sad and difficult for the recipient. One of his favorite words to use in these situations was *avanti!*

GRANDPA MARIO

The governor, who did some of his best work alone at his desk in the early hours before daybreak, took pen to ink one November day in 1999 just before the commercial Christmas descended, to write this gorgeous missive to his grandchildren. It's as lovely—and relevant—years later:

A New Millennium Letter to My Granddaughters

To My Granddaughters,

It will be a while before most of you are able to read these words and understand them, but what I want to tell you will be as true ten years from now as it is today and I want to be sure to write it all down while I have the opportunity.

Less than two months from now the world will celebrate the beginning of a new millennium. It's a good time to remind ourselves how quickly the days and years pass, and to think about what we want to do with whatever time is left. One of the things I want to do is to share with you as much as I can of what I have learned along the way. That's why I'm writing you this letter.

God can do anything. God could have delivered the world to us as a perfectly finished product, but He chose not to. Instead, He made it a work that changes from moment-to-moment and day-to-day. In recent years the changes have been more rapid and dramatic. Every day there are exciting developments: new ways to learn things, to communicate with one another, to cure illnesses, to travel in space—even new ways to give birth to human beings.

More and more, people are using computers for fun and for business, and they're replaced by more advanced models even before you have mastered the old ones.

Altogether the years ahead will create a dazzling new world of endless opportunity for you. But it will be a world that demands high skills, and if you don't have them you will fall behind.

You know how important education was to your grandparents. You've heard from us all the stories about how our parents came to America from other parts of the world with little or no formal education. How they worked day and night just to be sure their children would have the learning they themselves were denied. Because they did, we were able to educate ourselves, keep up with the changes of our times and provide ourselves—and your parents—with a reasonably comfortable life. The changes that lie ahead for you will be more rapid and more substantial, making your need for education even greater than ours was.

My advice is that you start early, work hard at learning everything you can, and never stop. Knowledge is power, and with that power you will be able to earn a good living, have a nice place to live, enjoy the finest music, art, literature, and gather much that the world has to offer.

But now let me tell you the most important thing I know.

It will take more than all those material things for you to have a really satisfying life. At some point, you will probably find that filling your own basket with goodies, satisfying your own wants and desires for personal comfort, will not be enough to make you truly happy. Chances are you will discover that to be fulfilled requires some fundamental belief, some basic purpose in life that gives you a sense of meaningfulness and significance and that answers the question: Why were we born in the first place? Without an answer, all the accumulating of material goods can become nothing more than a frantic fidgeting, a frenetic attempt to fill the space between birth and eternity.

It happens to a lot of people who spend their whole life so involved with the challenge of just staying alive in some decent condition that they don't get to think much about why they were born in the first place. Others get past the struggle then wander aimlessly as they approach the end, satisfying whatever appetites are left until there are no more appetites, or strength to feed them. They look for answers in the world around them, in the words of wiser people, in the leadership of some heroic figure. But the answers prove elusive, no Moses comes to them, and they die without ever having an answer.

Don't let it happen to you.

You don't need another Moses.

I think there is an idea that can give you all the direction you need, an idea simple enough for everyone to understand, sensible enough for everyone to understand, sensible enough for everyone to accept, sweet enough to inspire us. It's the idea that is the basis of the Judeo-Christian tradition that helped give birth to America and that helps sustain our nation to this day. It began with the Jewish people about four thousand years ago, who described it in two Hebrew principles—*Tzedakah* and *Tikkun Olam*. *Tzedakah* means that all of us, wherever we're born, whatever our color or accent, are children of one God, brothers and sisters who owe one another respect and dignity. And the second principle, *Tikkun Olam*, tells us we should find ways to come together in order to repair the universe, to make it stronger and sweeter. The Christians borrowed both principles. The first we call charity: the obligation to love one another. And the second teaches us—as it taught the Jews—that God made the world but did not finish it; that he left the world to us so that we could, side by side and working together, collaborate in completing the work of creation by making this world as good as it can possibly be.

Because God knows how grand the world is and how small we are, He is not going to expect any miracles from you. All he asks is that you do what you can. If you rise to great power and are able to end a war, or find a cure for cancer, wonderful. But if the best you can do is comfort a single soul in need of simple friendship—well, that's wonderful too.

If one does what one can to make things better, that's all God will ask.

It's a job you can work at every minute that you live, and it's a job that can make your life worth living, no matter what else happens.

So—Live. Learn. Love.

And have a Happy New Millennium.

Grandpa

It's no stretch to call Mario Cuomo a superb writer or to suggest he could have been a successful writer wholly apart from his political career in the public arena. Although well versed in the classic and timeless works of scholars, philosophers, and theologians, the governor admired the strong, muscular, passionate, on-your-sleeve contemporary writings of his pals Jimmy Breslin and Pete Hamill as well as the graceful columns of the sportswriter Jimmy Cannon. It should be remembered that a young Mario Cuomo did indeed spend time as a sportswriter on the staff of the St. John's campus newspaper.

We spoke often of the unique genius of Jimmy Cannon, the great Hearst and *New York Post* sportswriter (who died alone in his room near Times Square). Everybody knows Cannon's beautiful line about Joe Louis: "He was a credit to his race—the human race." But Mario and I loved Cannon's exquisite take on Sugar Ray Robinson when life turned sad and difficult for the greatest prizefighter of our time: "When a hawk falls, pigeons rule the sky."

And Cuomo the Wordsmith was also greatly taken by another haunting line from the pen of Jimmy Cannon when Sugar Ray was getting belted around late in his career by second-class pugilists. He described the sad spectacle: "Nijinsky is dancing in the hallways of Times Square to the sound of a kazoo."

I remember telling the governor after one of these conversations: "Yeah, and if *you* go down, we'll never forgive ourselves."

Mario treasured a signed first edition of *Christ in Concrete* by Pietro di Donato, a powerful narrative of the struggles and culture of New York's Italian immigrant laborers that his friend Breslin called "the greatest American novel ever written."

In later years and all during his political career he crafted his major speeches himself, writing them out by hand, as he did with his sensitive and touching personal letters and pronouncements. Sometimes he read early drafts of his speeches to members of his family and friends, including a white-haired Westchester broadcaster.

The power of Mario's speeches depended in great part on his presence and grace at the lectern, his poise, his personality, and on what Ted Sorensen would call "the skill of his movements and gestures." Also on his strong, resonant voice, what his friend the historian Harold Holzer called his "magnificent instrument." Like a maestro of vocabulary, he used rhetorical devices: alliteration and metaphor. He had a poetic literary sensibility, and like his idol Mr. Lincoln, Mario was aware of the right rhythm and pace and cadence and sound that infused his memorable public orations.

And yet, despite his considerable gifts, his facile mind, and the power of his oratory, Mario was gracious, self-effacing—and often uncomfortable—when accepting praise from his many admirers.

Once on taking the lectern after an extravagant introduction followed by prolonged applause, he uttered this gorgeous acknowledgment of all the encomiums and flattery directed his way: "You are among those who weigh my many faults, imperfections, and inadequacies less diligently than you assess what you may find commendable in my persona and stewardship."

I never heard him swear or curse or utter a profanity. Nor did I ever hear Mario, as the old saying goes, "take the Lord's name in vain." He could be rough under the boards on a basketball court, as his sons, Andrew and Chris—and a legion of young staffers and state troopers—have testified. And as a professional baseball player with the Brunswick Pirates, he once famously threw a punch at a guy who happened to be wearing a catcher's mask. Definitely not a smart move. And legend has it he once threatened to deck Mike Long, the Conservative Party chairman. There are abroad in the land some with a keen knowledge of matters pugilistic—and political—who will swear the actual plunking, the physical part of the altercation with Long, actually happened. Over the years I had several opportunities to delve more deeply into the contretemps with both the governor and the chairman. But I thought, on those occasions, that discretion was the better part of valor. So I took a pass—wisely, I think.

He could push (punch) back, but always in a civil tone. I recently found a note dating back to Mario's run for governor against Lewis Lehrman: "The Republican mailings play upon every unhappy chord that society knows. Show me a weakness, show me a frailty, show me a fear, and there is a piece of Republican literature to address it." Sound familiar?

Mario rarely let me get away with anything. When he heard about my "campaign" to ban clichés and business-speak phrases from our airwaves some years ago, he fired right back with a very funny rejoinder against my tongue-in-cheek and not at all successful attempt at censorship. Accompanying this text is a note we dispatched to our talk-show hosts, which found its way to the governor.

Once again I proved to be *absolutely* no match for the man.

———————————————

Mario and I spoke often of my Westchester neighbor Nelson Aldrich Rockefeller, the Great Squire of Pocantico Hills, who was one of his predecessors as governor. And my friends among the dwindling group of moderates who to this day still call ourselves "Rockefeller Republicans" will forgive me for noting Mario's intellectual prowess and facility and for comparing his scholarly inclinations to those of the great Rockefeller, who once famously, after reading a pithy quotation from the thirteenth-century Dominican friar Thomas Aquinas, instructed an aide: "Let's get this guy in; he sounds terrific!" (Despite this little vignette, which has grown in legend, I rush to tell admirers of the dynamic and magnificent Rockefeller that I am *still* very much with them—in name and spirit and affection and admiration—for Nelson. Mario understood and often referred to me as "a Rockefeller Republican who doesn't wear socks"!)

———————————————

The governor worked cocktail parties and receptions like a society maestro, and never once did I ever hear him "flunk the interrogatory"—for example, when someone inquired after his welfare, he would reply "I'm fine" or "Not bad for an old guy" . . . he then always came back with an "And how are you?" Unlike many contemporary politicians, he waited for an answer. But during Mario's twelve years as governor there were to be sure some slightly "uncomfortable" moments. I remember one such in about 1983 at Pocantico Hills near Tarrytown when the governor had to appear at a tony, upper-crust reception to "officially" accept from the Rockefeller family the

WILLKIE FARR & GALLAGHER

Mario M. Cuomo
212 728 8260
mcuomo@willkie.com

787 Seventh Avenue
New York, NY 10019-6099
Tel: 212 728 8000
Fax: 212 728 8111

August 1, 2003

Mr. William O'Shaughnessy
Chairman
WRTN and WVOX
One Broadcast Forum
New Rochelle, NY 10801

Bill,

  I write to commend you on intent of your vigorous new effort to refine and refresh the language of your on-air talent. But I must tell you that your method of enforcement – the rightwing draconian punishments you have imposed by ukase – is profoundly offensive to me as a matter of principle. Therefore, this is to state to you absolutely ($5) that I will do nothing to help you make it happen ($25) or in getting' it done ($35) and will do what it takes ($47) to create a win-win situation ($97) by defying your mandate while on-air and am requesting that you contribute the fines I will pay to the Catholic education of poor children. I'm never sure when I will be on your air so that you may take this to be a 24-7 ($172) commitment.

Absolutely ($177) yours,

Mario M. Cuomo

NEW YORK WASHINGTON, DC PARIS LONDON MILAN ROME FRANKFURT BRUSSELS magnificent gift of 1,233 pristine and verdant acres overlooking the Hudson River.

He arrived on a lovely afternoon to be greeted by several generations of the fabled Rockefeller clan: brothers Laurance and David (Nelson was gone by then), cousins, nephews, nieces, retainers, and local officials.

It wasn't exactly Mario's crowd, but he good-naturedly went with the flow, briefly hyperventilated, gathered himself, and gamely went into the tony, upscale gathering. He was very glad to encounter Nelson's widow, Happy, who, over the years, told many and all who would listen that she was "crazy about Mario and Matilda." They had a nice visit.

But accompanying this flash of *déjà vu* from that historic occasion, I also distinctly recall that every time Laurance—or his brother David— tried to engage the governor, Mario would pivot and move on to someone else. One moment he was having a heart-to-heart talk with the head groundskeeper of the Rockefeller properties while the senior Rockefellers tried mightily to get his attention. I even took it upon myself to put a shoulder into it to block his escape. Later I gently reminded Mario that he should have been perhaps a little "more attentive" to "The Brothers," as the senior members of the clan were known. Mario smiled and said, "Brother Bill . . . I forgot to brush up on my beetles (David Rockefeller was a renowned collector of the rare insects), and I was afraid he was going to go there," he added with a wink.

On this rare occasion, the gov may have been out of his comfort zone for the moment in the rarefied atmosphere of Pocantico Hills, but the wonderfully generous Rockefellers never noticed as several followed him to his waiting helicopter as Mario returned to Albany with the deed to those gorgeous 1,233 acres, which today constitute one of the nicest public parks in the Hudson Valley.

Over the years I often repaired to Mario's wisdom and counsel for help and guidance on matters of what we used to refer to as "faith and morals," which designation covered all manner of things and topics. For instance, I taxed his good and generous nature just a few years ago when I had to appear on October 1, 2013, before a packed house of supporters for a judicial candidate: New York State Appellate Supreme Court Judge Daniel Angiolillo. I borrowed so freely from the great man for my remarks that night, I thought surely he was going to sue me for plagiarism when he called the next morning to see if I was able to *comport* myself properly before a prestigious group that was made up of mostly lawyers and other judges. This is what I said:

First of all, permit me to thank you for the gift of your presence, as well as the generosity of your purse.

So many of you, as I look around the room, have been admirers and supporters of the judge for a long, long time; and I won't intrude for very long on your evening.

We've come on this beautiful Indian summer night because we need something to believe in. To hold on to. And to be guided by. Something wiser than our own quick personal impulses, and something sweeter than the taste of a political victory.

Our presence here tonight is a tribute not only to a gifted and able jurist. But it is a tribute as well, I think, to what one of the most graceful and articulate of your profession—Mario Cuomo— calls "Our Lady of the Law."

As the lawyers here assembled know, the Constitution, our more than two-hundred-year-old legacy of law and justice, has been the foundation, the rock on which we have built all that is good about America. For more than two hundred years "Our Lady of the Law" has proven stronger than the errors or sins or omissions of her acolytes, which is what lawyers are, and has made us better than we would have been.

But you know all of these things. They teach them in law school. And you practice them every day as officers of the court.

But you also know and are aware that the law does not apply to every single case or circumstance or even, perhaps, to every day and age. So judges must take a wonderful instrument, the Constitution—or statute or precedent—and try to lay them over and apply them to each case. They must try to fit the Law to reality.

To work well, the Law, in the care and keeping of a judge, has to have the restraint that comes with fairness, and it also must have tension to move and bend and be compassionate—firm, but flexible—to deal with each new circumstance.

What qualities, then, should we have a right to expect from the men and women we raise up from among us to interpret and define that Rule of Law?

They must have:

Experience
Intelligence
Integrity
Wisdom
and Compassion

So where do you find people with such qualities? Where must a governor who appoints them or those who elect them find such people? Not in every lawyer. Or in every judge.

To whom, then, do you entrust the power to restructure families? To take a business or diminish our purse and holding. Who maintains this Rule of Law? What protects it? Not a rifle or a bayonet or a prison cell. Only a good mind, accompanied by the precious, sound instinct of a judge who is both wise *and* good.

We found such an individual—albeit with too many vowels in his name—fourteen years ago.

And so here we are now in 2013 with another opportunity to reaffirm our confidence and admiration for an appellate judge with a collegial, compassionate, and loving touch, with a gentle heart to interpret the law, but with a firmness and power to apply it.

So, as I mercifully yield, I would ask again: Where do you find these qualities? Not in every lawyer, or even in every judge.

But we found all of it—and *more*—in the compassionate and caring heart of Mr. Justice Daniel Angiolillo.

And we must continue his brilliant service, *despite* the registration numbers, *despite* the political winds.

There is no Republican or Democratic way to interpret or dispense justice.

We've got to re-elect Mr. Justice Dan Angiolillo!

P.S.: We lost.

Mario touched more people than one could possibly count, in ways that often changed their lives. Such was his influence on people that his legacy will live on for many, many years. Rabbi Joseph Postanik, executive director of the New York Board of Rabbis, spoke of Mario's lasting legacy when he delivered "An Appreciation: Governor Mario Cuomo." These are his words:

> General Douglas MacArthur wrote the following spiritual legacy to his son: "Build me a son, O Lord, who will be strong enough to know when he is weak and brave enough to face himself when he is afraid, one who will reach into the future, yet never forget his past."

I shared those words with Mario Cuomo the last time I spoke with him. I told him the word for *inheritance* in Hebrew has as its root the word for *river* because we believe the real bequest of a parent to a child is not that which is transmitted upon death, but taught throughout life. Thus, Governor Cuomo and his loving wife, Matilda, were able to see a living legacy of commitment to community pass from generation to generation. He taught us to look forward, and still look back at a glorious past.

At the funeral, Governor Andrew Cuomo gave a moving tribute in which he spoke of the love and respect of a child for a parent. How touching it is when we hear [that] children are proud of their parents. It is said children want three things from their parents: "a hand to hold, a shoulder upon which to lean, and above all an example from which to learn."

When I spoke with the governor at the wake of his father, I mentioned that we spend much time expanding our professional résumés, but ultimately our kids remember most not the hours we spent in the office but the concentrated hours we spent with them. As the late Senator Paul Tsongas of Massachusetts said, "No one at the end of life ever says, 'I should have spent more time in the business.'"

Matilda Cuomo reminded me of her husband's close friend, the man the Roman Catholic governor called his "rabbi," Israel Mowshowitz, my predecessor at the New York Board of Rabbis, and Cuomo's neighbor in Queens—who was rabbi at Hillcrest Jewish Center. Cuomo gave him the title of special assistant for community affairs in the governor's office, where he negotiated issues between the state and religious groups. Matilda told me how much they miss the good rabbi, and how closely intertwined their families still are.

The governor's funeral was both simple and elegant, personal and yet far-reaching. I think each of us attending the funeral hoped our children would speak of us one day with the depth of love expressed at the service. Vice President [Joseph] Biden and Senator [Charles] Schumer came to the wake; Mayors Michael Bloomberg and Bill DeBlasio were at the funeral, as were the Clintons and other dignitaries, as well as the working people of New York Mario cared about so much.

It is said that at the end of our life, the question will not be how much have we *taken* but how much have we *given*; not how much have we *saved* but how much have we *served*—because the real measure of life is not *duration* but rather *donation*.

The world is a better place thanks to Mario Cuomo. I believe the lasting legacy of Mario Cuomo is that we should always have hope in a great tomorrow—remembering how he pulled the city together in the worst of times—and that we should have pride in glorious past accomplishments.

We will find that vision when parents and children walk together with love and loyalty for one another.

In early 2016, Chris Cuomo and *his* son and heir, young Mario Cuomo, "starred' in a touching CNN father–son video that went viral. The two of them sat alone in a small fishing boat as Chris explained to young Mario some of the lessons that he'd learned from his father, the governor. And then he revealed some of the life lessons he learned from his young son as well. Their conversation reveals how the governor's legacy will continue to live on in their lives, and in the lives of those they touch as well.

My son made me change in a way that made me who I am right now as much as any experience in my life. I'm not embarrassed to say that my relationship with my son is not how I wanted it. I wasn't doing the best for him. It wasn't making him the best that he could be. If you have to raise your voice with your kid every time you want him to do anything, are you really getting it right? Being intense and insistent works as a journalist. But it was not working for me as a father. Even as a baby, my little man literally ran the other way. Mario is who he is even at this young age. And he's always been completely sure of telling me that he doesn't like what I was doing. Sure, he knew that I loved him. But we ended up in frequent standoffs that were kind of funny. Really frustrating.

It's almost impossible for me to compare how it was for me and Pop with how it is for me and my kids. Times were different.

I realized my son and I were saying the same things, just in our own way. It was really hard for me to change what I thought was right, what I knew and how it was. He helped me do it.

CHRIS CUOMO TO HIS SON, MARIO: I used to get angry a lot more than I do now. I would say I'm sorry, I stink. I'll try to be better. How do you think you helped me become a better daddy?

YOUNG MARIO: You always were a good daddy.

CHRIS CUOMO: Do you think you'll always be my buddy?

YOUNG MARIO: Even when you're not on this earth anymore, you'll always be my buddy. *Always.*

Now I know when he says that, he's thinking about Grandpa being gone, and so am I. I think Pop would respect the effort I made for my family. He put inside of us what we need to stay together and stay true to what matters most. And that's all I want for my kids. Two Marios changed my life, I suppose. And my hope and prayer that matter most is he will live on in me, my girls, and the son who carries his name.

CHRIS CUOMO: Do you understand why it was important to name you after Grandpa?

YOUNG MARIO: No.

CHRIS CUOMO: Because Grandpa is gone, right. But his name lives on.

YOUNG MARIO: He's not gone, he's still in my heart.

5

Who Was Mario? Personal Stories

Since the governor's own departure on that sad January day in 2015, the Internet has been filled with reminiscences from people all over the country who were exposed to Mario Cuomo's wisdom and goodness, many who said he changed their lives by his words and by his example. For many of us, Mario had become a vessel that we poured our hopes into.

Some months ago Brandon Steiner, the baseball memorabilia mogul, was in a Westchester saloon telling us about flying in a private plane to baseball legend Hank Aaron's seventy-fifth-birthday celebration in Atlanta in 2009.

Steiner, who regularly pals with Derek Jeter, Mariano Rivera, Andy Pettitte, and just about every other modern-day baseball star, found himself seated next to Mario Cuomo on the jet. The ebullient memorabilia millionaire said it was the most "thrilling" ride of his life: "to have a two-hour conversation with such a great man—we talked about everything!"

Mario was also there to pray in a Westchester church for that young man, my stepson, whose name was Michael. And so too was his son Andrew, then attorney general of New York. After the funeral Mario sent that mother a simple note with the initials MMC engraved at the top of the vellum: "Sweetness eternally," and signed, "Mario."

I keep going back to Mario's relentless interest in matters spiritual. But it wasn't always all so lofty and soulful with the man whose brilliance was accompanied by a marvelous sense of humor. Some examples: When Mario lost to George Pataki, our pal Joe Reilly, at the time president of the New York State Broadcasters and chief Albany lobbyist for the radio and television stations in the Empire State, moved quickly—and appropriately—to ingratiate himself with the incoming Pataki administration. The defeated governor sent word, "Tell Reilly Mario says he is 'assiduously adaptive'!" Still broadcasting upstate at the age of seventy-five, Joe Reilly to this day wears the description as a badge of honor: "Mario Cuomo called me 'assiduously adaptive'!"

And speaking of George Elmer Pataki, it should be fairly noted right here that the Republican governor made several gracious and thoughtful gestures on the passing of his old political rival.

Mario loved to kid one Anthony Malara, who ran the most obscure television station in New York state in Watertown, up near the Canadian border. Tony Malara was a charming and beguiling Italian who also served as secretary of the local Republican Party—*until* he was discovered by CBS at a broadcasters' convention at the Otesaga, the old lorelei of a hostelry in Cooperstown, which led to his meteoric rise at the "Tiffany" network. And when Malara was elevated to a high, new estate as *president* of CBS Television, Mario was immediately on the phone trumpeting, "Tony is now the highest ranking *Italian* in network television! We can't let him get away with that! Should we tell people how, as an officer of the Watertown Republican Party, he would send personal checks to 'Friends of Mario Cuomo'? But he didn't trust the post office in Watertown, so he would give [them] to the Greyhound bus driver to deliver!"

Some years later Mario delivered a gorgeous tribute to Malara at a memorial service at 21, during which the governor said he didn't want any "eulogies" or tributes at his own funeral. Thank God his son Andrew wasn't listening to his old man this one time. "You can say just *one* word over me when my time comes. I got it from my son Chris: 'Finally!'" Other speakers that day for Tony Malara were Dan Rather and Phil Lombardo, head of the Broadcasters Foundation of America.

When he heard that a friend was visiting Litchfield, a tony town in the leafy hills of western Connecticut, Mario asked if his pal was wearing "lime green trousers with pink frogs."

And when he heard that same friend had taken a spill on his motorcycle coming out of the American Yacht Club . . . the governor rang me up: "I just had a call from the superintendent of the state police that there is a new pothole on U.S. Route 1 in Rye where your head hit the pavement!"

Call this one "A Tree Grows in Elmira." During a swing upstate, Mario's advance team scheduled a modest event in Elmira for the governor to plant a tree as part of a local conservation effort along the banks of the Chemung River. His advanceman, John Charlson, overnighted in my guest cottage in nearby Waverly; and as he was planning the event with the resident state trooper, I suggested we provide a "snack or two" for the attendees, which we estimated would be about fifty, mostly political types—"if the weather cooperates"—certainly no more than seventy-five. Meanwhile, we tipped off a reporter for the *Elmira Star Gazette* (which was the very first Gannett newspaper) that the governor would be in town the following day, and that everyone who attended the great tree planting would "be fed hot dogs, hamburgers, and Italian sausages."

However, when Mario arrived, more than 600 hungry upstaters were on hand to greet him! My friend Joe Valeant, a local restaurateur who catered the event, said, "You dumb bastard, everybody in the region is on food stamps," as he took off across town to round up more food. Mario made a gracious, impromptu speech and shook all 600 hands. But as he climbed back up into the state chopper, he winked at Charlson. "Boy, they love us here in Elmira!" He'd been tipped off about the newspaper story. And for years he kidded me about how "popular" he was in the southern tier.

NEW NEIGHBORHOOD

When the Cuomos moved to Sutton Place, a swell neighborhood near the river on the East Side of Manhattan, Mario quickly discovered that, upscale or not, the posh environs contained just as many colorful and endearing characters as existed in Queens, whence he had come: "I was driving Matilda crazy with the unpacking, and she sent me out for a walk. It was a beautiful day, I remember. And after a block or two, a lovely older man caught up to me: 'Look, I know who you are. Welcome to Sutton Place. But I have to tell you right now you won't find a good *bagel* anywhere around here. So prepare yourself for it. Nice neighborhood, but barren of bagels!' I could only thank my new friend for letting me in on the culinary offerings—or lack thereof—in our new 10022 ZIP code. But that was only the first bulletin. Every so often he would let me know of a 'new bagel emporium, just 20 blocks away, if you think you can make it.'"

LE CIRQUE

Here's another having to do with food, from my memory bank: A clearly apprehensive Governor Cuomo called a friend in Westchester to share a dilemma: "I have to go to dinner at Le Cirque. What do I order? What's the guy's name who owns it?"

The friend: "Great, it's long overdue; you *should* go and enjoy. Nixon was there last week, and Ronald Reagan the week before. Maestro Sirio Maccioni will take care of you. He knows you're coming; I've already talked to him. Just watch Matilda—she's been there often. It's about time you went. You'll have a fabulous evening!"

Late that night Mario called back. "You were right: the guy— Sirio—*does* look just like John Wayne! But who was our captain?"

"His name is Renato Palmieri, Mrs. Maccioni's brother. They call him Zio Renato!"

"Well, he was a darling older man and kept bringing out all this marvelous food. And before he brought the check and after furtively checking to see if Sirio was watching, he leaned over and whispered conspiratorially, 'Gubernatori! You gotta do-a something about-a the *racetracks*! Please!'"

FUN TIMES

One day the governor requested that I set up a luncheon at the Four Seasons restaurant with Neal Travis, the colorful, Runyon-esque *New York Post* gossip columnist and pal of Rupert Murdoch, who founded "Page Six," and Steve Dunleavy, his swashbuckling *Postie* compadre, both of whom were known to enjoy a cocktail of an evening, according to the proprietor of Langan's bar on the West Side, a Mr. Des O'Brien. "We'll take them to the Four Seasons, Brother Bill. And I, the governor, will treat. It's *my* check. And when Julian [Niccolini, the co-owner] comes over to take our order, I will announce, loudly, 'We're *not* drinking today, Julian!' And then you and I can just sit back and watch Travis and Dunleavy chew on their fingernails and munch on breadsticks!"

There was another marvelous lunch, some months later, this one at 21, during which Travis, the beguiling New Zealander, said to Mario, "Will you look at all the damn swells and moguls around here watching us. The whole room is wondering what the hell we're talking about. They'd never believe the governor and a *Post* columnist are sitting here in this high-class saloon talking about life, and about our bloody souls!" I would believe it.

A CASE OF MISTAKEN IDENTITY

Sometimes, "too many vowels" can lead to a case of mistaken identity. What did the former "Senator Pothole" Al D'Amato, the hero cop and popular Bronx congressman Mario Biaggi, and Chrysler's legendary Lee Iacocca have in common? Answer: They were all "setups" for Mario Cuomo's humorous asides about mistaken identity. Mario also swore that President Ronald Reagan came over to him at a White House reception and said, "Welcome, Lee Iacocca!" And Joe Spinelli remembers a woman who came up to the governor one night in Las Vegas and gushed, "Oh, I admire you so much, Senator D'Amato!" I myself well recall a night at Mario Migliucci's iconic restaurant in the Bronx when the governor told the proprietor that he was "constantly being mistaken" for Mario Biaggi.

Mario also loved to tell of introducing his mother, Immaculata, to Lee Iacocca at the Executive Mansion on Eagle Street in Albany:

"He's a very famous and powerful man, Momma. He makes cars."

"What's-a matter with you, Mario? You no know how to make cars!"

One of my favorites is this little vignette, which I call "Stamina on the Lecture Circuit."

The governor, with some regularity in recent years, would depart his prestigious Manhattan law firm, Willkie, Farr & Gallagher, to *debate* conservative icons George Will, Dan Quayle, and William Bennett before various trade groups around the country.

On one of those occasions, as the governor was taking his place on the stage for a "debate" with Bill Bennett, the blustery conservative educator-author, before some 3,000 midwestern grocers, Mr. Bennett leaned over (with the mikes off) and whispered, "Mario, I hear you're going to do some television with Bob Dole. Try to find out about the *effects* of *Viagra* when you see him."

Mario, adjusting his lapel mike, replied, "Bill, I'm an *Italian*. I don't need to ask about that stuff!"

Just then the curtain went up.

_____

The governor loved to tell the marvelous story of how he "recruited" Joe Spinelli. One day he put in a call to FBI director William Webster. The conversation between the governor of New York and the head of the FBI in Washington went down like this, according to Mario:

CUOMO: Judge, we're looking for a great lawman, a really stellar crime-fighter to become our inspector general in New York state. Right now it consists of one guy, with a badge, a gun, a secretary, and a desk. We really want to build it up and improve things, and I thought you might have some ideas. . . .

WEBSTER: Governor, we're flattered you would ask the Bureau. May I have until Thursday . . . ?

CUOMO: Take as much time as you like. We want to get this right.

On that Thursday night, right on schedule, the FBI director called the governor in Albany:

WEBSTER: Sir, we have a fellow in our New Haven office. He led one of our SWAT teams and was in six shootouts. He had a role in the ABSCAM investigation and helped bag some big politicians. . . .

CUOMO: Judge, stop right there. He sounds *great*. What's his name?

WEBSTER: Well, his name, sir—I have it right here—is Spinelli. Joseph Anthony Spinelli. S-P-I-N-E-L-L-I.

CUOMO: Uh oh, I was afraid of that!

WEBSTER: Something wrong, Governor?

CUOMO: No, no, he sounds just great. It's just that—why all those *vowels* in his name? Haven't you got a perfect guy like that with more of a Central Casting name, like for example somebody named Special Agent *Mark Conrad* or something *perfect* like that! Why all the *vowels*, Judge?"

Joe Spinelli was hired and did a complete makeover of the Office of New York State Inspector General, building it into one of the best in the country. It turned out one of his partners in that elite FBI three-agent squad were Louis B. Freeh, later a federal judge and FBI director. The third agent was John Pritchard, who would go on to head the Metropolitan Transit Authority police and serve as first deputy commissioner of the NYPD.

Joe Spinelli was also alone with Mario on board a New York State Police helicopter en route from New York to Albany just after the governor gave the late Art Athens of WCBS the biggest scoop of his life. As Mario was climbing up into the chopper, he turned to his inspector general. "Joe, I just made the announcement, via Art Athens, that I'm *not* running for president."

Lawman Spinelli, who hadn't heard the news, said, "Governor, it was a tough decision, but knowing you, I'm sure you gave it a lot of thought."

"Joe, I've just been re-elected by an historic plurality. It would be like cheating on my wife. I just couldn't abandon my responsibility to the people of New York." And then Mario Cuomo buckled himself in and spoke not another word for the fifty-nine-minute night flight up the Hudson River Valley to Albany.

But Spinelli, who also sat alone with the governor on another sad night—and, in fact, was holding his hand on the ninth floor at Columbia-Presbyterian Hospital just a few days before Mario left us— still remembers, with a rich admixture of sadness and admiration, that tears fell from Mario's eyes on that lonely flight to Albany on the historic night when he declined to run for president of the United States as so many had been urging him.

THE MIGHTY HUDSON

I recall yet another soaring moment when the governor came to Westchester to affirm the state's protection of the Hudson River. It was, as the Brits would call it, another brilliant day as Mario stood on a bluff in Tarrytown overlooking the mighty Hudson with the Palisades glistening in the background. The late actor-activist Ron Silver, a dedicated environmentalist, was master of ceremonies. Caught up with the bucolic setting in Sleepy Hollow country with the majestic river behind him, the actor launched into a stunning introduction of the governor. I mean it was absolutely riveting, the introduction. The brilliant Silver, who founded the Creative Coalition, spoke fluent Mandarin Chinese and Spanish. And his use of the Mother Tongue on that summer afternoon was nothing short of spectacular. After the actor's stem-winding intro finally came the governor to the lectern.

Looking over the greensward, Mario saw arrayed before him a local high school marching band, which took up the first five rows in the audience. Most of the youngsters, cradling their instruments, sat glassy-eyed as Mr. Cuomo tried to convey the importance of protecting an iconic resource like the Hudson. It was another brilliant Cuomo speech, which was kith and kin to the one at the Pine Barrens.

But the high schoolers, uncomfortable in their seats as the hot sun played down on their stiff, starched uniforms, were probably not the best audience. When Mario returned to Albany, he called for a critique. "Well, first of all, *never* follow Ron Silver to the microphone again!" he was told. But then the governor said, "Did you see the skinny kid with the tuba, the only one who kept his hat on? I think he *got* it. I could tell by his eyes—he *got* it."

I often wonder if that young man, now grown to adulthood, will remember the Westchester afternoon he sat there with the weight of the largest and lowest-pitched instrument of the brass family pressing on his lap as a graceful man named Mario Cuomo spoke to him and his bandmates about protecting some river for future generations.

———————

INSPIRING THE YOUNG?

There was one young man who definitely got it. Mario always took a keen interest in the sons and daughters of his friends. One November day in 1988, my own young son Matthew Thayer O'Shaughnessy volunteered to accompany me on a barnstorming tour with the governor, going with us from Queens out to the end of Long Island to drum up support for a controversial bond issue to rebuild roads and bridges. An entire trainful of VIPs, officeholders, and union leaders were aboard the special train as it paused for whistle-stop rallies in Jamaica, Hicksville, and Huntington before heading out to the Hamptons. As the train chugged into Suffolk County I started looking for Matthew. And after a nervous few minutes I found him chatting it up with the governor. Later that night Matthew asked me to get him some books by "a guy named Bacon . . . Francis Bacon. The governor said I should read his essays. He was a philosopher, statesman, and a scientist too, Dad."

Mario also took great pleasure in mentoring young staffers like Andrew Stengel. "I thought I was destined for a career in politics, and one day the Gov gave me some advice that changed my life. He sat me down and said: 'Andrew, you can do more than this. First go to law school; and second: marry a rich girl!'" Young Stengel took Mario's advice about law school. And accompanied by his trusty law degree he served with distinction as a prosecutor in the Manhattan D.A.'s Office and is now in private practice. He's still looking for a rich girl.

STAN LUNDINE

To replace our late Westchester neighbor Alfred B. DelBello as lieutenant governor in 1986, Mario chose Stan Lundine, an obscure congressman who had been mayor of Jamestown. Lundine entered the fray willingly, but he was clearly out of his comfort zone in a statewide race. So Mario, in effect, took over as Lundine's "campaign manager," taking the upstater with the twangy, nasal western New

York voice and inflection by the hand and introducing him to the power brokers as "*my* lieutenant governor."

To introduce Lundine to members of the prominent and influential Jewish community in the New York area, the governor enlisted the help of his dear friend Rabbi Israel Mowshowitz, the Conservative rabbi with a national reputation who headed the huge Hillcrest Jewish Center in Queens. The rabbi promised to introduce Lundine to some of his friends.

When the governor called the rabbi for a "how did it go?" report, he was told, "Mario, he's a very nice man, but he doesn't quite come across in front of my crowd."

Mario thought for a moment and said to his dear friend, "Rabbi, here's what we do—the next time, introduce him as 'my friend Lund*een*, Lun-d*een*,' as in *Levine, Levine*!" The governor and his rabbi had a great, good laugh!

And apparently it worked. The soft-spoken Lundine was elected as Mario's running mate in 1986 and again in 1990 and served with distinction as lieutenant governor of New York for eight years.

Mario's friend Rabbi Mowshowitz passed away in 1992. At a standing-room-only service for the beloved Jewish leader, Mario said, "*My* rabbi was a great spiritual leader, an eloquent preacher whose greatest sermon was his life. He was a man of God *too sensible to ignore the world and too wise to embrace it as the only reality*."

Stan Lundine was on a Buffalo radio station a few days after Mario died and said, "It caught me by surprise when he chose me to run for lieutenant governor. I never thought I had a chance because I'd backed Ed Koch, with whom I'd served in the Congress, in the primary. One thing I remember so well about the governor is his *capacity for work*. All my life I had never encountered anyone who worked as *hard* and diligently and with such devotion."

Although the governor was always drawn to the great, overarching cosmic issues, he was also, as Lundine indicated, very astute and diligent in dealing with all those nitty-gritty, recurring Earth-bound matters that face our state's chief executives: homelessness, public safety, health care, addiction, criminal justice, judicial matters, the courts, the arts, education, immigration, transportation, infrastructure, labor problems, energy, the economy. The list is long and daunting. Our workaholic governor, shaped by the example of his mother and father, found time for all of it. In other words, his public life wasn't all poetry. In truth, Mario Cuomo, he of great vision, brilliant mind, and gifted tongue, was also a hands-on administrative and policy wonk. I hate to admit it, but he was something of a perfectionist nerd who did sweat the small stuff, as anybody who worked for him will confirm. He applied himself with great dedication and a laser-like focus on domestic pocketbook issues.

The governor had considerable admiration for the Bush family. And vice versa. President George H.W. Bush always made a point to acknowledge any gracious reference or comment by Mario in one of his books or speeches. And I vividly recall a summer meeting of the New York State Broadcasters Association at the fabled Gideon Putnam, an historic old hotel in Saratoga Springs. William "Billy" Bush, who spent the summer with us as a news intern at our Westchester community station, "covered" the upstate confab, with broadcasters from all over the state, at which the governor was the featured speaker. After Mario's formal remarks, he opened it up for a Q&A session. The very first question came from the attractive young man in the back of the room: "Mr. Governor, my name is William 'Billy' Bush. I am an associate of your friend Mr. O'Shaughnessy. I'd like to ask you *why* must it always be 'us' against 'them' in the public discourse?" The room hushed and waited for Mario's response to the excellent philosophical question, which was right over the heart of the plate for Mario Cuomo. "Well, I can tell from the elegance of your question that you are indeed a Bush. . . ." And then Mario hit it out of the park with a beautiful ten-minute reply.

After the conference was over, I received a call in my car going down the Hudson River Valley. "Who was that attractive young man; is he really a Bush?" Mario asked. When I explained that Billy was the son of Jonathan Bush, Mario said, "Oh, I like his father very much. He's the one with the great personality, the one all the other Bushes wish they were like."

The governor and Jonathan Bush also had a lively correspondence about some of the great issues of the day. I received a copy of one such letter from the governor with a note: "I like him a lot."

(Jonathan Bush is a brother of President George H.W. Bush and an uncle of President George W. Bush. His father, of course, was Prescott Bush, U.S. senator from Connecticut. Jonathan's son Billy is today a television star and host of *Inside Edition*. And he may be on track for even greater things. Jim Griffin, the uber–talent agent, once proclaimed that Billy Bush "will be the next Johnny Carson." He is, even now, slated to take over the last hour of the *Today* show.)

LIKENESS

For years Mario Cuomo resisted the entreaties and pleas from the archivists of the State Capitol to sit for an official portrait that would take its rightful place among the fifty-one others in the great Hall of Governors. He found the whole exercise "pretentious." It took a while and a lot of behind-the-scenes maneuvering by his family, but he was finally persuaded to give at least nodding agreement that the well-known portrait painter Simmie Knox could do a likeness using photographs. Mr. Knox was the first African American to have painted a presidential portrait. He did both Bill's and Hillary Clinton's White House portraits.

At the unveiling, at which Mario was careful to show neither pride nor satisfaction nor pleasure, Governor Andrew Cuomo stole the show with his comment that trying to persuade his father in the matter was "above my pay grade." He assured his father he had "no knowledge" of the long-overdue gesture. "I thought they were giving him a *watch*," said Mario Cuomo's son and heir. Matilda knew better. And so did Mario.

RADIO DAYS

Among his many enthusiasms over the years was our own medium of radio. He took to the airwaves often. For many years he jousted on the air with Fred Dicker, the dean of the Albany press corps, and with Albany's brilliant Alan Chartock on a weekly program carried on public stations all over the Northeast; and on countless occasions he would favor our own WVOX in Westchester, during which he would have to submit to my own off-the-wall questions on life issues as well as current political and governmental developments and concerns. During these "lemon squeezes" we ranged far and wide, and transcripts of many of these memorable broadcasts appear in my four previous anthologies published by Fordham University Press.

In 1995, the Sony conglomerate tried to take Mario coast-to-coast and even worldwide via a Saturday talk show envisioned as something of a counterbalance to all the right-wing chatter. They even built a network around him: the SW Network. Sony spent big bucks on the effort, building a huge amphitheater-style studio at their corporate headquarters on Madison Avenue. But this noble experiment to provide a national platform and forum for the governor's genius was short-lived. Mario was great at answering questions and dazzling in the give-and-take part of it. But he was not at all comfortable with small-talk and meaningless chit-chat. Example: "How are you, Governor?" "Not bad for an old guy." And that was it. Idle, vacuous, casual, worthless dialogue was just not his thing. The Sony experiment lasted for about thirteen weeks.

But our WVOX broadcasts went on for many years after that. We would call the great man and put him on the radio live whenever one of the great issues of the day required his wisdom and interpretation. And in all those years—several decades, in fact—he never ducked or finessed a call from me or mine. Often, if we didn't initiate the call, Mario would ring us up! We always kept a studio "hot" for those calls. I mean, we talked about everything. Our audience loved it. And loved him.

AN UNLIKELY POLITICIAN

Leonard Riggio, the dynamic and colorful impresario of Barnes & Noble, who is still very close to the Cuomo family and has great expectations for Andrew's ambitions, was among those admirers who couldn't quite define or label Mario's unique genius. "Sometimes I think he's more like a monk than a politician," said the book baron. "Mario was very uncomfortable shaking the money tree, and he hated the rubber-chicken circuit."

REMEMBERING JAVITS

At seventy-eight, I'm at an age where *everything* reminds me of *something*. Like, for instance, the recent New York Auto Show at the Jacob K. Javits Convention Center. That fabled venue might today be known by a different name, but for Mario Cuomo.

One day the phone rang at the radio station. "Brother Bill, about that new convention center. Some people in my office want to name it for Sol Chick Chaiken: The Sol Chick Chaiken Convention Center. How does that sound to you?"

"Well, sir, forgive me, but who the hell is Sol Chick Chaiken?"

Mario replied, "You see, O'Shaughnessy, I didn't think a Republican from Westchester would have a clue. He's quite a great man: president of the International Ladies' Garment Workers' Union and a power in the AFL-CIO!"

"Well, with all due respect to you and the geniuses in your office, it just doesn't work. Somebody comes to New York on convention and says he's going to meet you at the Sol Chick Chaiken Center—it just doesn't sound quite right . . . ."

And then the governor got around to the *real* purpose of the call: "I agree with you. How about if we named it for Senator Jack Javits. You should like that; he's a Republican."

"That's a sensational idea! The Jacob K. Javits Convention Center! Go for it."

"Well, there's just one problem. We need Jack's permission, and not one of the guys in my office is brave enough to call Marian, his wife." (Marian Borris Javits was the senator's formidable and outspoken wife, fiercely devoted to Jack Javits.) "They're afraid she'll take over and try to fire the architect or rip up the carpet. Even my faithful Fabian [Palomino] won't call her."

It took me a while, but I finally got the message. "I'll call her."

Mrs. Javits could not have been nicer. She called back within twenty minutes. "A lot of folks have wanted to name things for Jack. He's turned them all down. But I just went into his bedroom [the great liberal lion was ill, in the late stages of ALS—amyotrophic lateral sclerosis, or Lou Gehrig's Disease]. Jack thinks this one would 'fit.' He thanks Mario for the gesture."

A few weeks later Senator Jacob K. Javits, father of the War Powers Act and one of the brightest men to ever serve in the Senate, passed into history—with a new convention center named after him.

———————————

Speaking of naming rights—or "rites"—there was yet another call to the radio station from the executive chamber in about 1993. I remember it all too well. "We want to name something for your friend Governor Malcolm Wilson." Wilson, a great orator, served in New York government longer than anyone, first as an assemblyman from Yonkers, then as lieutenant governor under Nelson Rockefeller, and finally as the fiftieth governor, filling Rocky's unexpired term for an entire year in 1974 after Nelson resigned. "Our people want to attach his name to the Liberty Scholarship Program, the first state-run effort to cover all college costs for low-income students. It was really thought of during Malcolm's time. Or they would like to do a vast tract of land in the Adirondacks in his honor."

Just then Nancy Curry, who also admired and loved Governor Wilson, interjected: "Why don't you name something 'important' for him, like a *bridge*—something like the Tappan Zee Bridge."

"That's not a bad idea, Nancy. Let me see if it will work." And so in 1994 the name of Malcolm Wilson was added to the bridge's name upon the twentieth anniversary of his leaving the governor's office, though to this day it is almost never used when the bridge is spoken of colloquially. I, however, always make it a point to refer to the span, soon to be replaced, as the Malcolm Wilson Tappan Zee Bridge. And as memory has it, at the dedication in Tarrytown, as the huge green sign with white lettering was unveiled for all the dignitaries there assembled on the Westchester side of the bridge, it was discovered that the name "Malcolm" was misspelled "Malcom." Everyone had a great, good laugh. Especially Mario and Malcolm.

Speaking of naming, I recall a fitting line written by Sir Terry Pratchett: "A man is not dead while his name is still spoken." From time to time, I would ask Mario what he would like named for him, because Malcolm Wilson, Ed Koch, Hamilton Fish, and Bobby Kennedy had their bridges and Hughie Carey had the Midtown Tunnel! And always the answer was the same: "Just put my name on a stickball 'field' in some alleyway in Queens. That'll be fitting enough. In fact, it's more than I deserve."

He talked often about returning to one's roots. In his writings and musings, Mario admired and often glorified intellectual strivers and truth seekers in matters religious and philosophical, but he also one day dispensed a none-too-subtle caution to those eager to bail out of the old neighborhoods in their efforts to escape urban blight, crime, and a deteriorating quality of life: "I know these people. I've seen them. I've talked to them. They leave Brooklyn and move over to Queens. Then they do a little better and settle in Nassau County, which gets a little 'crowded,' and they're off again to Suffolk County and a long commute. Next thing you know, they're doing well at work and they're in the Hamptons, thinking they've got it made. But they wake up one morning surrounded by traffic jams and rich weekenders from the city. So they move to Montauk. And they're faced with the sea! They don't know what do. And then it occurs to them: 'Maybe, just maybe, the old neighborhood wasn't so bad after all! I think I'll go back and try to build it up and return to my roots and my friends and where I came from.' And, incidentally, they find, after their frantic upwardly mobile odyssey, that they're not alone. . . ."

For this reason among others he openly admired the magnificent actor-activist Ossie Davis and his spectacular wife, Ruby Dee, who lived all their lives in New Rochelle, not far from where they had family in Mount Vernon in southern Westchester. "They're so successful they could easily live in some upscale, tony place like Greenwich or Bronxville or Scarsdale or Bedford. But they stay close to their roots and their friends."

And then, unable to resist a playful jab at me: "You're doing pretty good; why don't *you* move to Pound Ridge and become a Congregationalist?"

MARIO'S SENSE OF HUMOR

For all his profound, thought-provoking pronouncements at the lectern, Mario was also possessed of a marvelous sense of humor. Here are some examples.

In 1988 Mario told this story to a room full of Irishmen at a Friendly Sons of Saint Patrick dinner:

"The Friendly Sons of Saint Patrick want you to speak, Governor," Michael Patrick Joseph Finnerty, my budget director, told me, "Because although you're Italian you personally embody many of the outstanding qualities associated with Irish American politicians.

"You have Mayor Daley's looks, Ted Kennedy's luck, Jane Byrne's brains, and Hugh Carey's deficit."

Finnerty warned me, however. He said, "Governor, they won't make it easy. The Irish aren't happy unless they're confronted by dilemmas or creating them. They are people who enjoy swimming at the tops of waves they've created by their own turbulence."

To illustrate the point, he told me a story. It's about an old Irish fisherman who fished the lakes of Mayo and, no matter how badly anyone else did, always came in over the allowed quota of fish.

Nobody knew how he did it, least of all the Ministry of Fisheries in Dublin.

One afternoon, on the day before the opening of the fishing season, the old man and a brand new English-educated inspector from the Ministry of Fisheries found themselves sitting next to each other in the local pub.

The old man looked over at the young inspector and said, "And would you like to start the season with me tomorrow?"

The inspector said, "Do you know who I am?"

The old man said, "Yes, I do."

The inspector said, "Well then, I'd love to."

The old man picked up the inspector the next morning, put him in his rowboat, rowed out to the middle of the lake, put down his oars, looked over at the young fellow, reached under his seat, took out a stick of dynamite, lit it, and threw it overboard. Boom! Dead fish came floating to the top of the lake. "Good grief, man, you can't do that!" the inspector said; "you've violated three statutes and six regulations with me looking right at you!"

While the consternated inspector fumed and reeled off violations, the old Irishman leaned down, took another stick of dynamite, lit it, held it a second or two, leaned over, handed it to the inspector, and said, "And tell me now, do you want to *fish*, or do you want to *talk*?"

I have chosen to talk. I hold no grudge against the Irish because, in 1929, a stockbroker named Jeremiah Aloysius O'Grady ended my father's career on Wall Street.

O'Grady, you see, was a Fordham graduate who apparently knew more about Jesuit philosophy than he did about arithmetic *or* the stock market. And so he jumped out a window one day . . . and landed on my father's pushcart!

Before he passed away, however, O'Grady swore he had nothing against Italians . . . and was just aiming for the street!

———————————

In the well-heeled audience of more than 1,000 Irishmen were the legendary federal judge William Hughes Mulligan and former New York Governor Malcolm Wilson, both renowned Fordham orators who insisted they had never heard the O'Grady story before. They roared.

He was in rare form perfect early one morning after a breakfast at 21.

WILLIAM O'SHAUGHNESSY: Governor, at the 21 Club breakfast this morning, with all the moguls here assembled, they called you the "great philosopher-statesman of the American nation." One of the fat cats said that, but they also let slip that it is your *birthday*. How old are you?

MARIO CUOMO: I'm much older than I was when I was born, you see, because that's when I was beginning. Now, I'm beginning to hit my stride. So, I'm old enough to *know* better, and probably, because I've learned to *know* better, this is the last interview I'll ever do with you, O'Shaughnessy! [*laughter*].

I once told Mario I fell in love at a horse sale in Elmira. Mario immediately replied, "Well, I hope with a *horse*, Bill!"

———————————

Mario loved to joust with my former father-in-law, the late B. F. Curry Jr., a prominent Westchester car dealer, one of the best-known in the nation. "Papa" Curry, as Mario and everyone in our family called him, was, shall we say, quite conservative politically. Make that *very* conservative. But he very much liked the governor on a personal level. Mr. Curry would often refer to Mario as a "modern-day Robin Hood"—a nice guy who takes from the rich to give to the poor. Mario, when they first met, immediately dubbed him "Paul Bunyan." "Papa" Curry was a strapping six-foot-five-inch-tall man with a big, booming, resonant voice. (He was also a 2-handicap golfer at the fabled Winged Foot Golf Club, something the governor also kidded him about on several occasions.) They loved to have a little "sport" with each other.

One day my phone rang.

"Brother Bill, you've got to hear this. I called 'Papa' Curry and said, 'This is the governor. I'm in Albany working on bills the legislature sent over for the governor's signature. I thought you'd like to know that I'm *vetoing* that one the car dealers were lobbying against because it's flawed.'"

"Papa" took a moment to respond. Then he said into the phone: "Well thanks, Mario, but you're still a foul ball, *politically.*"

The exasperated governor said, "I'm trying, Brother Bill, I'm trying."

We had a hell of a laugh about that one. And here is a little clip from one of our radio interviews:

WILLIAM O'SHAUGHNESSY: You've given me one unsettling bit of news though: that Andrew was a *rugby* player as a youngster. Is that a sport young Italian guys from Queens take up? Rugby?
MARIO CUOMO: I don't even know how you *say* "rugby" in Italian, O'Shaughnessy!

[99]

Mario sometimes started a speech in this way:

I received a marvelous and memorable introduction the other night as I was preparing to give a speech.

Actually it was by the mayor of a city in upstate New York who was—to put it mildly—unhappy with my state budget.

He referred to me as a "Gov-er-nor." Then he slowly read for the audience a dictionary definition: "Gov-er-nor: a device attached to a machine to assure it does not achieve maximum efficiency!"

Well, at least the crowd loved it!

———————

Sometimes, actually quite often, the governor liked to joke at my expense:

I don't know how many people know Bill O'Shaughnessy, but he provides outstanding evidence and represents a perfect example of the extraordinary opportunity allowed in this country. All you need is a good face, a head of hair, you don't even have to wear socks, and you can make money in Westchester County. Here's a man who, with good looks, goodness, and a 1920s suit, has won himself prominence in places like 21. Only in America. That was just one of the many success stories I was thinking of as I saw the Statue of Liberty—talk about your teeming refuse!

———————

Not everyone was over the moon about the man. Our Westchester radio stations once lost a lucrative fast-food advertising account when we received word from its Madison Avenue ad agency that "We're sorry we have to cancel your advertising, but one of our major franchisees is not exactly 'crazy' about the governor, and they've informed us, in no uncertain terms, that this individual doesn't want to do anything to 'help' Mario Cuomo."

And on another occasion, during the chaos of the Elliot Spitzer–David Paterson era in Albany, we lost another pretty substantial chunk of advertising support—after an eighteen-year relationship—from a New York state entity for much the same reason.

I view these episodes as a small price to pay for Mario Cuomo's friendship. In fact, I them as a badge of honor.

6

The Best of Mario Cuomo

In Governor Andrew Cuomo's recent memoir *All Things Possible,* which came out in 2015 amid political turmoil and distractions (everyone expected a "campaign" book, but there are actually some very candid, revealing, deeply personal—and honest—passages!), Mario's son and heir has a fascinating chapter about the tension, uncertainty, and preparation leading up to the famous keynote address at the 1984 Democratic National Convention. The current governor recalls that his father's legendary San Francisco speech, subject to many rewrites and much massaging by Andrew, Tim Russert, and Mario himself, was "The Best of Mario Cuomo," an opinion shared by many. Mario never thought so. I heard him say countless times, "It wasn't one of my best." But the great James Reston was among those who were greatly taken by what is undeniably Mario's most famous speech. Scotty Reston called it a "brilliant speech . . . with every word, gesture, expression and pause in harmony."

William Safire, in his excellent collection *Lend Me Your Ears: Great Speeches in History,* chose the Iona College speech of June 3, 1984, when the governor spoke over the heads of the graduates to their parents. "We have for a full lifetime taught our children to be go-getters. Can we now say to them that if they want to be happy they must be go-givers?" Safire, a Pulitzer Prize winner for the *New*

York Times, thus elevated this address above the governor's better-known "Shining City" speech at the Democratic convention and his brave and controversial Notre Dame talk about abortion and the responsibilities of Catholic public officials.

My candidate for The Best of Mario Cuomo occurred on an early spring day in 2005 when Mario addressed the prestigious Omega Society at the New York Sheraton (site of many of his campaign kick-offs and victory parties).

On that April day, the governor faced a ballroom full of brilliant and thoughtful "thinkers, searchers, and seekers." They weren't disappointed as he took the lectern. Listen again to his observations about the Roman Church that he loved. It's almost as if ten years ago Mario was predicting the coming of Pope Francis. Here is the entire speech, "Meditation on Ultimate Values."

When I was asked by a representative of Omega to give the closing remarks following the galaxy of distinguished individuals you have already heard, I said I probably could not add much to the intelligent, subtle and splendid articulations they were sure to deliver.

The representative said, "You probably can't, but as a former three-term governor and still-active political voice, you may be able to tell us something about how politics and government might affect our search for meaning, truth and a sustainable future."

I agreed to try.

Actually, I attempted to do something similar some years ago when we were in the midst of another troubling period that created greater-than-usual uncertainty, agitation and anxiety. Another period when people's search for meaningfulness intensified.

On that occasion the title of the conference was "Who (or What) is God?" with "God" being the undefined and undefinable label given to ultimate meaning and direction.

I addressed the question then, as I do now, certainly not as a scholar, or a theologian, or an apologist, but as an ordinary New Yorker—from Queens, from asphalt streets and stickball, from a poor and middle-class neighborhood—who made a living, helped raise a family, and found his way, somewhat improbably, into the difficult world of politics.

I do it as a person who struggles to keep a belief in God that he inherited; a Catholic raised in a religion closer to the peasant roots of the simple Sunday Mass practitioners than to the high intellectual traditions of the Talmudic scholars, elegant Episcopalian homilists, or abstruse Jesuit teachers.

The simple folk of South Jamaica, Queens, who came from the tenements and attached houses on Liverpool Street, perceived the world then as a sort of cosmic basic training course, filled by God with obstacles and traps to weed out the recruits unfit for eventual service in the heavenly host.

The obstacles were everywhere. The prevailing moral standard was almost impossibly high: If you liked it, it was probably a sin; if you liked it a lot it was probably a *mortal* sin.

Their fate on Earth was to be "the poor, banished children of Eve, mourning and weeping in this vale of tears," until by some combination of grace and good works—and luck—they escaped final damnation.

For many, if not most of them, their sense of who or what God is was reflected in the collective experience of people who through most of their history had little capacity to learn from the exquisite musings of philosophers and theologians, and little chance to concern themselves with helping the poor or healing the world's wounds.

They were the poor, the wounded.

It was a cold voice these people heard from God on Beaver Road, next to a cemetery across the street from St. Monica's Catholic

Church, where a famous ex-jockey, one of the homeless winos, froze to death sleeping in a large wooden crate.

No doubt there were others in America—millions indeed—who felt content with the world as they found it.

But for most of the people in my old neighborhood, it was hard to see God's goodness in the pathetic faces of the customers in our small grocery store who pleaded with my father for bread, and maybe some cold cuts—until the next relief check came in.

It got harder still, during and after the Second World War, when the best we could say about victory was that the new terror was put down . . . for a while.

And a gold star in a window announced that someone's son had been killed, his mother's prayers at St. Monica's never answered.

It was hard for them to believe God spoke at Hiroshima either.

Who could blame these people for feeling that if God was not dead, he must surely be looking in another direction?

Others reveled in what they believed was the cultural liberation and enlightenment of the sixties, but for most of the people of Saint Monica's the sixties were remembered for Vietnam and the sadness memorialized by Simon and Garfunkel: "Where have you gone, Joe DiMaggio—our nation turns its lonely eyes to you. What's that you say, Mrs. Robinson? Joltin' Joe has left and gone away."

No more John F. Kennedy, no more Martin Luther King. No more Bobby Kennedy. Nothing to believe in. Nothing to grab hold of. Nothing to uplift us.

People weren't asking, "Who is God?" They were asking, "Is there a God?"

The same question many were asking after 9/11 and after a preemptive war in Iraq in the name of liberation that killed more than 40,000 human beings, most of them innocent civilians; and after Rwanda and the grotesquely lethal tsunami.

The same question many ask today when a child dies in a crib—inexplicably.

Many of us find a way to go forward resigned to a world that has no answers to the biggest questions.

For some of us, however, the burden becomes intolerable; the absurdity of a world without explanation is almost too much to live with.

Our intellects push to find a rationale, an excuse ... anything to take the place of despair ... some fundamental belief or belief system, some dominant purpose in life—an absorbing activity, a benign crusade, a consuming passion for romantic sex, or music or art, something larger than ourselves to believe in.

If the answer cannot be compelled by our intellect, we plead for an answer that, at least, we could choose to believe without contradicting that intellect.

We yearn for more than just a God of prohibition. More than just a God of guilt and punishment.

More than John Calvin's chilling conclusion that God loves Jacob but hates Esau.

For us, it must be a God like the one that was promised in the New Testament: a God of mercy, a God of peace, a God of hope.

In the end, to make any sense, it must be a God of love!

Mostly, we want a God because we sense that the accumulating of material goods and the constant seeking to satisfy our petty appetites—for a flash of ecstasy or popularity or even temporary fame—is nothing more than a desperate, frantic attempt just to fill the shrinking interval between birth and eternity with *something*!

In my old neighborhood, despite the doubts, the simple and sincere preachments of the pre–Vatican II Catholic Church, and the prodding of uneducated parents whose moral pleadings and punishments were as blunt and tough as the calluses on their hands, were still given a degree of apparent respect. Probably this was only because there seemed to be nothing more intellectually satisfying to put in their place.

In the fifties, some of us were suddenly gifted: We were presented with the enlightened vision and profound wisdom of an extraordinary man.

A scientist, a paleontologist. A person who understood evolution. A soldier who knew the inexplicable evil of the battlefield. A scholar who studied the ages. A philosopher, a theologian, a believer. And a great priest.

Teilhard de Chardin heard our lament, and he answered us. He reoriented our theology and rewrote its language and linked it, inseparably, with science. His wonderful book *The Divine Milieu*, dedicated to "those who love the world," made negativism a sin.

Teilhard glorified the world and everything in it. He taught us to love and respect ourselves as the pinnacle of God's creation to this point in evolution. He taught us how the whole universe—even the pain and imperfection we see—is sacred. He taught us in powerful, cogent and persuasive prose, and in soaring poetry. He integrated his profound understanding of evolution with his religious understanding of the "Divine Milieu." He envisioned a viable and vibrant human future: "We are all foot soldiers in the struggle to unify the human spirit despite all the disruptions of conflict, war and natural calamities."

"Faith," he said, "is not a call to escape the world, but to embrace it." Creation is not an elaborate testing ground with nothing but moral obstacles to surmount but an invitation to join in the work of restoration; a voice urging us to be involved in actively working to improve the world we were born to—by our individual and collective efforts making it kinder, safer and more loving. Repairing the wounded world, helping it move further and further upward to the "Pleroma," St. Paul's word for the consummation of human life. The Omega point, where the level of consciousness and civility would eventually converge, having infiltrated the whole universe, elevated to the highest level of morality. A new universe, a peerless one; one we could help create by our own civilizing behavior.

Teilhard's vision challenges the imagination, but it has achieved sufficient scientific plausibility to be given cautious but respectful attention by celebrated intellectuals like Robert Wright, a scientist and a declared agnostic. (See his book *Nonzero: The Logic of Human Destiny*.)

Actually, I would have been less influenced by Teilhard's exquisite and moving enlightenment if I thought it was reserved for people like Robert Wright who are equipped to understand the scientific complexities and nuances that he weaves through his theology.

In fact, if one looks closely, some of the most fundamental of Teilhard's principles are equally available to me and to all rational human beings whatever their level of formal education.

They are instructions of what has come to be called "natural theology" or the "natural law," which is to say they can be ascertained by using evidence that is there for all of us to see and feel with nothing more than the gift of consciousness and exposure to the world around us.

Without books or history, without saints or sermons, without instruction or revelation, three things about our place in the world should occur to us as human beings.

The first is that the greatest gift we have been given is our existence, our life and the power to help procreate.

The second is because as humans with the gift of consciousness we are unique parts of creation—sharing the same principal needs, desires and threats against us—our intelligence inclines us to treat one another with respect and dignity.

The third is the inclination to work together to protect and enhance the life we share.

The Hebrews, who gave us probably the first of our monotheistic religions, made these ideas the foundation of their beliefs. *Tzedakah* is the principle that we should treat one another as brother and sister, children of the same great source of life. And *Tikkun Olam* is the principle that instructs us to join together in repairing the world.

Rabbi Hillel pointed out that these two radiantly logical principles together make up the whole law. "All the rest," he said, "is commentary."

Jesus confirmed it was also the whole law for Christians. "The whole law is that you should love one another as you love yourself for the love of truth, and the truth is God made the world but did not complete it; you are to be collaborators in creation."

I know of no religion recognized in this country—God-oriented or not—that rejects these ideas.

If, then, as seems to be the case, politicians today are looking for guidance from religions in learning how to create a sustainable future or looking for the best wisdom to govern by, day-to-day, the answer is apparent: To deal effectively with our problems and to make the most of all our opportunities, we must understand, accept, and apply one fundamental, indispensable proposition. It is the ancient truth that drove primitive people together to ward off their enemies and wild beasts, to find food and shelter, to raise their children in safety, and eventually to raise up a civilization.

Now, in this ever more complex world, we need to accept and apply the reality that we're all in this together, like a family, interconnected and interdependent, and that we cannot afford to revert to a world of us against them.

It is the one great idea that is indispensable to realizing our full potential as a people.

This is true whether we are considering the sharing of the wealth in the economy of the richest nation on Earth; deciding what we must do to relieve the economic and political oppression of people all over the world; or deliberating over how to join in protecting millions of Africans against the ravages of AIDS or the barbarism of warlords.

Each of us is presented with a choice to act or not to act in a way that will move the world in a different and better direction. A brilliant agnostic, Chief Justice Oliver Wendell Holmes, echoed Teilhard's call for the vigorous involvement of all of us in the management of the world around us and added a warning. He said, "As life is action and passion we are required to share the passion and action of our time at the peril of being judged not to have lived."

Teilhard would have augmented Holmes's remarks with his promise of glorious attainment. "The day will come when after harnessing the wind, the mind, the tides and gravity, we shall harness for God the energies of love and on that day for the second time in the history of man we will have discovered fire."

I wish I had a recording right now of a lot of people's one favorite piece of music.

Reflecting on Teilhard's vision and importunings, it's easy to hear in the background Beethoven's wonderful message to humanity which was his ninth symphony.

With its unforgettable ending . . . .

The single moral principle he wanted to share was the need to see the world as a family. Listen to it again. It begins dark and threatening; disaster and confusion loom because of clashes of will, misunderstanding and alienation. It moves into the frenetic hunt for resolution seeking an answer that will comfort and reassure humanity.

Then in the final movement it swiftly presents again the initial picture of disunity and discord, only to dissolve into the "Ode to Joy," using the words of Friedrich von Schiller's poem, ending in ecstatic jubilation—the chorus rejoicing at the convergence of the world's people through maturity, brotherhood . . . and love!

Simple, and simply wonderful!

So, "Who or What is God?"

I have grown old enough to understand the vanity of trying to define fully the infinite and eternal.

But I also understand that I'm not required to eliminate any possibilities just because my intellect is not acute enough to make them irresistible.

In the end, I can choose to believe—and call it "faith" if I must— if that promises me meaningfulness.

So, it may not be easy to understand Teilhard or believe that God commits us to the endless task of seeking improvement of the world around us, knowing that fulfillment is an eternity away.

But it's better than the anguish of fearing futility.

Better than the emptiness of despair.

And capable of bringing meaning to our most modest and clumsy efforts.

That's a useful consolation for any of us still struggling to believe.

Wow! A few days before the governor delivered this stunningly brilliant homily (and that's what it was), I received a copy of the working transcript with a "What do you think, Bill O'S?" note attached. As I've acknowledged, I would occasionally take pen in hand to weigh in with my brilliant two cents, which he usually—and wisely—ignored. However, after reading this riveting talk that literally took my breath away, all I could do is write, "Wow!" Wow . . .

As governor, Mario Cuomo had many formal speechwriters and self-styled "communications specialists" on the public payroll as would-be ghostwriters. They included Bill Hanlon, Stephen Schlesinger, Harold Holzer, Peter Quinn, and the estimable Tim Russert.

But the great man rarely used the product of their considerable genius, except in the case of Harold Holzer; their Lincoln book relied heavily on Holzer's scholarship and genius. My own meager contributions over the course of thirty-eight years rarely, as I've indicated, made the final cut. Mario's soaring and thoughtful speeches were from his own heart and mind. The governor himself famously said, "I am not capable of delivering an important speech even reasonably well unless its content, style and language are mostly my own. I've discovered over the years that as long as I am strongly committed to the message I am trying to deliver, my mind and voice and body will find ways to help people understand what I'm trying to say."

In *More Than Words*, a stunning collection of Mario's most memorable speeches published by St. Martin's Press, the governor of course included his famous and soaring "A Tale of Two Cities" speech at the Democratic National Convention in San Francisco in 1984. That speech, as I just mentioned, mesmerized a nation and catapulted him to a worldwide reputation as an iconic liberal champion.

But perhaps because it was a purely political speech, it was never one of his favorites, and that's why I have not included it in these pages. Also in the same beautiful collection of his speeches was the thoughtful, soul-searching Chubb Fellowship Lecture delivered at Yale University on February 1, 1985, which he titled *E Pur Si Muove*.

The speech dealt with the counterproductive tendency we have to exalt glib ideology over good, time-tested ideas. In a packed New Haven amphitheater, Mario reminded Yale's best and brightest and many New England political and civic leaders that "while programs and policies change, our principles don't."

In its most memorable passage, Mario begged the audience—and the nation—not to abandon its principles, even in the face of the sweeping national Republican victories in the previous year.

He reminded the scholars, students, and politicians there assembled on that winter night that "the great Italian astronomer Galileo faced a similar situation as he questioned abandoning his own long-held belief." The audience paid rapt attention as Mario reminded them:

> Galileo described the world as he saw it, a world that circled the sun in constant orbit. But many people had trouble accepting this for they were taught that the *Earth* was the very center of the universe and never moved. Galileo had challenged their perception of the universe, which came dangerously close to challenging the very basis of their faith. This occurred during the terrible time of the Inquisition and Galileo was actually forced to kneel before a high tribunal of elders, royalty, scholars and theologians and renounce and retract his ridiculous assertion, bordering [on] heresy, that the Earth moved. With the elders of the tribunal looking down, they made him say that the Earth was stationary because God had created it that way.
>
> Galileo knelt and with great pain and reluctance spoke the words they forced him to speak: He denied [that] the Earth orbited the sun. But ... as he arose ... those around him heard him say in a quiet voice, "*E pur si muove.*"
>
> "But still ... it moves ..."

Just as Mario uttered these words, a student in the upper balcony, unable to contain himself, leaped to his feet and shouted: "Bravo, Mario!" The stunned audience froze for a moment and again cast their eyes on the lectern, where Mario, without missing a beat, screamed back, "Thank you . . . Bart Giamatti!" Giamatti was president of Yale at the time and later commissioner of Major League Baseball (a position the governor himself was widely rumored to have been at least "considering" or "interested in"). The audience erupted with laughter and cheers!

I've also not included in this memoir the governor's famous and controversial (to this day) "abortion" speech, "Religious Belief and Public Morality," delivered at Notre Dame in 1984. Mario worked on the Notre Dame speech for more than a month. The governor had been invited to tackle the difficult question of Catholics in the public arena, which had been put to him by the great modern theologian and Notre Dame scholar Father Richard McBrien. The point he was trying to make is simple: "I think it's already apparent that a good part of this nation understands—if only instinctively—that anything which seems to suggest that God favors a political party or the establishment of a state church is wrong and dangerous." As he said on another occasion, "I protect my right to be a Catholic by preserving your right to believe as a Jew, a Protestant, or nonbeliever, or as anything else you choose."

Incidentally, little known is the backstory told by the governor and confirmed by Matilda Cuomo about the harrowing trip out to South Bend, Indiana. Almost from the moment the small jet carrying the governor, Matilda, columnist Jimmy Breslin, and Tim Russert lifted off and headed west, the plane encountered rough air. As Mario sat alone polishing the speech, the jump jet took a sudden dive and plummeted for several minutes before the pilot regained control and found some smooth air. At which point Jimmy Breslin said, "Mario, maybe God is telling you something. Maybe he doesn't really want you to give the damn speech!"

The governor never acknowledged the sudden jolt and kept concentrating on his speech and polishing his prose. But Matilda well remembers that as a result of the sudden turbulence a large glass of orange juice on the governor's tray table was up-ended, spilling all over Mario's master copy of the historic speech.

When the intrepid flyers arrived in South Bend, they were taken directly to the president's residence, home of Father Theodore Hesburgh. As soon as they were alone in the guest room, Matilda retrieved the soaked original master copy of the famous speech and dried it with a hair dryer as she held it aloft.

Controversial though it may have been, Mario always felt that the Notre Dame speech on which he labored for many, many weeks helped turn the abortion discussion toward a more constructive and reasonable phase.

THE IONA SPEECH

Another speech that brought Mario great personal satisfaction was his 1984 Commencement Address at Iona College in Westchester. One of the graduates that year was Mario's luminous and beloved daughter Maria, now married to the designer-philanthropist Kenneth Cole. But the governor didn't aim his remarks at Maria or her classmates. Instead, he addressed himself to the parents: "How do we tell our children not to be discouraged by the imperfection of the world and the inevitability of death and diminishments?"

His Catholic faith meant a great deal to him in every season. But the governor never had quite the same kind of relationship with John

Cardinal O'Connor that he enjoyed with the present archbishop of New York, Timothy Dolan.

And yet despite some public contretemps and an oft-reported "tension" between Cardinal O'Connor and the governor, Mario had enormous respect—and considerable affection—for the outspoken prelate.

As John O'Connor lay dying, Mario wrote this beautiful piece reminding New Yorkers to look beyond the labels and headlines when assessing the whole canon of the cardinal's life work.

Greeting marchers from the steps of St. Patrick's Cathedral in his bright red skullcap and cape, or delivering a homily from its lofty pulpit, John Cardinal O'Connor is an instantly familiar face, a figure who exudes charm and grace.

Most New Yorkers, however, have little knowledge of his complicated and nuanced character as a priest and as a religious leader.

As a Catholic public figure who has felt the force of Cardinal O'Connor's strong advocacy on the subject of abortion but who knows the rest of the cardinal's work as well, it seems to me a sad irony that at a time when we have grown accustomed to learning more about most of our public figures we should know so little about this distinguished prelate.

Throughout fifteen years of indefatigable public ministering and advocacy he has carried the Church's banner in high-visibility campaigns against abortion and homosexuality. In the process he has earned a reputation as one of the Vatican's favorite conservative dogmatists and attracted a host of strident critics.

But his equally vigorous efforts on behalf of the rest of the Catholic agenda have received less attention. Over the last decade and a half the archdiocese he leads has educated, housed, cared for, comforted, and counseled hundreds of thousands of Catholic and non-Catholic New Yorkers. None of the great American philanthro-pies have done more for the most vulnerable among us. And in some cases the archdiocese has led the way for the rest of the private charities. One example in particular comes to mind.

In 1983 when HIV and AIDS suddenly struck New York like a plague, our great city nearly panicked. Frightened and confused New Yorkers began attacking "homosexuals" as the cause of the problem. People thought to be HIV-positive or suffering from AIDS were treated as pariahs. It was difficult to get bed space and doctors and nurses to accommodate victims as patients. With no need for prodding from government, the cardinal made St. Clare's Hospital in Manhattan a haven for AIDS victims. His example helped relieve the anxiety of the caregiver community and encouraged its aggressive response to what was then our most severe health crisis.

The cardinal has also advanced classic American Catholic social policy by being one of the last undiluted and proud advocates of the union movement, committed to assuring dignity and economic equality to all working men and women. And his gentle but insistent importuning has advanced ecumenism significantly, particularly with the Jewish community.

Altogether, his attempts to repair and strengthen the social fabric should have earned Cardinal O'Connor a reputation as one of the Vatican's favorite social progressives, as well as one of its premier conservative dogmatists, especially since the course he chose was such a difficult one. Both in his conservative theological approach and his more liberal position on social issues, the former admiral found himself constantly sailing against the prevailing winds in a nation that has become more material, more sexually permissive, and less willing to offer collective support for social needs.

All of this can be found in the public record, but only his advocacy against abortion and homosexuality have been memorialized in the headlines.

And there are many things not published anywhere that tell us even more about this extraordinary American spiritual leader. Things like unpublicized visits to AIDS patients and others to comfort them in their last hours; long personal letters to Catholic leaders filled with humble admissions of his own imperfection, and gentle attempts at saving people in authority from committing what he believed to be grave and dangerous errors of judgment; scores of homilies to small groups of communicants at daily Mass in the "Lady Chapel" at the rear of the great cathedral. All of these were private acts of conscience and compassion by a "Prince of the Church" who has always been a priest first.

Speaking of dying, here is how Mario thought of it. His words are also a fine tribute to his mother:

My mother was a magnificent woman. She came from another place and faced this tough new world defenseless, except for the heart of a lioness protecting her cubs, and the shield of her deep, unflinching faith.

She lived nine decades through two great wars and a number of smaller ones, through depression, recession, and several personal calamities. And then, she left us. Exhausted, wanting not to leave her children, always the lioness.

Someone saw a different picture of this kind of leaving and sent it to me and I found it to be both moving and consoling.

Here is the picture as my mother saw it:

"I am standing on the seashore. A ship at my side spreads her white sails to the breeze and starts for the blue ocean. She is an object of beauty, and I stand and watch her until at length she hangs like a speck of white cloud just where the sky and sea mingle in the mist. Then someone at my side says, 'There! She's gone!'"

Gone where? Gone from my sight, that's all.

She is just as large in mast and hull and spar as she was when she left my side, and just as able to bear her load of living freight to the place of her destination. Her diminished size is in *me*, not in her, and just at the moment when someone at my side says, "There! She's gone!" there are other eyes that are watching her *coming*, and other voices ready to take up the glad shout, "Here she comes!"

And that, dear friends, is dying.

But the playwright John Patrick Shanley observed recently, "As long as you're alive and on your feet, you have a shot at the title."

Mario would have loved the line.

7

Echoes of Greatness

WORDS OF WISDOM

Over the years, Mario came up with a number of graceful, memorable phrases that he called upon many times in order to press home an important point. His wisdom and goodness linger in these wise and pithy pronouncements and observations dispensed over the years:

Franklin Roosevelt rose from his wheelchair to lift this world from its knees.

This nation was born in gunshot and flames.

We should show a little creativity in selecting a president. Let's choose, not a hawk or a dove—but an owl who is strong enough to fight but wise enough to know when it's necessary.

New York has never been and never will be one of those quaint, restored, historic villages frozen in time. Change—constant, dynamic, unpredictable, exciting change—is part of the rhythm of New York!

You are among those who weigh my many faults and inadequacies less diligently than you assess what you may find commendable in my persona and stewardship.

Don't let us forget who we are and where we've come from. We are the sons and daughters of giants.

Instead of capital punishment . . . the taking of another life . . . I'd say, "That's it, Charlie, you're going to be by yourself for a hundred years!"

You campaign in poetry. You govern in prose.

We believe in a government strong enough to use words like *love* and *compassion* and smart enough to convert our noblest aspirations into practical realities.

We believe in a single fundamental idea that describes better than most textbooks and any speech that I could write what a proper government should be: the idea of family, mutuality, the sharing of benefits and burdens for the good of all, feeling one another's pain, sharing one another's blessings—reasonably, honestly, fairly, without respect to race, or sex, or geography, or political affiliation.

We believe in encouraging the talented, but we believe that while survival of the fittest may be a good working description of the process of evolution, a government of humans should elevate itself to a higher order.

The Republicans believe the wagon train will not make it to the frontier unless some of our old, some of our young, and some of our weak are left behind by the side of the trail. We Democrats believe that we can make it all the way with the whole family intact.

Lincoln isn't a man with ingrown toenails, he's an idea.

A shining city is perhaps all [President Ronald Reagan] sees from the portico of the White House and the veranda of his ranch, where everyone seems to be doing well. But there's another part to the shining city. In this part there are more poor than ever, more families in trouble, more and more people who need help but can't find it.

For me to make lasagna would be a desecration of a great Italian dish.... I don't mess with sacred things.

Every time I've done something that doesn't feel right, it's ended up not being right.

When you've parked the second car in the garage, and installed the hot tub, and skied in Colorado, and wind-surfed in the Caribbean, when you've had your first love affair and your second and your third, the question will remain, where does the dream end for me?

I watched a small man with thick calluses on both hands work fifteen and sixteen hours a day. I saw him once literally bleed from the bottoms of his feet, a man who came here uneducated, alone, unable to speak the language, who taught me all I needed to know about faith and hard work by the simple eloquence of his example.

We must get the American public to look past the glitter, beyond the showmanship, to the reality, the hard substance of things. And we'll do it not so much with speeches that will bring people to their feet as with speeches that bring people to their senses.

How simple it seems now. We thought the Sermon on the Mount was a nice allegory and nothing more. What we didn't understand until we got to be a little older was that it was the whole answer, the whole truth. That the way—the only way—to succeed and to be happy is to learn those rules so basic that a shepherd's son could teach them to an ignorant flock without notes or formulae.

In this life, you should read everything you can read. Taste everything you can taste. Meet everyone you can meet. Travel everywhere you can travel. Learn everything you can learn. Experience everything you can experience.

The American people need no course in philosophy or political science or church history to know that God should not be made into a celestial party chairman.

The beauty of America is that I don't have to deny my past to affirm my present. No one does. We can love this nation like a parent and still embrace our ancestral home like cherished grandparents.

I love bunt plays. I love the idea of a bunt. I love the idea of the sacrifice. Even the word is good. Giving yourself up for the good of the whole.

I don't want to be a big man. I know who I am.

Life is motion, not joy. If the way you measure success in life is by how much joy it brings you, you're measuring inaccurately. Life is also sadness, defeat, striving.

I am the one who believes that the world goes from the slime to the sublime. And you can take Darwin and all your philosophers and all your ontologists, and that's the direction.

What would you say on your tombstone? I know what I would say: "Mario Cuomo, 1932–" and, "He tried."

Religion is extremely important in this democracy—so important that it occupies a prime position in the Bill of Rights.

Lincoln had bad press, too. He wasn't appreciated until after he was gone. My favorite thought about Abraham Lincoln is [that] he believed in two things: loving one another and working together to make this world better.

I love immigrants. Legal, illegal—they're not to be despised.

Decide exactly what you want to achieve. Do you want to help people, or do you want to be powerful?

I have no quarrel with people seeing me as a sinner.

I talk and talk and talk, and I haven't taught people in fifty years what my father taught me by example in one week.

America was born in outrageous ambition, so bold as to be im-probable. The deprived, the oppressed, the powerless from all over the globe came here with little more than the desire to realize themselves.

I am a trial lawyer. Matilda says that at dinner on a good day I sound like an affidavit.

The price of seeking to force our beliefs on others is that someday they might force their beliefs on us.

Most of us have achieved levels of affluence and comfort unthought of two generations ago. We've never had it so good, most of us. Nor have we ever complained so bitterly about our problems. The closed circle of materialism is clear to us now—aspirations become wants, wants become needs, and self-gratification becomes a bottomless pit.

Tell me, ladies and gentlemen, are we the ones to tell our children what their instructors have tried to teach them for years? That the philosophers were right. That Saint Francis, Buddha, Muhammad, Maimonides—all spoke the truth when they said the only way to serve yourself is to serve others; and that Aristotle was right, before them, when he said the only way to assure yourself happiness is to learn to give happiness.

An unborn child is, at the very least, potentially human and not to be treated causally.

I'm a good man in the ontological sense.

CUOMO ON THE FAIRNESS DOCTRINE

Mario Cuomo was always quite a glorious champion of free speech and the First Amendment. Over the years we had countless conversations on the subject. He used to accuse me of being a First Amendment "voluptuary," an appellation I proudly embraced. When the Congress, driven by Democrats, came close to reviving the so-called "Fairness Doctrine" with legislation that had previously been vetoed by President Ronald Reagan (at the urging of my dear friend of many years, the legendary Midwest broadcaster-statesman Ward Quaal), MMC spoke boldly and bravely against the doctrine's reimposition or any other incursion against free expression that the Congress or government bureaucrats might dream up.

> Broadcasting has such immense impact on our lives: it is important to our politics, our governance, our economy, and our culture. We must protect it.
>
> Underlying and supporting our system, and the entire Constitution that built it, is a specific working principle: the people who will always remain the ultimate authority must have freedom of expression. Now, from the beginning, it's been clear this extraordinary gift—the right to speak, to advocate, to describe, to dissent, to sing—is not just a wonderful privilege that makes this democracy the miracle that it is.
>
> The Founding Fathers gave us this freedom of expression—not tentatively, not embroidered with nuances, not shrouded and bound up in conditions, but plainly and purely.
>
> The government that seizes First Amendment power from the people develops an appetite for power that can be sated only by consuming more of the peoples' liberty.

This nation was born in gunshot and flames, driven by a passion for freedom. For two hundred years we have fought for freedom and given up lives for it. But we are a rational people as well as a bold people, and we know that freedom brings with it responsibilities. The marvelous self-correcting instincts of our exquisite separation of powers insists on balancing these two: freedom and responsibilities. And where freedom is abused, laws and rulings will spring up to correct the abuse, by diminishing the freedom. And let broadcasters or journalists be guilty of excessive bad taste, dangerous incitement, reckless reporting, pervasively biased opinion and analysis, yes, palpable unfairness, and they will be inviting laws and rulings the Founding Fathers would have abhorred.

I would urge broadcasters and journalists to remember that you have the ability to uplift. But that implies the capacity to demean. You can unfold for us the majesty of Creation and humanity's masterpieces. But you can also teach a child a taste for violence or encourage a fascination with perversity and inflicted pain. You have the power to instruct, but it implies the power to distort. You can make things darker, meaner, uglier than they are. Or broadcasters who reach millions and millions with your sights and sounds and words can make us fuller, surer, sweeter than we are. As long as you continue to treat your power and privilege with the respect it deserves, you'll preserve for yourselves the freedom to help us develop the richest and wisest culture ever.

LADY LIBERTY

Mario loved the Statue of Liberty. He used its wonderful symbolism and shining example in many speeches. One of his loveliest tributes to Our Lady in the Harbor was written thirty years ago in the form of a letter to his then-sixteen-year-old youngest son, Christopher. *New York* magazine printed the entire piece when the statue was given one of its periodic refurbishments.

Our youngest son, Christopher, recently asked me why everyone was making such a fuss over the Statue of Liberty. I tried to explain it to him the way my parents explained it to me.

My mother and father came from another country. My mother came here by ship from Italy, and her first glimpse of this great country was when she sighted the Lady of Opportunity, steadfastly lifting her torch.

My mother understood immediately the meaning of that beautiful symbol. To her, the Statue meant freedom and opportunity, a chance to earn one's own bread with dignity. The Statue told my mother that if she and my father were willing to work hard and care about this nation, they would be able to share in its incredible bounties. And this new country would not ask them, or force them, to give up the culture of their parents. Lady Liberty said, "Welcome. You are welcome, and the culture you bring with you is welcome, to blend with all the others into this beautiful mosaic that is America."

America was made into steel and stone by the flesh and bone and muscle of people like my parents, from every corner of the world. Guided by the beacon of hope that the Statue of Liberty represented, they settled across New York state and throughout the five boroughs of New York City. To the Lower East Side, to South Jamaica, to Hell's Kitchen, to Williamsburg, to Brownsville and the South Bronx, these "strangers" came to this strange land and quickly made it their home, investing the equity of their labor in their new communities.

Our neighborhood in South Jamaica was then poor and lower middle class, made up of Irish, Italians, blacks, Poles, Jews—a classic polyglot community: immigrants and the sons and daughters of immigrants from Europe, the East, the South; people who had come to New York for opportunity but were only beginning to find it.

We had an Italian American grocery store on the corner of 150th Street and 97th Avenue, and on the other corner, down the block, there was an Orthodox synagogue. And between us were Lanzone the baker, Rubin the roofer, and Kaye the tailor. We lived in rooms behind the store in a building owned by the Kesslers. The Kesslers taught my mother how to count, and she taught Mrs. Kessler how to make tomato sauce—à la marinara, without meat.

Together, we taught one another, learned from one another, shared tears when a neighbor down the block passed away, felt joy at each bar mitzvah, Holy Communion, or wedding our friends celebrated. We were family, sharing burdens and benefits, birth and death, good times and bad.

We had—from different lands, with different customs—come through the Golden Door, beckoned by the same beacon of hope, the same promise of opportunity.

We were family, and although we were aware of our differences, we didn't think so much about them. Instead, there was a commonality among us, a commonality of need and concern and striving that helped form us into the American mosaic.

The Statue of Liberty will always remind me, and millions of others, of that striving, of that commonality of need, of the responsibility we have for one another's welfare. It reminds us that together we have bridged rivers, put up buildings that pierce the sky, elevated the arts to new levels, defeated depressions, and reached down to lift up millions of immigrants who came to this country with little more than the clothes on their back and the children in their arms.

In celebrations across New York state and throughout America, we commemorate the restoration of the Statue and the reaffirmation of that spirit—the dream that brought our ancestors past the Statue's lamp to Ellis Island and then into this magnificent land.

What's all the fuss about, Chris? It's about a struggle by millions who came before us to create a new society of opportunity and tolerance. It reminds us how, beginning with nothing but their hands and their hearts and their minds, they built this beautiful country and gave it to us and left us the obligation to make it a better one.

"YOU ARE THE SUN"

Before he became governor of New York, Mario Cuomo served as lieutenant governor under Governor Hugh L. Carey, and prior to that he was New York's secretary of state (1975–78). Few people will recall, but he also ran for mayor of New York City back in the seventies. At each stage of his political career, Mario Cuomo dazzled audiences all over the state. Here are some remarks delivered at the New York State Labor–Religion Coalition Conference in Albany on February 22, 1982.

For too many of us, there are no more noble causes, nothing beautiful to believe in. "Where have you gone, Joe DiMaggio?"

But now we see the beginning of a new period, an awakening, a reminder of old lessons temporarily forgotten. We remember with pride that we are a nation that believed in justice and love— unashamedly and relentlessly; that we fought wars in the name of virtues. We fought them abroad and even among ourselves.

We are beginning to see again more clearly what has always been true: that these are the things our religious leaders have been trying to tell us from the beginning. What else did Buddha, Maimonides, Christ, Gandhi, and Martin Luther King say but "justice and love"?

Some of us now appreciate more fully what John Courtney Murray meant when he told us involvement in the issues of the day was a better road to sanctification than the basket-weaving done by contemplatives to fill the grim interval between birth and eternity.

The unions carried the tablets into the mean streets and valleys and, holding them on high, struggled for recognition. They embodied—probably for the most part without suspecting it—what Teilhard de Chardin later called the "Christian perception of human endeavor." For them, whether they would accept its theological implications or not, they demonstrated what Chardin urged when he said, "God is waiting for us in our work of the moment. He is at the tip of my pen, my spade, my brush, my needle, of my heart and of my thought. Work is the truth."

No one ever said it better than that great French priest who reminded us that what we do today we do in and for God, by whatever name we call Him.

Teilhard said it this way: "Lift up your head. Look at the enormous crowds of those who build and seek. All over the world men are toiling—in laboratories, in studios, in deserts, in factories—in the vast social crucible. Welcome humanity! Accept the burgeoning plant of humanity and tend it, since without your sun it will disperse itself wildly and die away."

How perfect a marriage you have made: the world of religion and the world of labor.

You are the sun.

Try to cheer up, you guys! (*Left to right*) The author, the governor, and the author's son David Tucker O'Shaughnessy, now president of Whitney Media. (Wendy Moger-Bross)

When once giants worked the land of politics! A rare photo taken at the Executive Mansion on Eagle Street in Albany. (*Left to right*) Former Governor Malcolm Wilson; Perry Duryea, the Montauk lobsterman who became the powerful speaker of the New York State Assembly; the governor; and Sol Wachtler, chief judge of the Court of Appeals. (Don Pollard)

Mario's last hurrah! Celebrating Andrew's election to a second term as governor with Matilda at the New York Sheraton in 2014, one of Mario's last public appearances. (Don Pollard)

Party labels don't matter. The governor always had high regard for the affable Jonathan Bush. Brother of President George H.W. Bush and uncle of President George W., Jonathan is also the father of TV host William "Billy" Bush. (Wendy Moger-Bross)

For many admirers of Mario Cuomo, this is their favorite photo. It was taken at the Hotel Syracuse after an exhausting all-day visit to the New York State Fair in 1986. (Don Pollard)

The governor and New York State Inspector General Joe Spinelli, a Cuomo favorite. Executive Chamber staffers beat the State Police (just barely) 7 to 6 in the game. Mario hit two home runs. Shortstop Spinelli made a dazzling play at second base. Mario yelled from the mound, "You're so short . . . I thought you were going to miss that!" (Don Pollard)

"I know how to spell 'Malcolm.'" Mario and Malcolm Wilson share a laugh at the naming of the Tappan Zee Bridge for the great Westchester orator and former governor. Mario said of Malcolm, "He would defeat you in English . . . and finish you off in *Latin*!" The sign misspelled Wilson's first name as "Malcom"! It was quickly replaced.

Confab at one of our WVOX studios. (*Left to right*) The governor, the author, and New York State Supreme Court Justice Samuel George Fredman, an early Cuomo supporter and a towering figure in Jewish affairs and the Democratic Party.

Our first radio interview. "This guy was so damn bright, I wanted to get the hell out of the studio." At this precise moment we were discussing capital punishment. "Vengeance doesn't work . . . it just doesn't work," said Mario. After the program, I started calling Democrats, "Who is this guy? Who the hell is he . . . ?"

Stickball champ! "Don't name a bridge or tunnel after me—just a remote stickball alley somewhere in Queens!" (Don Pollard)

"Is this the way they dress in Westchester, O'Shaughnessy? I want this coat! I mean I *must* have it!" (Don Pollard)

Bill,   May 2001

When you glance at this from time
to time, remember how grateful we
are for all you have done and meant
to me.

        With love,

                    Mario + Matilda

A personal note, one of many that I treasure—as I do his generous friendship. And Matilda's of many years.

Mario had some fun at my expense during one of our earlier book parties. "That face, that face . . . ! I can't stand it!" The governor always said *he* had a face for radio! (Whitney Media Archives)

SPEECH AT ST. JAMES CATHEDRAL

This stunning thirty-year-old talk delivered in St. James Cathedral in Brooklyn was praised by Notre Dame's Father Theodore Hesburgh, who found it better even than Mario's historic speech at Notre Dame. Could any bishop, cardinal—or even a pope-have done better? This, I respectfully suggest, is one of the governor's very best. I was there in Brooklyn that day, October 2, 1986, to witness its power and beauty.

It's a great privilege for me to be asked to speak at St. James Cathedral.

The truth is, we all need guidance, and I come here tonight not so much to instruct as to learn.

Certainly, I do not come here as a theologian: I do not have that competence.

Nor am I competent to speak to you as a philosopher.

I am here as an old-fashioned Catholic who sins, regrets, struggles, worries, gets confused, and most of the time feels better after Confession.

And I am here as a politician and public official who has found that trying to be both, as a Catholic, has raised some questions.

I started to think seriously about being a Catholic right here in Brooklyn—at St. John's Prep and later at St. John's College, where I first began to regard my faith as something worth struggling to understand more fully.

And later, as I moved into other phases of my life, it was in Brooklyn, too, that I married Matilda, we had our first child, and I worked at the practice of law—at a time when the Church, through the deliberations of the Second Vatican Council, was moving into another phase of *its* life.

Amid all the changes in the Church's life, and my own, Brooklyn changed too, in many ways.

Real estate development, demographic patterns, and changing attitudes took their toll. Some parishes merged or closed. Congregations dwindled.

There is no secret to St. James's success. It has utilized the oldest and most obvious strength of Christianity—a broad, deep emphasis on a life of love. It has committed itself to what a cathedral church was in medieval times: the symbol of a city that belonged to all people, a place where the blessings of life were celebrated and the burdens shared.

St. James has worked as hard as any parish in this city—or, for that matter, in this state and nation—to love the world. To marry its mission to all the needs of its people—their need for physical as well as spiritual sustenance, for song, celebration, beauty, and art.

We are living through a time of turbulence in the Church's history.

This is a time of disagreement, public dissent, and debate.

That debate has been in two areas principally.

Recently it has involved dissent from Church doctrine between and among theologians and members of the hierarchy.

A second—and distinctly separate—part of the public debate involved the Church and politicians.

The more difficult debate for me is the theological discussion on Church doctrine and on teaching authority in the Church—on questions like the role of theologians and pastors and their relationship to those who exercise juridical authority over the area of doctrine.

It is not uncommon for people who share a great deal—people even part of the same family—to find themselves sometimes at odds, their closeness sometimes marred by suspicion or distrust.

As my opportunities and experiences broadened, my father, especially, feared that I was moving away from his world. And despite all his ambitions for me, despite the pride he felt, I think that troubled him.

He never said so, but I could sense it. I could see it in his face, hear it in his voice.

It took him a while to adjust to what were for him new ways, new emphases, different truths.

But gradually I realized that whatever success I had, however many degrees I obtained, whatever money I earned, however comfortable in my new identity I seemed, the deepest part of me belonged to him and my mother, and what they were.

I carried in my heart their values, their sense of family, their faith.

And those things were more profound, more important, more enduring than the differences that developed over the years.

Only gradually did my father come to understand this, to know that his son in a suit and tie, with the big desk and the office, the son who seemed so at home in another language, another world, was bound to him and my mother in ways that could never be broken.

Bound to them by love for them, for whom they were and what they stood for.

The Church is a family, like mine, like yours. After all the headache and the heartache of the moment's contentions, that will prove to be the greater truth.

The early Church was a church journeying through history with a still-forming sense of its identity and mission. Ambiguity, restlessness, incompleteness, an eagerness to probe, refine, to deepen understanding, did not cause the "gates of hell to prevail against the Church." In fact, they led to a deeper, more vibrant faith.

So, while the Church struggles to discern where the spirit is leading it, on questions like the role of the laity, particularly of women, church–state relationships, even the precise meaning of subtle doctrines, we should be neither surprised nor unduly threatened because people disagree about what the answers to these questions are.

In my own experience, I was part of a discussion over how we, as Catholics, having *agreed* on what we believe as doctrinal truth, were called upon to relate our belief to our political world. More specifically, we were asked to consider how a Catholic politician should exercise political judgment in an area where the Church's moral teaching is clear.

The question I, and many others, struggled over was to what extent my belief, my full acceptance of Catholic moral teaching—in such areas as birth control, abortion, divorce, capital punishment—bound me to work to make my belief the law in a pluralistic society such as ours where millions of decent and good people believed differently than I.

At Notre Dame, I stated my belief that as a Catholic I was a partner in the Church's salvific mission and was bound by its moral teachings, but that the Church did not require me to pursue that mission according to a precisely defined political plan or strategy.

Nor did it require me, as a matter of doctrine, to engage the political system in a struggle to have it adopt every article of its belief as part of public morality.

The Church has often made the decision to abide by the civil law on questions of moral conduct where the law's direction ran counter to the Church's teaching.

On birth control, for example, and even capital punishment—one area where the Church's instruction was pointed directly at government—the Church had decided *not* to insist that the moral values it teaches be the law of the land for our pluralistic society. Even on the question of slavery in the 1850s a barely established Church thought it prudent *not* to make a political fight over the elemental moral proposition.

At Notre Dame I did not suggest, however, that the freedom to disagree with the Church's political strategy on the abortion question would excuse doing *nothing* to proclaim our belief. I urged that, in the present climate, where not everyone accepts what Catholics and others believe, we must begin with ourselves, proving the beauty and worth of our instruction.

The central truth—the Church's *principal* teaching—is that Christ calls on us to be centers of his energy by working not with force or wealth to change the world but by using the weapons of the Word and of love.

He calls us to share our truth—not just by legislating its acceptance—but by being living examples of it. By accepting the terrible risk of loving each other the way he loved the world.

This is the simple, astounding truth that is the greatest mystery of our belief. This is the great mission of the Church, a mission that has endured through all the tumult of 2,000 years.

We are called to be the salt of the earth, the light of the world, entering the world as He entered it, not to sit in judgment, not to condemn, but to heal and enlighten. To bring the light of His hope into all the arenas of our lives—social, political, economic, and cultural.

To affirm with our lives the revolutionary idea that we are our brother's and sister's keeper. And that the responsibility to love is higher, wider, deeper than any of our differences.

We all agree on that: cardinals, bishops, priests, nuns, brothers, the lay people. From the beginning until now.

And the Church's work of love goes on, day in and day out, in thousands and thousands of places, unnoticed by the unconcerned, unnoted by the media.

When a priest, in the twenty-fifth year of his ministry to the people of the South Bronx, climbs up into the pulpit this Sunday to offer his congregation the message of a God of joy and hope, there will be no network coverage of this miracle of one man offering his life to all these others—in the name of Christ's love.

When a thirty-year-old Sister of Charity makes her rounds this evening in the hospice where she tends victims of AIDS abandoned by the world, there will be no reporter inquiring as to how the call of Christ's love brought her to this place and this service.

When the Franciscans fill the plates and cups of the scores of shivering, homeless, hungry souls who come to St. Francis of Assisi on 31st Street in Manhattan, where love is measured by the things that permit survival, no pictures will be taken for the next day's centerfold.

There are a thousand times a thousand wonders being worked in this city by people bearing to the world the outrageous belief we share. And none of them will be in tomorrow's news.

We have dissent and argument enough to occupy us. But there is no dissent on the obligation to feed the hungry, to shelter the homeless, to care for the ill, to educate the young, to work to provide everyone with the dignity of a job, to find ways to console those who are broken in body or soul, and to dedicate ourselves to the vision of a society that is as inclusive as the kingdom that Christ came among us to found.

That—more than the complex and nuanced differences among theologians—is the fundamental strength of this amazing institution we call the Church, which has survived the 2,000 years since the message was first heard, the message it will be uttering and living until prophecy becomes eternity.

Teilhard de Chardin, himself the survivor of a lifetime of contention and debate, in just a few magnificent sentences said it better than I and most of us ever could. Talking about what truly matters, about our obligations to involve ourselves in things of this world, he wrote these words:

> Lift up your hearts! Look at the immense crowds of those who build and those who love.
>
> Over the world they toil—in laboratories, in studios, in factories—in the vast social crucible.
>
> Open your arms and your hearts, like Christ your Lord, and welcome the flood and the sweat of humanity.

Accept it all, be part of it all, Teilhard said. For without becoming part of it, what hope have we of the kingdom?

Teilhard's words and the lively, world-loving faith of St. James's parish are worth thinking about as this diverse family that is the Church struggles toward that kingdom.

DIVERSITY IN AMERICA: "THE NEW IMMIGRANTS"

This speech about diversity in America and the new immigrants, delivered June 7, 2000, resonates even now, sixteen years after Mario stood at the lectern in the great ballroom of the Waldorf Astoria in New York. Even the captains, waiters, and busboys applauded.

One of our greatest gifts is the rich diversity we are allowed as Americans.

And despite the world's skepticism two centuries ago, it certainly has proven to be a good prescription for building a new nation.

The world said it couldn't be done. A great nation could not be assembled from fragments of other cultures, joined together permanently by the idea that human beings are *inalienably* entitled to life, liberty, and the pursuit of happiness.

But in 1776 the call went out from a small group of immigrants in a new and wild land, struggling against a powerful oppressor. And ever since, people from all over the world have responded.

Millions left their birthplace to join in building a unique republican democracy—freer than any nation on earth, and still remarkably well-ordered by an extraordinary legal system.

Now, after 200 years, we have made our nation the world's most powerful economy, military force, and engine of opportunity.

We could not have done it without the immigrants.

Nothing was built. *No* war was won. *No* new level of progress ever reached, without them.

Immigrants from Europe claimed the new land, rejected the foreign oppressor, and participated in writing the documents that established a unique new nation.

Immigrants from all parts of the world have supplied workers, entrepreneurs, soldiers, judges, artists, philosophers, scientists, and religious leaders.

They shared with us their culture as we worked to create our own.

And as they have been vital to our past, they are indispensable to our future.

That's especially evident here in New York, where *so many* of us are from other places that it's hard to think of *any of us* as an alien.

Immigration has been the protein of New York's life, giving it sustenance and strength and growth.

The continuous new waves of immigrants have nourished this multi-layered, polyglot, pulsating crowd of humanity. Together, we've built the great World City.

Many of the immigrants stayed a lifetime.

Others spread from here to the rest of our nation, reseeding it with their twin cultures, relishing America's unique prerogative: *here* you can affirm the *present* without having to deny your *past*.

New York needs the immigrants now more than ever, and so does the rest of the nation.

Our Social Security and Medicare systems depend upon today's workers paying for today's elderly. At the current rate at which we are producing native-born Americans, we will soon not have enough workers to support our growing number of elderly.

At the same time, our education system has not produced enough high-skilled workers to meet the needs of our high-tech industries, so this year we will seek 200,000 more computer engineers from other nations.

We will continue to rely on immigrants.

And they will come.

They will not be exactly like my parents' generation.

They won't be part of the "huddled masses."

The color and accent of most of them will be different.

And their skill and education level will almost surely be higher.

But they will come, *yearning to breathe free* the air of opportunity.

And they will come bearing gifts.

In addition to skills, the replenishment of our work force, and the willingness to work hard, they will provide a *fresh appreciation* of the glorious good fortune all Americans enjoy, and an *eagerness* to contribute at the highest level they can reach.

The honorees can describe their gratitude and pride, eloquently, *in the English language.*

My mother and father would have not been able to do that. They were immigrants too, but they came speaking only the rough dialect of their small community in the mountains of Salerno, and they were never given a chance to be educated here.

They arrived as the Great Depression began to drag down the nation and soon found themselves with two children, no money, and no work.

There was no welfare or unemployment insurance or Medicare or Medicaid or housing vouchers.

And in their poor neighborhood of South Jamaica, Queens, on the other side of the tracks, there were no charities either.

They were rescued by a couple who owned a small grocery store, other immigrants from Poland, Harry and Ruby Kessler.

Harry had to run the store but suffered a heart attack and needed someone to do the physical work. In exchange, he provided a large room behind the store with a toilet, a black tub, a coal stove, enough to eat, and a few dollars a week.

Harry and Ruby Kessler saved Momma and Poppa and their kids.

But they weren't able to teach them to speak, read, and write any kind of decent English.

Or to appreciate more fully the world around them.

Indeed, Harry's and Ruby's own command of the language was a limited one. And in those years before television and the computer, their understanding of the culture that surrounded them hardly reached beyond the simple daily patterns and lifestyle of their own tenement community.

The Kesslers and the Cuomos of the early twentieth century in South Jamaica, Queens, accomplished more than anyone had the right to expect of them.

But it pains me to think of how these bright, proud, ambitious, God-fearing, family-loving, hardworking new Americans were stifled by a lack of education.

How it tied their tongues and imprisoned their intelligence.

It hurts to think of what they might have been, what they might have given, what they could have enjoyed, if only someone, somehow, had taught them the language.

With the language they would have taught themselves all the rest.

A thousand volunteers—many themselves immigrants—teach thousands of immigrants every year the English language and American culture.

Empowering them, enriching their contributions to our society, enhancing their enjoyment of the gift of life in America they cherish, and deserve.

For all the celebrating and even exultation in this room tonight, there are other people in other places, deriding immigrants as fragmentors of the American culture, and pledging to use their political and economic strength—in the words of one of the more prominent of them—"to stem the flow of foreigners into our great country."

People like that have been with us from the beginning.

Their own forebears were immigrants: they themselves may even have been.

But once they were safely ensconced here, they decided America should take up the gangplank and lock the gates against all but temporary visitors, lest they be required to share our abundance with people not lucky enough to have been born just a generation or so sooner.

There were people like that even before the Know-Nothings and Nativists of the nineteenth century.

Later, in the 1950s, they talked about "mongrelization" by Slavs and Mediterraneans.

And after that they warned America was being overrun by people of color.

They tried to bar, then oust, the Irish.

They cursed and mocked the Jews.

They treated my parents with snide condescension at best.

They talked ominously about putting "America first."

Their negativism persists and it is distasteful, but it affects our politics.

And us, to this day.

HELP THE WORLD REMEMBER

This beautiful speech on October 25, 2000, before the Westchester Holocaust Commission was widely heralded by Jewish leaders across the nation.

Some months ago one of our newspapers requested a letter to my grandchildren. They had asked me to offer my grandchildren a perspective on what they can anticipate in the life that stretches out before them in the new millennium.

I wrote some predictable things, things most people would write to their grandchildren, and I tried to share one basic idea that I, like a lot of other people, have struggled with for most of my adulthood. I told the grandchildren, or tried to at least, that if they paid attention in school, learned all about computers and the other wondrous tools of technology being created it seems almost every day, and worked very hard, they would probably do very well, materially, in life. They'd certainly make a good living, have all the day-to-day necessities and probably a lot of the luxuries, too.

And then I added that for many people all the accumulating of material goods proved not to be enough to make them truly happy, that at some point in your life, after you've won the struggle for survival, just filling your own little basket of appetites with goodies may leave you feeling empty. You may discover that to be fulfilled requires something else, some fundamental belief, some basic purpose in life that gives you a sense of meaningfulness and significance, that answers the question for you, "Why was I born in the first place?" And "What is my mission in life?" Without an answer to that question, all the frantic gathering of material goods can become nothing more than a frenetic fidgeting in an attempt to fill the space between birth and eternity.

I told them how hard it was, for me and for most people, to find the answer they need. Many of us look for it for a lifetime and die without it. So I offered them the thoughts I had been able to put together for whatever they were worth, and this is what I said.

The older grandchildren found most of the letter familiar, because we had discussed these things before. I told them more than once how all my life I had witnessed Jewish people living the principles of *Tzedakah* and *Tikkun Olam* and helping my own immigrant mother and father survive the Great Depression and earn a living that allowed them to give me and their other children the benefit of an education and a good life they never had themselves; and how for years I had watched the children and grandchildren of Jewish immigrants, who have received abundantly from this miracle called America, giving back even more abundantly, building a stronger, sweeter American community, for the Jewish people, certainly, but not just for the Jews—for all of us together as Americans, supporting education and art and music and health care and research and human rights and civil rights.

I told my granddaughters that the Jewish people are one of the best examples we can find of the idea of community, people coming together to share benefits and burdens for the good of all. I told them that is the only way we are able to finish the work God left us to do, by sharing our strengths to combat our weaknesses.

One of my grandchildren listened carefully and, for the most part I thought, approvingly. But then in the middle of the discussion she asked a question which will occur to all of them eventually, the question which has tormented today's Jews, and many of us who are not Jews, for a lifetime. She said, "But Grandpa, if the Jewish people have been such good people for so long, why were so many of them killed in the Holocaust?"

I was silent. I reached for an answer or an explanation for why. I had no answer. I tried to change the subject but she asked again, "Why did they kill them, Grandpa?" You scan your recollection for all the vague responses you've thought of or heard before: it was a religious thing, it was a political thing, it was because the Jews have always insisted upon being different and some people are frightened by different. None of these things seem persuasive enough to share, so you tell her, frustrated by your inability to do any better, "We don't really understand, sweetheart. What we do know is that the Holocaust was one of the most horrible things that ever happened, and we must never let it happen again. Grandpa will talk to you about it again when you get older."

And you wonder if you'll ever get old enough to learn a better answer. Then you go over it all again in your mind. You remember how hard it was even to get New York state, the great liberal bastion of America, to face up to the reality of the Holocaust, how they refused to teach it in their schools until finally a law was signed in

1994 requiring it. Why is so much of the world so ready to pretend that this enormous horror never happened? I know there were some good people who in many ways, including risking or losing their life during the war, came to the aid of the Jewish people. I know that. But why were so many willing to turn their back on millions victimized and martyred by Nazism, so willing to obscure, to diffuse, to deny the reality of the war against the Jews, to forget the lessons of the Final Solution? And why does anti-Semitism persist—a disease which seems to be immune to destruction, waning, perhaps, from time to time, but never quite disappearing, always capable of reasserting its malignant presence, in terrorist attacks on the streets of Paris and swastikas smeared on the walls of synagogues on Long Island—Jews accused of being Jews, singled out, vilified, threatened, and not just by the Nazis?

Those who staffed and operated the machinery of genocide were not just black-booted Nazi soldiers or monsters like Eichmann, whose very name still echoes a kind of blasphemy. For every murderer with blood on his or her hands, there were thousands of others whose day-to-day cooperation made the act possible—those who had a mouth but did not speak, ears but did not hear, eyes but did not see: the typists who typed the lists and inventories, the clerks who filed them, supervisors who initialed them, a vast number of ordinary people doing ordinary jobs, acting as though genocide was an ordinary occurrence.

The truth is that the barbarians by whose hands the atrocities occurred were aided and abetted by armies of people who chose not to oppose them, as barbarians almost always are, aided by those who refused to notice or refused to care or refused to speak up, those who chose not to resist the annihilation of human decency, of mercy, of love. God bless the good people who helped: the Christians, the nonbelievers, the righteous Gentiles.

But why were there so many who failed to help? Was it weakness? Was it ignorance? Some of us have been asking these questions, and my granddaughter's question, for half a century since the end of World War II and the first revelation of the Holocaust. For a time, as a society we tried to put the memory away. It was simply too terrible to contemplate. It was not that we forgot. For any of us alive then, the impression on our minds created by the great horrors of the time is indelible. Whether we experienced the Holocaust firsthand, God forbid, or learned about the atrocities through radio or newsreels or the stories of survivors and liberators, no one of my generation is in any danger of ever forgetting it. But it seems that some distance was required before our society as a whole could face the whole truth of what occurred. In the intervening years, two generations have been born and grown now to adulthood. They're raising a third generation, like my grandchildren. Not having borne witness to this terrible event, those who have come after us can have only a small inkling of what the Holocaust was, and for that reason ways have to be found to preserve the truth—all of it. The truth about the pitiless slaughter of millions of human beings, the truth about the valor and dignity of those who somehow survived. Ways have to be found to teach it as it actually happened, not in some dry, aloof history-book way but in a vivid, memorable way, so the world does not forget that the words "Holocaust" and "Jews" are inseparable.

To neglect the truth would be a grievous sin against the memory of those who suffered and died and those who suffered and survived, a sin against a people persecuted across thirty centuries because of the God they worship.

Judge Sam Fredman and the rest of you who do the work of your commission and support that work by being here tonight understand all this. You understand that if we fail to convey to our people, especially to our younger people, the meaning and magnitude of the Holocaust, they may never comprehend the full implications of the worst human impulses of hatred, racism, and anti-Semitism. They may fail to understand that using an ethnic slur and planning a Final Solution are links in the same terrible chain. They might not be able to recognize the seeds of new terror if they don't understand what was done in modern Europe to the Jews. The good people that run the commission understand that until the hatred disappears, until we no longer hear the horror stories of bombings and murder, these are lessons we must never dare stop teaching. And they understand there is another lesson in the Holocaust that we must not allow to fade, this one an inspiring lesson demonstrated magnificently by the heroic souls in the Warsaw ghetto, in the Minsk ghetto, in Auschwitz, in Treblinka, in a thousand unrecorded places: the indomitable human spirit that cannot be crushed by any tyranny or oppression.

This, too, must be taught, for the agony and glorious courage will probably never grow too distant to be felt by Jewish children. We must help all our people, especially our children, Jewish and non-Jews, feel history's pounding heart. That's what this commission does. It reaches out in a special way to the people who would probably not be hearing about the Holocaust from their families, and perhaps not from their schools either. But the leaders of the Westchester Holocaust Commission have asked us all here tonight to assist in this vital effort to help the world remember those who stood up in history's darkest, most abysmal corners and fought back against hopeless odds in the Warsaw ghetto, in the Minsk ghetto; the squads of Jewish partisans, the nameless freedom fighters, who kept their proud, passionate spirit alive until machines and sheer numbers ground them into the earth, fallen but still uncrushed, scattered but not obliterated—the seeds of a new and ancient nation unconquered, unconquerable.

They have us here to help them, to help the world to remember the shame of the people who might have stepped forward but did not, and the glory of the people who chose to help because justice was more dear to them than even their own safety. The story the commission is telling is unique. It is precious to everyone, Jew and non-Jew alike, and everyone who cares about the survival of freedom, about the values that make us human, about the destiny of this earth we were given to repair.

And the remembrance will be more than resurrected grief or recollected sorrow, more than ritualist speeches or even prayers. The lessons of the Holocaust can create a new respect for life and for that which resists hatred and needless bloodshed, the slaughter of innocents, and all of the evil harbingers of a failed humanity. Thanks to all of you, the commission will teach more and more of our people the meaning of *Tzedakah* and charity and *Tikkun Olam*, the need to be collaborators in the creation of a better world so that the sacrifice made by all the victims of the Holocaust will renew in us a belief in the promise that Isaiah heard for the whole: "I create in Jerusalem a rejoicing and in her a people, a joy. And I will rejoice in Jerusalem and joy in my people. And the voice of weeping shall be no more heard in her, nor the voice of crying."

Shalom.

GOVERNOR MARIO M. CUOMO AT THE CATHEDRAL OF SAINT JOHN THE DIVINE

On Sunday, April 13, 2002, Mario stood in the magnificent Cathedral of Saint John the Divine in Manhattan to welcome a new rector to the famous Episcopal church. He touched on many subjects.

9/11.

In one horrifying moment on that tragic day all our petty desires and concerns, and much more that we thought was important, went up in a giant cloud of black smoke that rose to the heavens above New York like a terrible lamentation.

Thousands were killed or injured: millions have been spiritually wounded.

It is a heart-searing page that will never be torn from our calendar. *Two* images were forever burned into our nation's memory on 9/11.

The first, foreign assassins who hated us so much they were willing to give up their own lives to take ours. And the second, heroic Americans who loved humanity so profoundly they charged into the flames and smoke, risking their own lives to save the lives of innocent victims who were strangers to them.

Hate and love—in a war to the death that will continue for years to come.

Then, as we struggle to reorient ourselves to the ordinary chores and challenges of our life, some of us are fortunate enough to hear a *voice* reminding us that with all of the sadness and confusion, *one* thing remains certain: the greatest treasure we have is the breath we are still able to draw, the life that is still ours—however depleted, however scarred.

The chance still ... to think, to feel, to act. The opportunity to use every precious moment well, clinging to a gift that we know may be taken from us in the very next instant and cherishing.

Moved by that inspiration we resolve to *come together* to do everything we can to fight hatred and make this world safer, stronger—sweeter than it is, if only a little sweeter.

I know believing that we have an *obligation* to love is not a comfortable position to be in. It can haunt us. It can nag at us in moments of happiness and personal success, disturbing our sleep and giving us that sense of guilt and unworthiness that used to be so strong and that the modern age is so eager to deny.

It can accuse us—from the faces of the starving, the dispossessed, and the wounded, faces that stare back at us from the front pages of our newspapers, images from across the world that blink momentarily on our television screens.

A French priest, a Jesuit, in just a few magnificent sentences, captured everything I've tried to say here:

> We must try *everything* for God. Lift up your head. Look at the immense crowds of those who build and those who seek. All over the world people are toiling—in laboratories, in studios, in factories—in the vast social crucible. The ferment that is taking place by their instrumentality, in art and science and thought, is happening for your sake. Open your arms and your heart like Christ, and welcome the waters, the flood—accept the juice of humanity—for without it you will wither like a flower out of water. And tend it, since, without your sun, it will die.

To some of us that is the echo of God, at God's most eloquent.

Not an easy matter, believing that God commits us to the endless task of seeking *improvement* of the world around us, knowing that fulfillment is an eternity away. But better than the anguish of *futility*. Better than the emptiness of *despair*.

And capable of bringing meaning to our most modest and clumsy efforts. A useful consolation for any of us, and especially for those of us still struggling to believe.

JACK NEWFIELD EULOGIZED
BY MARIO M. CUOMO

He gave many eulogies for his friends—John Aiello, Bill Modell, Michael Modell, Tony Malara, Kitty Carlisle Hart—and this one for the legendary reporter and author Jack Newfield, at Riverside Memorial Chapel, New York City, December 22, 2004.

I'm one of Jack's older friends who strived to stay on his good side because I expected to receive rather than give his eulogy.

Staying on Jack's good side was prudent for politicians, too; it might not provide immunity, but it might offer a little clemency.

And I'm sorry for all of us because we lost one of our era's most courageous and compelling journalists, a champion of justice when we needed one most.

After forty years and thousands of conversations about politics, sports, and mutual friends, I came to know Jack about as well as you can know a person.

And in recent years, when he was preparing his memoir, we even talked a little about religion.

Jack was intrigued by C. S. Lewis's famous *Screwtape Letters*, a description of the subtleties of the Devil's mind and how evil can overcome you in simple and familiar ways. Lewis writes, "What Hell wants is a man to finish his life having to say, 'I now see that I spent most of my life not doing either what was right or what I enjoyed.'"

The Greeks believed the gods' most valuable gift is the gift of passion, and Jack's life bubbled over with it!

His passion infused his life as an investigative reporter, author, commentator, and political analyst. And it forged an enduring bond with his friends and colleagues.

His passion intensified his loves and hates. His love of the city, his country, baseball, music, and his idols, Jacob Riis, Jackie Robinson, and Robert Kennedy.

And his hate of racism, economic injustice, the wars in Vietnam and Iraq, the death penalty, corrupt politicians, and fickle friends.

The gods did indeed bless Jack Newfield. And they blessed us, too, by allowing us to share his passion for sixty-six years. For that I think we should all say, "*Deo Gratias*."

8

WVOX Radio Interviews

My portfolio as a broadcaster and trustee of a daytime community radio station endowed with only 500 watts but uniquely located in Westchester County, New York, has given me access not only to hundreds of thousands of upscale local residents and those of standing, stature, and influence but also to countless politicians and business leaders who came over the years to what has been called "The Golden Apple," drawn by the influence and money herein. It seemed like everyone peddling a new idea or ginning up a political campaign came through our home heath seeking support and affirmation. Those meager 500 watts have drawn many heavy hitters and political personages—those who aspired to high estate in the political world as well as those who were already in the national spotlight—to our Westchester studios. Our microphones have amplified the voices and pronouncements of John F. Kennedy (and his son John Jr.), Bobby Kennedy, Nelson Aldrich Rockefeller, Daniel Patrick Moynihan, Tip O'Neill, Malcolm Wilson, John Lindsay, Ed Koch, Gerald Ford, George H.W. Bush, Jacob K. Javits, Hugh Leo Carey, Alfonse D'Amato, Ogden Rogers Reid, Nancy Pelosi, and many others somewhat lesser known outside of our local turf. Some stellar ones—many of them down-home "townie" politicians—also come rushing back to me: Edwin Gilbert Michaelian, Frederic B. Powers, Alvin Richard

Ruskin, Andy O'Rourke, Tony Colavita, Samuel George Fredman, Bill Luddy, Dick Ottinger, and Richard Daronco. But the most vivid, compelling, and memorable of all those I've encountered as a community broadcaster is the "failed baseball player with too many vowels in his name."

In recent years, I had a number of wonderful on-air conversations with Mario Cuomo about the great issues of the day. Aside from the back-and-forth "banter," these interviews helped our listening audience—and now our readers—know what a wise and articulate man the governor was. Many times we discussed difficult topics. But often our conversations occurred during moments of triumph or great elation.

A NEW MILLENNIUM CONVERSATION

Over the years, I would ask Mario Cuomo for his thinking on current issues. In this conversation of January 2000, we talked at length about the new millennium.

WILLIAM O'SHAUGHNESSY: What's the secret to a good life, Mario?

MARIO CUOMO: Never give up trying to follow your dream, whatever it is. Poppa taught me you're never too young or too old for dreams. Every time I thought I was going to fail—in politics particularly, or when I failed a test and I was crushed—all those moments when you want to hide and you don't want anyone to see you, all those times when I wanted to quit, I thought about Poppa and how he would never quit on a dream.

WO: Mario Cuomo once said, "When the people say 'Send me a president,' they are really saying, 'Send me a *moral* leader.'" But you told some friends, "I don't *want* to be the *moral* leader of this country."

MC: I would tell the children of America what I would tell a child about his or her father. What we hope for in our father, our mother, our heroes, our presidents is somebody perfect. Someone who is so good, so correct, so right that whenever we're confused about life we can go and put our arms around him or her and say, "Thank God for the Truth, and there is the Truth." Unfortunately, that has happened only once in my experience and knowledge. Only once have we been given such a person, and even then we didn't recognize it. That was the beginning of the Christian era. Since then, and before and maybe forever, we're going to have imperfect creatures. And we will *all* sin, according to the good Jewish book and the good Christian book, seven times seven times a day! That's true even of presidents, of popes, of great rabbis. Some day in another universe we will achieve perfection. That is called Nirvana, Heaven.

You have to hope for institutions that can survive the weakness, the venality, the short-sightedness of leaders, as we have for many years. This is not to confuse what is *real* with what is *desirable*. Nor to suggest that we shouldn't continue to aspire for more excellence—and insist on it.

The presidency should be a place where you send signals to people about how they should behave, about how to be civil: You shouldn't hate someone because the other guy is Jewish or black or a female or gay; honor your relationships, live up to your contracts; don't mess around with interns in the back room. We all have an obligation to put out these signals of civility. Everybody is a parent or role model to somebody.

We have two things going against us, O'Shaughnessy. The first is our humanity and vulnerability, our concupiscence: just because Adam and Eve bit that darn apple all those years ago. And the other thing is *freedom*. Because we are a relatively *free* society, because we insist on giving ourselves a lot more room than most other successful nations ever have, we are free to make mistakes and bad choices. We are free to be disgusting and even mean in our language. We are free to lie about public officials as long as we don't do it maliciously. We're free to have all the sex we want. We're free to do a lot of things a lot of people regard as not good for the making of a healthy society.

wo: Governor, you're not blaming all of Bill Clinton's problems on Adam and Eve, are you?

mc: I blame *everything* on Adam and Eve, Brother Bill!

wo: A few weeks ago out on the West Coast you addressed 2,000 people, and at the end of the program some nut in the back row screamed out, "Why don't *you* run for president?" He brought the whole damn gathering to their feet. Why don't *you* run?

mc: I think my moment has passed, Bill. I think there was a time when I might have been able to make the case. I think the party has enough quality to make the race, and I don't think there is a need for me. If I believed there was a need, I would consider it. There are other people who run not because they think they are the very best but because they think they would like to be president. That has never been enough for me. Would I like to be president? Yeah, but I don't think I'm anywhere near the best available, and so I'm not even considering it.

I do miss the opportunity the governorship gave me to do good things. I described it once this way: Every morning you are lucky enough to wake up as the governor of New York, you have an infinite number of opportunities ahead of you to do good things.

It is a great gift to be in a position to help a lot of people to make their lives a little bit better. The private sector has many rewards, and I have been luckier than I deserve to be, but I do miss the opportunity to be useful to a lot of people. The test is not so much what you achieve, although we all strive to achieve; the test really is *how hard you try*. So I'll keep trying as long as I have the energy to do it.

Try to make this place as good as you can make it. And don't ask how. God says, "I've sent you rules, I've sent down the tablets: don't take someone's spouse, don't take someone's goods, don't kill anybody. That is all you need. The rest you have to work out for yourselves. You know what sweetness is, as distinguished from bitterness. You know what fairness is, as distinguished from unfairness. You know what it is to be good. And to be bad. Just do the right thing. That's all I'm asking."

And if you think that's not a good enough answer, show me another one!

And that's what Islam believes too.

And God also admonishes us, "And don't be telling me you don't have the capacity to change the world. I know you don't have that capacity. But you have the capacity to *try!* I *know* how grand and complicated a place this is. And I know how *little* you are. And so if the best thing you can do in your lifetime is find one other human being along the way and comfort her in her moment of distress, then terrific! I'll settle for that. Don't worry about fairness when judging your effort. *I'll* know when you tried and *I'll* know when you didn't."

That's what I tell my grandchildren. And if you understand that, then you can live *justified*.

They ask me, as they ask every politician, I guess, "What do you want on your tombstone when you die?" That's easy for me. I always give the same answer, "Just put: 'Mario Cuomo, 1932– . . . fill in the blank. He *tried.*'" Tried what? Just forget about that. He *tried.* That's all you have to do to make yourself successful. In this life and the next, Brother Bill.

WO: Whew! You're being very profound this morning. Governor, what does it mean to be an Italian American?

MC: You say it accurately when you say, "Italian American." If you had said, "What does it mean to be Italian," I would have had difficulty because I'm not really Italian. I'm an American born here. Momma and Poppa were born in Italy and came here. They were born in a place called Salerno, in the *Mezzogiorno*, one day's journey from Rome, in the *south* of Italy from which most Italian American people came. They didn't come from the north—and this is important to remember when you're thinking of Italian Americans. Milan and Florence are where the industry has always been—the money, wealth, and high culture, if you're talking about literature, literacy, and the arts. The South has always been the poorer part of Italy with fewer educated people, fewer successful people, more poor people and strugglers. That was true for all the [twentieth] century, and it's why so many people came from Sicily and the lower part of Italy to America, and my people were among them.

WO: It's part of the popular culture, Governor, that your parents were very poor.

MC: They were poor in Italy and that's why they came here. And they were poor here because they chose, unfortunately, just before the Depression as a time to come. My father and mother were never educated in Italy. They never went to school a day in Italy. And whatever they learned about Italian writing and words they learned from their families and from the streets in Salerno. When they came here my father had no skills other than labor.

He was a small man, not big and powerful. What he did was use a shovel. He was a ditch-digger, literally, in Jersey City. He was able to make a living. He had no friends, no money, no family here. He was able to make a living until the Depression stopped the construction work, and then he was desperately poor. My mother came over a year after my father did, which was the established pattern. You'd get married, the woman would become pregnant, you'd go to America, and a year later she'd come over to America with her first child. So they were poor and they were saved in the Depression by a gentleman from Queens County by the name of Kessler, who owned a grocery store but couldn't run it himself because he was ill and needed someone to run it. He put them in a back room of the grocery store in South Jamaica and taught them what they needed to know. It is hard to say we were poor because, although my father wasn't paid in the beginning, we had food and shelter and probably did better than most people in the neighborhood.

wo: Governor, you mentioned Mr. Kessler, the owner of the grocery store. I've heard you speak of this to Jewish groups. Are there similarities, I wonder, among Jewish people and Italian Americans?

mc: I think, Bill, as I've grown older—and this is true of a lot of people I know—you arrive at two conclusions about *values* in this society. One is that it is harder and harder to look to the collectivity, to the American culture, and say, "This is going to supply me with all the values I need." Especially at a time like this, given the current argument: What is it that we believe in that truly uplifts us? And because we're troubled by a lack of heroes and a lack of *clear* values, we tend to turn more and more toward our ethnicity, toward our *roots*. I'm probably more distinctly Italian American now than I was when I was fifteen.

When I was fifteen or sixteen, it didn't mean as much to me. For some immigrants, and this is a shameful thing to admit, if you were poor and your parents couldn't speak the language and you weren't particularly good at it yourself, there can even be an embarrassment factor at being Polish or Jewish or Romanian or Greek or Irish (not the Irish as much because they were literate in this language). But then as you grow older you come to appreciate your roots. If you happen to be an Italian American, then part of your heritage is Italy itself. Notwithstanding [that] my mother and father weren't educated and never visited a museum in Rome and never knew who Cicero or Caesar was, it's in their blood to some extent. They share that culture, and, therefore, you inherit it to some small extent. And that's meaningful. You come from a people thousands of years old.

You see this in the African American community very vividly. They're going back to their roots. Remember [Alex] Haley's book *Roots.* And when they go back they are reminded that however badly they're treated here, they have an immense contribution to give. They have been left a tremendous legacy of intelligence and accomplishment from Africa, and so these things take on much greater value.

I think of myself as an Italian American, and I feel that I have the culture of the Italian American. I have the *values* my mother and father brought over that are centered and distinct. These they have in common with all the other immigrants of their generation, whether they were Irish, Polish, or German. And these values were a willingness to work very hard, a total commitment to *family*, an instinct for *religion* though no philosopher had taken the time to teach them the nuances and subtleties of one God and three Persons. But they had a general sense of a God to whom we owe loyalty and obedience and who in one way or another would save us when it's all over. They had that religious commitment. They also had incredible patriotism, and so they developed this very powerful commitment to the United States of America. People who came here as immigrants appreciate it better than those who were born here, the difference between this place and all others; and, therefore, they had a fiercer love even than some of the native-born people. All these things I inherited in common with the Podales who were Greek Americans, the Svitliks who were Czech Americans, the Fosters who were Jewish Americans (I think there was a name change! They were from Russia originally). These people lived in my neighborhood in addition to a lot of African Americans.

WO: Mario Cuomo, who are some other Italian Americans who have made great contributions to this country?

MC: My mother and father were truly great people! If you take the little they had against what they accomplished—raised a family of four, one died, for those children to grow up reasonably straight and well situated in this country—[it] was a fantastic accomplishment. If you want to talk about "historic" Italian Americans who achieved great fame in this country, there are the scientists and inventors like Fermi and Marconi; great athletes like DiMaggio; artists like Sinatra, Toscanini, Cavore; great politicians. Incidentally, there are great Polish Americans, Irish Americans, Greek Americans, Jewish Americans, African Americans—we all have our pantheon of heroes. But I must tell you, Bill, as great as they were, the two things I notice when I look at the range of great people all across the board is, none of them are greater than my mother and father.

WO: But is it fair to say that Italian Americans have a stronger sense of *community*? No one has spoken more eloquently about Jewish people than Mario Cuomo, but what about your own tribe?

MC: I'm not sure that isn't a conceit. I can say for sure that the Italian American culture I was born to was very strong on family. And the respect for your mother and father, and for your spouse, whether she liked you or not—the respect for your *obligation* to one another, toward your children, the *loyalty* to the blood—was a very powerful part of my upbringing and of the genes that make me whatever it is I am. I am not sure that distinguishes me from the Svitliks or the Podales or the O'Rourkes in my neighborhood or even the DeSilvas, who were Portuguese. I think that has a lot to do not so much from the place from which they came but with their situation here. They were close when they came because that's all they had.

When my mother and father were in Jersey City, before the Depression struck, and then in South Jamaica, in 1929–32, there was no welfare, no worker's compensation, no unemployment insurance, no Social Security, no Medicare, no Medicaid. There was charity, but we didn't belong to any groups that would have a settlement house for us. You were on your own and had to learn how to make it on your own. You're cooped up in one room behind a grocery store because a man by the name of Kessler, who can't speak your language, or even appreciate your *food*, provides for you. You get the sense you are in an alien place. You're lucky to find this wonderful man who reaches out for you. That vulnerability creates a desire to cling together. You could be primitive cave people. When that lightning strikes, the lightning you don't understand—when the storm comes from gods you only imagine—your instinct is to cluster together for heat, for warmth, for protection. I think that has a lot to do with the idea of family.

This is dangerous ground for me because I haven't thought it through, but I suspect as you go from that condition of privation and desperation and the struggle for survival—as you add to it layers of generations and growing wealth and ease—I suspect

the idea of family deteriorates. One of the great ironies in my own experience as a lawyer is how many families started as immigrants, like my mother and father, and made a ton of money, and then you're working on the estate and you discover that brother won't talk to brother and sister won't talk to sister and everyone is cursing everyone else as they rack up the wealth. I'm not sure it's a matter of wealth as much as a matter of circumstance.

The answer someday, for more intelligent people than our generation or all the generations we have had in this country, is to realize that the consummation, the perfecting of this world, which is what we're all supposed to be striving for, will occur only when we appreciate *all* of us. That we're *all* family. That we're all connected to one another, with some of us a little bit closer than others, but all connected, all in the same struggle. Not just to survive in this place but to make it the most beautiful place possible, to make this the most decent, fairest, safest, the most civilized country in the most civilized world that has ever existed. Only when you understand that is your *mission*, as grandiose as it sounds. Your mission is to play whatever role you can. You may be only a foot soldier in the army here, and the war is not going to be won or lost because of your efforts. But only when you appreciate the pride of being a foot soldier and marching with the army in the right direction for the right cause. Only then when you think of yourselves as family. That's the word we get from our God. When you appreciate your brothers and sisters with one Father—only then will you achieve anything like you're supposed to.

WO: Governor Cuomo, with all your magnificent words, I'm reminded that the Irish had some trouble when they came here: "No Irish need apply!" I just wonder if the Italians faced that too.

MC: "Guinea," "dago," "WOP," "greaseball"! Those are the words *we* heard. The Irish heard "micks," "potato eaters"; "*manga batana*," a bigoted Italian would have said of the Irish. We all took our turns being victimized by this stupid language and snide condescension. The tragic thing about that is we never seem to learn. One wave of immigrants after the other was abused by the one who was here before it. And when your turn comes, and the Hispanics move in behind you and the African Americans are finally being given an opportunity to emerge, a lot of us tend to forget what happened to us and our people. And how much we hated it and how unfair it was. And we become guilty of the same kind of bigotry to the group that is coming behind us. We're still *learning* this game. We're still a work in progress as a people and as a culture. But oh, yes, we took our turn at bigotry, and we still do. More in the old days than there is now. The Jewish people? Do we have to even talk about the discrimination they've felt? The anti-Semitism. Racism: Is there any question the African American has been treated badly in this country? Can you really allow yourself to forget they were enslaved, denied the most *basic* liberties? And many of them are still suffering from that, still way behind. Our history, unfortunately, has been to take diversity—people from all over the world who are different—and put them together and mold them into the greatest country in history, and so we have learned to make a *strength* of diversity but it is a *vulnerability* at the same time.

WO: When you sit in your ivory tower at the Willkie, Farr & Gallagher law firm in Manhattan, or go around the country making those magnificent speeches, does your mind drift back to that one room behind the grocery store?

MC: When I am all finished with my speeches, O'Shaughnessy— whether they are bombs or passable—when I'm all finished with the day's work, advocating whatever I'm advocating, what I think of—the truth, Bill—is a plate of good pasta, and a good glass of red wine, a nice piece of bread. That's enough for me.

WO: Mario Matthew Cuomo, give us some predictions for the new millennium.

MC: Predicting what one thinks will happen in the new millennium gets easier when you remember it's going to take a thousand years for anybody to prove you were wrong, O'Shaughnessy! And I'm comforted by that reality. The change that has been so dramatic over the course of my own lifetime is going to continue, and it's going to change the way we play, the way we look, the way we think, the way we relate to one another, and it will present us with immense challenges: to our intelligence, to our political wisdom. And it will present challenges to our *soul*. Physicians are going to be able to operate on people on the other side of the world, through robotic hands, by using computers, without ever moving from the great hospitals here in New York. The computers are still in their infancy; they will grow more intelligent and more effective. Artificial intelligence will allow a computer to beat us at chess, or even rotisserie baseball—all the time, without ever lagging, without having a headache, or a bad hair day, or a fit of depression. The newspapers will probably become obsolete—not totally obsolete, but less needed because of the Internet and computers. You won't be able to work unless you're computer literate. The computer will shrink the universe. Space travel will become so frequent it will drop out of the headlines. They'll be going back and forth to the moon. There may be colonies there. The cascading of new possibilities constantly says to the intelligent person: you can't rule *anything* out. The interconnectedness and interdependence of *all* people will become clearer, and that will have its consequences. It will spur more and more linkages and mergers of political groups.

The European community will be well established within the first quarter of the new millennium, and so will the euro. The French and Italians will have to stop arguing with one another about their wine and their romance and all the other things that have divided them. And in that first part of the new millennium it will be the dollar and the euro, a bipolar economy. And you'll have to figure out how to stabilize these things, and that will remind you of your interconnectedness and your interdependence. NAFTA will become AFTA, the *American* Free Trade Agreement. Inevitably, it will take *all* of Latin America, all the way down to Brazil and Argentina and everybody else. They'll all be in one grand trade zone.

The ability to destroy one another with even newer and more powerful devices, unfortunately, will continue. We're not going to get smart enough over the next millennium to stop progressing in the ability to demolish one another. Our insecurity, our imperfection, will be sufficient so that we'll keep guarding against the enemy. We need to have it because *we're* good, *they're* bad. And we need to protect ourselves. And because they think they're good too, everybody will have this lethal force. More and more we'll be aware that we can destroy one another very easily. Thirty years ago we said, "That's what will bring peace to the world," and it hasn't, and it won't over the next century. But what it will do is remind you that you had better *talk*, you had better communicate with one another, or you may just *destroy* yourselves. And so the United Nations will continue. The World Trade Organization will be more meaningful than ever.

Thanks to television, the computer, and other technological marvels, we're already the most knowledgeable people in history. Kids will sit in front of that Internet, as they do now, and get information from all over the world that you didn't dream of when you were twenty-two. It's frightening in a way. We're going to be much more knowledgeable; *will we be wiser?* Does it follow that because kids or adults *know* a lot they *understand* a lot? Or will you confuse *facts* with *philosophy*?

How will we deal with our ability to clone life? We're so afraid of the issue now we're saying, "Don't mess with it. Don't even *look* at it." You can't tell the scientists and the world, "Don't study it. Don't explore it. Don't see what it *means*."

I did an article a hundred years ago at St. John's Law School for *Catholic Lawyer* magazine, as a St. Thomas More scholar. And we had a priest who was a sociologist, a canon lawyer, and a regular lawyer. And we did an article on artificial insemination, and I thought the dean would go crazy. So I said to the dean, "It's coming and it's *real* and we have to think of the *morality and* the *legality* of it." He said, "That will *never* happen!"

I'm very good historically, better than I am projecting, because I've been around so long.

Will our computers become our soulmates, withering our relationships with humans? Person to person, people to people, community to community? Will we fall in love with our computers? Will we become too introverted? Or will chat rooms that make us disembodied conversational companions to people all over the world draw us closer together? Because now you can talk to anybody. But you can't *feel* them, you can't touch them, you can't smell their breath, you can't kiss them, you can't hug them. But you can talk to them. Will that make you closer?

We'll certainly be stronger and smarter. But will we be better? Or sweeter? Ever since Adam wondered why the fruit was forbidden, and Einstein struggled with the meaning of energy, thinkers have been forced to admit there are more *questions* than *answers*. But because it's true that where there is no *vision* the people perish, we have to continue asking ourselves these questions. We should be practical and constructive about preparing for this future or we risk a world run by computers, which would be a grotesque intensification of the *Frankenstein* fable.

The politicians, very silently, are saying to us, "Don't mess with this economy. Don't try to make it any better for people. Because if you do, you're only going to *spoil* it." Using economic language: the economy has to do with the *production*, the *distribution*, then the *consumption* of goods. What does it have to do with the *condition* of *people*? Zero! That's *sociology*. So you have to ask a separate question here: What is the condition of people? You have more millionaires, more billionaires, more people making over $100,000 [than] in our history. About 5 percent of the American people now are in that shining city on the hill above $100,000 a year. That's very good.

I remember being in the Executive Mansion with Momma, before she died. On a coffee table, she saw a *Fortune* magazine with Lee Iacocca's picture on it. She said, "Who is that?" I said, "Ma, that's Lee Iacocca." She said, "What does he do?" I said, "He makes $15 million a year, and he says it's not enough." She said,

"What does he *do*?" I said, "He makes *cars* for Chrysler." I was governor, my second term. I thought I was doing all right. She looked at me and said, "What's the matter, you don't know how to make a *car*, Mario?" For her, the idea that you could make $15 million and think that's not enough, that was incredible. She couldn't read, she couldn't write, she came from a very poor neighborhood, her son got lucky and got to be a governor. But as far as she was concerned you go all the way you can in this country as long as you don't cheat, you don't steal, you don't hurt anybody—that's the American Dream. And so we have more people in the shining city than ever—that's great.

But there's a *second* city where the glitter doesn't show. Forty million poor people. We have 16 million children at risk of malnutrition, under-education, teenage suicide, teenage pregnancy. For the new millennium you have to conclude: Look, things are great. But they could be better. Unless you're willing to conclude that there is no more room in the circle of opportunity.

One last thing, more important than anything. And that is something that I don't think that we can be taught by our computers. And that is that no matter how much cloning we do and how fast we do it, we're never all going to look alike in America. Thank God there'll always be tremendous diversity of race, of color, of sex, of sexual orientation, national origin, economic class—there'll always be great *differences*. That's *what* we are. We're made up of *differences*. And we continue to be nurtured by it. We're not endemic. The people who lived here first, we destroyed virtually. Those were the Native Americans. Them we killed and brutalized. All the rest of us came from somewhere else. One of the great strengths of the City of New York, the in-migration of people from Asia, the Caribbean— people with strength, with will, with values, with family—that's going to continue. And no matter how hard we try to widen the distribution of opportunity and success, there'll always be winners and losers, the well-to-do and the strugglers, the people who can afford to *give* and the people who desperately *need*.

And how will we deal with that as a society? That's the *question* for the new millennium. Above all things, we should be sure that Americans and New Yorkers remain fully *human*. We should make ourselves masters of the technical universe without ever forgetting a truth thousands of years older than our computers and infinitely more powerful: that we will find our greatest good as individuals in the good of the whole *community*.

SEPTEMBER 11, 2001

It was a soft, gauzy September morning with high, thin clouds floating over Westchester and drifting toward Long Island Sound. And as one of the great, simple pleasures of my life has always been washing my own cars, I was out in the driveway early on this beautiful Indian summer day.

The former Nancy Curry appeared at the side door and said, "Billy, I think you should come and take a look at this." Some idiot, so we thought, had flown a small plane into the World Trade Center. As serious as it was, I went back out to finish washing my car, wondering, What was that jackass doing up there? and What next?

A few minutes later I found out, when Nancy reappeared to announce that yet another plane had struck. I immediately called my office at WVOX and WVIP. They were already on the story with bulletins and live, firsthand reports from lower Manhattan.

I jumped into my dripping-wet car and raced down Pinebrook Boulevard to the Whitney Radio Network studios and began to assemble a series of interviews with some leading New Yorkers and ordinary citizens.

I've sat before our microphones during earthquakes, race riots, a tanker blowing up in the Hudson River, and blizzards. And on every one of those occasions we found that a community radio station, if you do it right, can play a very useful and essential role by serving as a platform or forum for our listeners, many of whom were confused, frightened, and eager for information and also for the reassuring voices of their neighbors.

We fielded thousands of calls from all over the metropolitan area. While other radio stations "adjusted" their programming somewhat, I'm immensely proud that we at WVOX and WVIP threw ourselves totally and completely into those terrible events as they unfolded.

Our listeners heard raw, unfiltered dialogue (we're the only station in the area without the infamous seven-second delay, preferring to fly without a net), and they were exposed to the confusion and apprehension abroad in the land on this terrible day that changed our lives forever. You could also hear the sweet strength, courage, and hope of the indomitable people of New York as they roused themselves from their initial shock and disbelief. But before we opened up our microphones, we put in a call to Willkie, Farr & Gallagher.

The terrible events of September 11 have been called a "television story." But tens of thousands turned to local radio as the day wore on. And one of our first interviews was, of course, with Mario Cuomo, that morning at 10:30:

WILLIAM O'SHAUGHNESSY: Now on the line from Manhattan, a former inhabitant of the World Trade Center. He was governor of New York when the previous attack occurred [in 1993]. His office, the office of the governor, used to be there. Governor Mario Cuomo, good morning, sir.

MARIO CUOMO: Good morning, Bill. Well, of all the inappropriate greetings, I guess yours and mine set a record: "Good morning." If anything, it has been a terrible morning.

WO: Governor, you are a sensitive and deeply religious man. What are you thinking about all this?

MC: Well, I'm thinking what you're thinking, Brother Bill, and what everybody is thinking at the moment, and that is the *details* of the tragedy: how many people have been lost, *whose* people, how many of *my* people, how many of my family. I think that is what everybody is fixed on now. And that's not surprising, and that is as it should be. And I suspect the next few days we will spend measuring the extent of this brutal, brutal act of damage. But after that, I think we will come to analyze the situation and discover that it is even worse than it appears today and will appear tomorrow. It's worse because you will not have an identifiable enemy to defend yourself against. It won't be as though some nation had declared war on you. We can fight a *nation*: we can defeat any nation, and we can protect ourselves in the process. This will be about unnamed people. And worse than that, we may not understand their grievance, what it is that fuels the hate, that inspires the acts of terrorism, and we will be in the frustrating position of not being able to defend ourselves, because the truth is there is no way, militarily or through the use of your police, to protect yourself against madmen who are willing to sacrifice their own lives to take yours. That's what this proves. We've been warned over and over that they were going to make this kind of attack. They even got quite explicit in their warnings about airplanes and other ways to do it. But you just can't protect yourself against it. So the real anguish will come, Bill, after all the personal tragedies, that will keep us crying for many lifetimes. The real anguish will be, how do we defend ourselves in the future? And I am afraid, Bill, that our society, at least yours and mine, at least for our lifetimes, is changed for the worse—permanently. We'll be more militaristic. Of course, we'll have to be to protect ourselves. We'll be more bitter than we should be and have been. We'll be more afraid. We'll be more concerned about protecting ourselves. And we will be angrier.

wo: Governor, even these days, at airports in Rome and Paris, you see troopers with sawed-off shotguns and Uzis. Do you think we will ever get to resemble almost a police state?

mc: That's what I mean about being more militaristic. You'd have to. The people will demand it. The people will demand, first of all, that you do everything possible to protect yourself, to find these people, to punish them, to execute them. That is the natural and almost certain reaction. You do have to do everything you can to protect yourself.

wo: You told me once, Mario Cuomo, vengeance doesn't work.

mc: It won't be for vengeance. Many people will want to take vengeance, but there won't be anybody to take vengeance *against*. That's the problem. You won't know the enemy. You won't know who it is. You can't say, "Well, it's every Islamic person, or every Arab, or everybody from the East." That's not rational. So you wouldn't know *whom* to take vengeance *on*. And so what you do know is you have to *protect* yourself. And in the process of protecting yourself, you will go to extremes. These are your children. This is your life you're protecting. So you can expect, Bill, and we can expect, like it or not, more militarism in our society.

wo: Governor, is it too far a stretch to suggest that people might now be saying, "We paid a hell of a price for supporting Israel"?

mc: Oh, God forbid. God forbid. I think it would be simplistic and unfair to Israel and unfair to the Jewish people to say this is all

because of Israel. I think, Bill, that would also be a little bit
arrogant of us. You know what that would leave out? That we
have never done anything as a nation to offend anybody. I don't
think that's true. I think there are a lot of people in this world
who think we have offended them and who feel offended. People
who think that you ignored their poverty, you ignored their
despair, you ignored their begging for help, while we lived in the
lap of luxury. You ignored your obligations. We have had
evidence of that. This is not to say they're right, but that is not the
question, right or wrong. We *know* this was wrong. This couldn't
be *more* wrong. So, you know, there's no need to quibble about
who's right, who's wrong. *They're* wrong. But, you also have to
understand what it is that is motivating them. And to say, "Well,
it's *Israel*," that's too easy, because all you'd have to do then is
betray Israel and you'd be safe. But that would be wrong. That
would be unfair. And it would be arrogant. We have to study the
relationship between us and the *whole world* to see whom we
might possibly have offended. To see whom we might be
provoking. Now, that is something we'll not do easily. But I think
it is necessary.

wo: Did you ever think you would see, when you looked out the
window from your office, that anything like this could ever
happen in your city?

mc: Yes. As a matter of fact—I certainly never *predicted* this, but I
said often that when people would talk about threats, the great
threat is *ideology*. Ideologies that think that *our* ideology is evil
and wrong. And there are a lot of people who think that about us.
And we are vulnerable as a nation because we can't protect
ourselves against that. I said that many, many times. I certainly
didn't predict this, but if you think about it, Bill, this should not
really surprise us. We have been warned over and over by

terrorist groups. I think if you can get an FBI or a CIA
representative to tell you the truth, and you ask him on your
program, "Did you ever get any threats?" he would say, "We get
them *every day*." And we know they're capable of it because we
saw what they did before at the World Trade Center [in 1993].
How did they get in? How did they plant the bomb? And if they
could plant that small bomb—it was sizable for its time—then
they could do bigger ones. And that's what they've done. Can
they seize an airplane? How many movies have you seen in
which persons took hostages on a plane? Fifty? I mean, there's
nothing that's happened here that's surprising. What's happened
psychologically is we're the only place in the world that's never
been subjected to a war. That was never attacked in a war. This is
like being attacked in a war. But to say we never imagined this
could happen, well, I'm not sure that's true.

wo: Governor Mario Cuomo, on this awful day when our airliners
are falling out of the sky, crashing into symbols of our national
power and prestige, the psyche of America has taken a pretty
good hit.

mc: Yes. And it will be worse as we think about it over the first few
days.

wo: What do you mean?

mc: We will think about this and we will become angry. And we
will become more and more angry. And I think, in the end, the
only solution, if there is a solution to this madness, is what
we've understood from the beginning: that you have to replace
hate with *understanding*. In a perfect world, you'd replace hate
with love, and everything would be ideal. That's too much for
us to ask in this life. What is *not* too much to ask is that you at
least abate the hate and replace it with understanding and
conciliation and compromise and figuring out a way to get

along. That is the only way we can make it, by creating a sense of *community* that is worldwide. It's the only way you keep peace in your own family, to create a sense of community, involving your children, your spouse, yourself. The only way you keep peace on your block, in your village, in your state, is to create a sense of *community*. We're all in this together, *all* of us: the black ones, the white ones, the ones who wear turbans, and the ones who wear hardly anything. We're *all* in this together. Now, that sounds like poetry. It's not. It's fundamental, *essential* common sense. And we're not good at it. We're not good at it, Bill.

wo: Governor Mario Cuomo, I don't know anyone better to ask this question of: You once wrote a letter to your granddaughters; what, Grandpa Cuomo, what would you now say to those little girls? They're gonna see this on television.

mc: I would say, when you see what happened and you listen to the adults around you, you will hear some of them cursing, you will hear some of them saying, "We'll get those SOBs!" You will hear some of them saying we need tougher laws and stronger armies. And don't be surprised, that's what they will say. But if you listen to them closely over the weeks and months ahead, you'll see that the *wisest* of them are saying something else. And they're saying, "Look, we have to remember those *principles* we talked about starting 5,000 years ago." If we want this place to work, there are *two* things you have to believe in. One, we are all *equals* on this planet. No matter who has the money and who does not. No matter who is big and who is little. We are all equals. The Jews called it the principles of *Tzedakah*. The Christians have other words for it. And the *second* principle: We're supposed to lock our arms, all of us, and try to make a better world. And by *better* world, we mean fairer, more intelligent, and even sweeter. Now,

all people are impatient when you talk that way. People don't
want to hear it, especially Americans. That's too unreal; it's *too*
sweet; it's too soft; it's too poetical. You've got to get *tough*. Well,
we're the *toughest* nation in the world, and we just lost probably
. . . probably . . . *thousands* of people.

WO: Governor, thank you for a few moments of sanity and
enlightenment on a terrible news day.

MC: Let's say a prayer, Bill.

9/11 ONE YEAR LATER . . . TERRORISM . . .
AND, AGAIN, WHY HE DIDN'T RUN
FOR PRESIDENT

And then, on September 11, 2002—one year later—we again turned
to the governor. A stunning reflection on a sad day . . . and more:

WILLIAM O'SHAUGHNESSY: Governor, you were with us exactly one
year ago, almost to the sad moment. Your words, which once
lifted a nation, also inspired us on that terrible Indian summer
day. And so we turn to you again. We can't figure out, Governor
Mario Cuomo, if this is a day for rage and retribution or for
remembrance and reflection. How should we *feel* today,
September 11, 2002?

MARIO CUOMO: I'm not sure we know yet, Bill. And I'm not at all
sure *I'm* equipped to provide a formula that our leaders haven't
found yet either. That's probably why they decided to recite the
words of other leaders at other times in the past, because it's
such a daunting—even impossible—challenge to rationalize this
for people. And I'm not sure the people *want* the rationalizing
now. I think what they want today is what you want at any wake,

[179]

any funeral: You want sympathy, you want reaffirmation. You want to have an opportunity to feel your catharsis, to feel your grief, to feel sorry for yourself, to feel sorry for others. I think that's exactly what we're doing. I think that's perfectly appropriate. It's what we did right after 9/11. I think what happens, however—and it happened after 9/11—is that after a while you return to normalcy. After a while, despite all the pledges you made while you were on your knees and touching his cold hand for the last time before they closed the casket and took him away—or her, or whomever—you made *all* these pledges about doing things to better yourself and not making the same mistakes you had in the past . . . . What you do, in effect, is you remind yourself of the value that you have left in your life that is the only *sure* value. And that is the next breath that you are going to draw, the life you still have to lead. And you just absolutely make up your mind that you are going to lead it better. And for a while you do. And then, for most of us, you forget and you lapse back to the old ways, for better or for worse.

And I think a lot of that has happened in the country. It hasn't completely erased those first feelings. And there's still a lot of residual commitment to making more of your life. That's visible all around us. People are staying home more, doing some of the old-fashioned things like hugging their children and making up with old friends.

I think we're still confused, as a people, about what more we should say by way of the significance of this event. All those unanswered questions are still unanswered—the *big* one being, Why would any good God let this happen? That still torments us. And the others, the practical questions: Who are these people? Whom do they represent? How do you deter people like them if they're willing to give up their own lives? If they're willing to give up their own lives, then you can't stop them with a threat that you're going to take their lives. In some cases, it might even *encourage* them. How do you deal with that? And why are they so angry to begin with?

That question, in the first days, was a legitimate question, but you couldn't utter it, because if you did you would be called disloyal or you would be denying people their rage. Well, that's not true. We have a right to be angry. We have a right to use force—we're using force—and we've used it with lethal effect, even against some innocent people, inadvertently. And so we're fighting the war against terrorism. It's absolutely clear that it's not a war that is going to end in a pact or a parade. It's not a war that's going to end like other wars do. It's a war that is going to go on forever—like the war against drugs. And the war against crime. And the war against disease. How do you *deal* with that? Don't you have to do something other than bring force? Don't you have to look for *another* explanation? And shouldn't we start answering that question?

And finally, Bill, and this is what really staggers me, I saw a poll that said 61 percent of the people now say they're ready to go to war with Iraq. What? Ready to go to *war* with Iraq? Are you sure? Ready to condemn Saddam Hussein? Well, absolutely! Ready to say he's a threat and should be gotten rid of. Absolutely. But three or four hundred thousand human beings on the battlefield. Your brothers. Your sisters. Your children. Your loved ones. If that poll is anywhere near accurate, then I'm staggered by it.

So what do I have to say? Nothing inspirational, I'm afraid. I'm still trying to think this thing through. I'm still at the point of trying to remind myself that the *one* sure value is the value of the life I still have. And making the most of it with Matilda and the kids and the people I love and the people who love me. And the little good things I can do if I can find them in a twenty-four-hour day. And trying to do them a little better than I used to. But beyond that I don't have much to offer.

wo: Governor, sometimes I think we put too much pressure on you. I hope these radio stations are not always taking advantage. But in *New York* magazine this week, Walter Shapiro, a great writer, said he wasn't happy that [Mayor Michael R.] Bloomberg was going to read from Lincoln [during the September 11 anniversary memorial at Ground Zero] and that there are no wordsmiths who can lift us up. He said, "Where is Mario Cuomo when we need him?" What would *you* say today if you were standing there at Ground Zero, at the Pentagon, or in the field in Pennsylvania?

mc: I'm not sure I would have been able to say anything, Bill. If you thought very hard and concluded that you were required to offer an interpretation, then I think there are a number of things you might address. I think the one still puzzling question to me that needs discussion and ventilation deals with the subject of solidarity. There is one thing we all agreed on after we agreed on the heroic quality of the people who were at Ground Zero and who ran into those flames and smoke to save the lives of people they didn't know and weren't even sure were there. But they were willing to risk their own lives because they loved humanity so profoundly. The fire people, the emergency people, the police, and all the other New Yorkers and others who came together— the so-called togetherness that we're all so proud of and still demonstrating by holding hands and chanting and crying together. *That* solidarity.

Let's deal with that. What *was* it? Well, it was a magnificent coming together of the variety of people in this country for a *single* purpose: to express our anger, to some extent; our sadness, of course; and our commitment to protecting that way of life that [the terrorists] were challenging. All of that is beautiful, Bill. But something like that happened after the Second World War was started—on December 7, 1941. Something like that happened in all the great catastrophes looming that threaten you and your life in any substantial way. You cling to one another.

What happened in the *intervals* between the crises? Where is that feeling of togetherness and solidarity when you come to the day-to-day catastrophes—the quiet catastrophes like elderly people who can't find enough wherewithal to take care of themselves in their nursing homes or with prescription drugs. A middle class that's struggling *desperately* to stay in place. Police and firemen we lionize and iconize and cheer and hug and kiss and give them reverence, not being paid a decent wage in New York City. Imagine not having the best equipment! And we make a $90 *billion* budget that doesn't have a penny for *any* of them. It says go to your city, go to your state, *et cetera*. What happened to togetherness when you have a $500 *billion* tax cut? Forget about politics. Forget you're a Democrat, a Republican, a supply-sider, or a mushy-headed liberal. You have $500 *billion* you're about to give to the one million *richest* people in America! People like the people we have as clients at Willkie, Farr & Gallagher! And meanwhile, you have people struggling to make ends meet in this country. How can you call that togetherness?

wo: Governor, you're not going to be pleased that I remind you of this, but as we listen to you we're aware that a *lot* of people in this damn republic, in this country, wanted to see Mario Cuomo as president of the United States, and I remember Nancy Q. Keefe, a friend of yours and mine, a gifted writer for Gannett for many years, said, "I hope he doesn't. You can't have a good man like that as our president." When you see all this, are you glad you didn't do it? How do you feel now, years

[183]

later, when that could have been you down at Ground Zero, called upon to reassure the nation?

MC: When I hear things like that, I immediately think about checking the *water* in Westchester! And suggesting to people like Nancy and other good Republicans maybe that you should drink the *wine* instead, because there's something about that *water*!

WO: You can try to be glib about it. But people still stop you on the street. It happens every day. They don't exactly berate you. They just say, "Why the hell didn't you run?" I've seen the frustration.

MC: Bill, the question about running—I wouldn't even try answering it again, even for you, because I've answered it a thousand times and nobody ever listens to the answer. The truth is, the only time I ever took seriously the possibility of running was in 1991. I *did* announce that I would "look at it." I *did* look at it, for two months, as you remember. I did go to the Republicans in Albany who were running the State Senate and say, "Look, if you will make a budget, I will be *out* of here and I will run for president, and you *can't* lose, because *if* I win then you have a New Yorker in the White House, and that has to be good for New York. And if I *lose*, you're rid of me here in New York, and that has to be good for you Republicans!" And I thought for sure they would say, "OK, let's make the budget!" And they didn't, as you know, and they wouldn't, as you also know, and I announced at a press conference that if a budget weren't made and we were in trouble in that year with a recession and real problems balancing the budget, I said I couldn't possibly leave. So I had no chance to run. Do I regret that? No, I can't say I regret it, because I won't allow myself to say I have *any* regret about the circumstances of my life, because, overall I've been so lucky.

Would I have looked forward to an opportunity to serve at the highest level? I looked forward to serving at the highest level in

New York state and did it for twelve years and wasn't concerned about the attacks it makes on you, or the inevitability of your failure and therefore your unpopularity at moments in time. I *enjoyed* public service. I was never, however, someone who felt that I am the *only* person around who can do this job. With the governor's race, as you recall, I said in 1982 that if Paul Curran, the Republican, had been the Republican candidate, then I wouldn't have run. I said, I think he's *better* than I am! But these *other* guys, including [Ed] Koch, I think I'm better than they are. And so, O'Shaughnessy, that's why I ran for governor.

WO: We're going to have Ed Koch on the radio in just a few minutes. Governor, my point was that CBS has asked you to comment today. The *New York Times* has asked you to prepare a piece. The *Daily News* invited you to prepare an essay to explain this day, to put it in perspective. Cindy Adams, the columnist, asked you where you were a year ago. You said in yesterday's *Post*, "I was in Manhattan walking to work, and then in a horrifying moment of terror, all that was normal went up in a giant cloud of black smoke. You ask yourself, *Why could any good God let this happen?* You conclude there is no answer." And, said Mario Cuomo "You must believe in the next day. Your next break. You have to live and continue to love the people you love. There is *no* alternative!"

MC: Well, that's a kind of rough-and-ready and simplistic summary of much of our philosophy—those of us who are trying to claim to believe in a single, powerful source and purpose and call it God. There *is* no answer to the question of why good people suffer bad things in this life. There never has been. And the answer you come to, the *only* answer you can come to, is that the surest value you have in *life* is life itself. And making the most of it. And incidentally, Bill—to say something that you're probably tired of hearing, with all this confusion about religions and wars in the name of religion and some Muslims feeling that the enemy are the Christians and the Jews, and with people talking about the Crusades, *et cetera*—the *two* ideas that are common to *every* major religion and *every* ethical humanist, every ethical secularist, every atheist group I know, the *two* main principles are *Tzedakah* and *Tikkun Olam*.

And incidentally, these two principles you would come to, I suspect, if we all were on a desert island, if we never saw a book, never met a rabbi, never had any instruction from our history, if we were just 200 people on a desert island. You would conclude that O'Shaughnessy and I, and all of the rest of us who are human beings, are different than the rocks, different than the fish, different than the trees, different than all the other sorts of life, and we ought to cling together to take care of ourselves. That's called *Tzedakah*. *Tzedakah* is brotherhood. We owe one another respect and dignity as human beings. Call it charity. The ultimate in charity is *Tzedakah*. And what do you do with this relationship? Well, let's lock arms and try to make our lives better, because we have in common the ability to reflect, the ability to feel, to love, to think, to act. So let's get together and try to make the place more comfortable, fairer, stronger, more productive, *sweeter*, if we can. That's called *Tikkun Olam*. That's the Christian truth. That's the whole truth. It's the truth of the Qur'an. It's the truth of Hinduism. It's the truth of Buddhism. And of ethical humanism. And secularism. And intelligent atheism. It's the basic principle. There is *no* intelligence that goes much beyond that. Except very good *guesses* about what happens when this life changes form into some spiritual existence.

What I said to Cindy Adams and what I said on the street is just a summary of *all* that. In the end, that's the whole game: living your life in a way that makes this place a little bit better, and understanding that your limits in trying to change things are very, very drastic. You're very small. But to the extent that you can make a difference in this big world, for the better, you do it. For the better. That's life.

WO: Mario Cuomo, we're going to be on the air for most of this sad day. We've got a lot of rabbis, judges, mayors, journalists—including the great [Jimmy] Breslin—coming up next. I doubt—nay I'm *sure*—we won't have anything as inspiring or as eloquent as your words. Thank you, Governor. We're very grateful to you on this, another sad September morning.

TWENTY YEARS LATER

We again took to the airwaves on July 26, 2004, the twentieth anniversary of the famous "Shining City on a Hill" keynote address at the Democratic National Convention.

WILLIAM O'SHAUGHNESSY: Governor, remember when you stood in the spotlight and gave that keynote in 1984?

MARIO CUOMO: I do remember, Bill. This is the twentieth anniversary.

WO: Were you nervous standing there? Do you remember that now-historic speech?

MC: I remember it extremely well. And I wasn't nervous because I resigned myself to utter failure! The speech wasn't something I wanted to do. As a matter of fact, I told Walter Mondale to get Ted Kennedy. And I had spoken to Kennedy about it, and he was willing to do it, but Mondale didn't want Kennedy. And when he asked me, I was shocked, and so was Tim Russert, who worked for me at the time, and my son Andrew. All three of us thought it was a bad idea. I resisted, but Fritz Mondale insisted.

And when we came to the podium, nobody appeared to be paying any attention, including John Forsythe, the actor; President Carter; and Ed Koch, the mayor of New York City. And I remember John Forsythe saying, "Well, just look at the light; keep your eye on the red light, Mario; that's the television camera." So when I started the speech, I was prepared for the worst. I said a silent prayer, "Oh Lord, please don't let me screw up too badly here."

WO: "There is another shining city on the hill, Mr. President." Did that line just fly into your head?

MC: Actually, when we reluctantly agreed to do the speech, I didn't know where to start. So I took my inaugural speech from the previous year in Albany. And then there was a story in the paper about President Ronald Reagan referring to the country as a "shining city on a hill." And I got to thinking about that and the story of the shining city. And it just came naturally, the next line: yeah, it is a shining city on the hill, perhaps, but there are people in the gutter, where the glitter doesn't show. And there are people halfway up the hill who are sliding back down. So the allusions came very easily after the president himself painted the picture.

ELECTION DAY 2004 RADIO INTERVIEW

MARIO CUOMO: I think a lot about how *lucky* I am. And the older and closer I get to the ultimate accounting, the more I think about how good this country has been to us, to our family. I think about how I can make my contribution. I am all over the country; I do give speeches—and they are not all for money, incidentally, O'Shaughnessy. But I do give as many as I can. I do speak my piece and try to make my case in the hope that it will help a little to advance the dialogue in this country, and be a contribution. I want desperately to be as useful as I can be.

I don't think I had the stuff to be a president. I really don't. I know what I am good at, and I know what I can do. The notion that you are smart enough, wise enough, and strong enough to run the whole place, to do the most powerful job in the world . . . George [W.] Bush had the confidence for that position. John Kerry certainly did. But not all of us feel that way about our own abilities.

WILLIAM O'SHAUGHNESSY: You're picking Kerry. I am picking Bush. Do you want to make a bet right now?

MC: What do you want to bet, O'Shaughnessy?

WO: Well, I don't know . . .

MC: If *I* win, I want to interview *you*! And I want you to answer all my questions the way you expect me to answer all your questions. How is that?

WO: All right, sir.

MC: Prepare yourself for some real shots, O'Shaughnessy!

A RADIO CONVERSATION ABOUT CHRISTMAS . . . AND LIFE

In this December 2007 interview we spoke about growing up . . . and life.

MARIO CUOMO: In our circumstances, Bill, let us think about big issues: What is life? When did it begin? What about God?

For most of us, for much of my life, and certainly for all of my parents' lives, they didn't have the time for that. They needed to put bread on the table and raise their kids. And so most people are driven by necessity and don't have the opportunity for conversations like this one.

I've been gifted with the time, and the situation, to think a lot about those issues. In politics, they come up all the time. A governor interacts with the private sector to help people lead fulfilling lives. But to do that, you must define a "full life" and determine how to distribute the resources of the society.

And, yes, deep down inside me, even as a child, I had questions about life. And I think they derived from my early introduction to books.

My mother and father were never formally educated and read only a little bit. They ran a grocery store, and I was sheltered indoors during my early years because my older brother was hit by a car and badly injured.

So I listened to the radio and read books. My older brother brought them home from the junkyard in the war years because they were separated from the other paper due to their disproportionate weight.

And sometimes it was an old Bible. Sometimes it was an interesting book on lesbianism or homosexuality, an otherwise forbidden topic.

I read a lot, Bill. And I also became a *shabbos goy*. Our grocery store was on one corner, a synagogue on the other. And on the weekend, a *shabbos goy* performs tasks forbidden to Jews on the Sabbath, such as taking out the garbage or other chores.

And you listen to their chants and witness their liturgies. And then on Sunday morning, you're an altar boy in the Catholic Church, and you compare the two.

They both speak a foreign language: Hebrew and Latin. And you ask yourself, "Why?" And you conclude there's a "mystique." We can't know everything about God with our puny intelligence. God is indescribable, and that's what Christian encyclopedias say if you look for a definition.

With a start like that in life, those thoughts are constantly with you, and you can spend a lifetime mulling them over. And I have. And sometimes, you share your struggle with others, and they find it interesting.

WILLIAM O'SHAUGHNESSY: You still have an amazing facility with words. Any regret you didn't do more with that?

MC: [*sigh*] I regret, the way many people do, I wasn't better at what I did. Not in the first half of my life, where everything was trying to put bread on the table for five children, living in a furnished room, and then a walk-up apartment. But then, after that, you can write books, as you have, Bill, brilliant books, and give speeches, as you have, Bill. And you are probably unsatisfied as well.

You write the book because you think you have something to say. You give the speech because you think you have something to say.

People don't listen. Yeah, they will applaud. But the purpose is to move people to a different level so they make different decisions.

WO: I'm glad you're a friend of WVOX and WVIP, sir.

MC: How could I not be? They're wonderful, wonderful always to listen to. And so are you.

THE MORNING AFTER:
"MY SON, THE GOVERNOR"

This WVOX interview was broadcast November 3, 2010, the morning after Andrew was elected governor. It was one of the good days.

In this conversation we hear one of Mario's best-known utterances/observations, which many political candidates of both parties, most recently Hillary Clinton in 2008's presidential campaign, have appropriated: "You campaign in poetry, but you govern in prose." Many years earlier President Richard M. Nixon said, somewhat less elegantly, "Politics is poetry, not prose." And a British journalist, Beverley Nichols, who although he wrote fifty books is mostly remembered for his essays on gardening, once famously said of marriage, "It's a book in which the first chapter is written in poetry and the remaining chapters in prose." But Mario Cuomo's succinct and graceful observation is the one that carries down through the years.

Is it possible my friend Donald Trump heard the interview? When you read the transcript, you'll see what I mean.

WILLIAM O'SHAUGHNESSY: This is, in every telling and by every account, an historic day for the state of New York, for last night Andrew Mark Cuomo became governor-elect of the Empire State. We've talked many times to his father, the fifty-second governor of New York. And it's fitting, proper, and appropriate to talk to him once more on this "morning after." How did you feel last night when the returns came in?

MARIO CUOMO: Well, it was almost anti-climactic, Bill, because we had been listening to polls and they consistently said Andrew was going to succeed by a comfortable margin.

There's great relief for his mother and family, including myself. It's not pride. People keep insisting you must be proud. I think *gratitude* is a better word. We're grateful for the good luck that gave us the opportunity to serve, the good luck that gave Andrew all the wonderful gifts he was born with—a good mind, a strong body—and we were lucky he's made the most of that good luck, and we admire him. That's the way we feel this morning, and I believe that's the way we will feel for every day of his long governance.

WO: Governor, why do you take yourself out of this? Don't *you* believe genes rule? Didn't *you* have something to do with the man he's become, with his priorities?

MC: No. It's hard for me to say, Bill. Frankly, I don't like the gene game. I have two sons who are startlingly good-looking men— and they remind me of that constantly—and my biggest disadvantage according to my sons was that I appeared on *television* and allowed my photograph to be taken too often!

WO: I know where you're going with this, but he was raised at your knee, with your example. Andrew spoke movingly about you last night, about the integrity and decency you bring to the political arena.

MC: Now, that was nice. But there are two aspects to the experience he had. Yes, he was there from the very beginning—from my sudden decision after twenty years as a lawyer to go into politics and government, he was there. He was a part of it from the very beginning. And sure he learned a lot, some of it good and positive. But then he also learned about mistakes that can be made. And I, like every other human being, am subject to mistakes and sometimes significant ones. So there were two things he got: an education in how to do the *right* thing—some very good moves we made, especially economically—and a

warning he ought not make the kinds of mistakes I made. So he
learned from the negatives, and he learned from the positives.

wo: The morning papers, Governor, say you were the hero of the
liberal wing: an icon of liberal persuasion. And that your son and
heir Andrew is more of a centrist, a moderate, a technocrat. Does
that sell him short?

mc: I think it is a very serious mistake, Bill, to give theoretical
political ideology a high place in our legal and political
discussions. I don't believe you should put together a bundle of
principles the way they do for the platforms of the parties.
Incidentally, in every election cycle there's always a platform in
which they say we believe in this or that. I don't believe putting
them all together—and calling them liberal or independent or
Republican or conservative—I don't think that is useful. I think
we should be clearer about our governance, clearer about what
we want as president of the United States, as Members of
Congress, as governors, as members of the state legislature.

   You have to answer the following questions: Is what you are
attempting to do something government *should* be doing
because you can't get it done privately? Now with education, for
example: A long time ago, the Founding Fathers had the
opportunity when they put the Bill of Rights together to say
everybody in the nation should get a reasonable amount of
education and the government has that obligation to provide it.
And they had the opportunity to say, as Founding Fathers, that
everybody in the United States should have the right to health
care. OK. And they had that opportunity at the founding to put
it into the government. But they let it pass, notwithstanding we
as a state, for example, put in our Bill of Rights that we will
fight poverty using government. OK, but the federal government
didn't mention health care or education. And so we had to do

them privately. And we did health care privately from 1789 until 1965. And a lot of people died because they didn't get health care—especially old people who couldn't work died before their time because they didn't have the money to take care of themselves. And, finally, after all those years passed, they said this is something we *must* address through our government. And we did, with Medicaid, Medicare, Social Security.

And that's what we should do again. You want to spend money on something, well prove to me you can't get it done through the market system or through independent means, and you can't get it through the benefactors, *pro bono*, the charitable foundations. Do you want a tax cut? Well, do you *need* a tax *cut*? You want a tax *increase*? Well, do you *need* a tax *increase*? And that is where our process should be. That is what Abraham Lincoln instructed us to do. Lincoln said: Look, don't make this complicated. He said we're a government, a coming together of people—O'Shaughnessy, Cuomo, and all the rest of us—in this particular state and this particular country, to do for ourselves what we could not do as well or at all, privately. If you can do it privately, Cuomo . . . and O'Shaughnessy . . . then do it. But if we need it and can't get it done privately, then consider, as a last alternative, government.

wo: Governor, I think what I am trying to find out . . . is Andrew going to be more like his—if you will forgive me—his magnificent, soulful, visionary *father*, or is he going to resemble pragmatic, "gettin' it done," . . . "doin' what it takes" Bill Clinton, for whom he once worked?

mc: He's going to be smarter than his old man was because he won't make the mistakes his old man made, because they made him bleed when he first witnessed them, and he's going to avoid those. So he'll be smarter than I was. He'll learn from what I did that didn't work well, and he will also learn from what I did that did work well.

For example, Centers for Advanced Technology. If there is anything this state needs and this country needs, it is to get back to the business of making *things* and selling them to people in the rest of the world and to our own consumers. And those things should involve high technology, because there is no limit to high technology. Think of a rocket that will make it through the atmosphere, and you keep going until you think of ways to build communities in space—oh my God, there is no limit to it. And so we did Centers for Advanced Technology on imaging and on other things. That's all in a book I wrote: *The New York Idea*. He should pick that program up and follow it, and he *will*. And he will *use* it. He'll profit from both the things I did right and the things I did wrong.

wo: You said earlier no feelings of pride have invaded you this morning after the historic election. But surely it's not lost on you, great student of history and things political, that none of your predecessors—Franklin Roosevelt, Theodore Roosevelt, Charles Evans Hughes, Nelson Rockefeller—none of them ever had a *son* who became governor.

MC: Let me tell you what the most beautiful thing about that is. It's not Mario Cuomo, and it's not Andrew Cuomo at all. It's Immaculata Cuomo and Andrea Cuomo who, in 1927, came to this country, uneducated in their Italian country where they were born, without a whole lot of money, without any particular skills. He, a laborer. She, doing what a woman could do—raise children, do the cooking, do the sewing, *et cetera*. And they lost a child by the name of Mario, incidentally, who died at the age of two, because they didn't have health care. They didn't have a clinic. They didn't have friends around them. And they were helped by a

Jewish owner of an Italian American and Jewish grocery store in a place called South Jamaica, Queens. And they put my mother and father and an infant behind the store, and they worked there for seven years. And Mr. Kessler, the owner, turned it over to them, and so these poor Italian immigrants who did everything right, everything they were capable of doing at the simplest, most fundamental level, got a public education for their kids. And one of them became a governor! Oh my goodness! But now it's the next generation, and a *second* one of them will become a governor, as he did last night! What it means is that this is a spectacular *place*, this is a spectacular country. This is a magnificent, unique home of opportunity for *everybody*: no matter how humble, no matter how miserable, no matter how little they come with, if they work hard, say their prayers, and get a little lucky, they can go *all* the way! That's what this says. It's not me. It's not Andrew. It's not the Cuomos. It's America I celebrated last night.

wo: Governor, it's become part of the popular lore that when your mother, Immaculata, heard about Lee Iacocca, she reproved you and said: "What's the matter? You think you are very successful, you don't know how to make a car?" What do you think she would have said to Andrew this morning? Or your father, Andrea, after whom Andrew is named? What would they think?

mc: Well, they would probably start talking about *auguri*, their way of saying "pride." They would be proud, and *they* would talk to everyone around them and say, "See my son, see what he's done!" They would be very, very happy about it. Unfortunately, only one of them was around when I got to be governor, and even then she was a little disappointed. Early on, when I went to my parents and said, "I am no longer going to be a lawyer; I want to be a politician," they were very upset because they didn't know anything about politics—except politicians were not to be trusted; it was a terrible business, *et cetera*. "All your life you've been good and decent. You are a nice lawyer, why should you do this thing?"

And I felt so terrible they were hurt and had to think of a rationale. I said, "Mom, listen: by being a *politician*, this is the way you get to be a *judge!*" Aha, you see the notion of the *judge* is something they understood! The judge wears a *robe*, the judge sits up high and looks down at the people he's working with—it was always a *he* in those days. And so she said, "OK, not so bad. Not so bad, he's thinking more intelligently than I thought. He's going to use politics to get to be a judge." Well, years later, after a couple of tries, I won an election. In the [1982] primary I defeated Ed Koch, and it looked like I might have a good shot to go all the way. And so somebody got at the mic on election day and said, "In addition to everything else, Mario Cuomo will be the first Italian American governor in the *history* of the state of New York!" And I looked down at my mother standing next to me, and I said in Italian, "Ma, what do you think of your baby now?" And she looked up at me and said in her wonderful broken English, "This is no so bad, but when you gonna be *judge*, Mario?"

wo: The talk is already started that your son and heir Andrew may run for president, that he could go *all* the way with his gifts. So say people who've seen him on the stump. Do you think you will live to see Andrew in the White House?

mc: The most significant thing I have said this morning, Bill, is how I feel about all of this ceremony we are having about his ascending to the governorship. He has many gifts, no question about it. And if he performs well as governor, then one shouldn't be surprised that his name will almost automatically be thrown into the hopper. They're talking about [George E.] Pataki, a good man who was governor for three terms, and he's thinking about being president. We're a big state and a leadership state. That's why they called us for a long time the Empire State, So, yeah, there is always that possibility here in New York. However, I think we should be looking for *better ideas*. Now, we are not sure what the Republicans stand for. We are not sure what the independents want. We are not sure what Obama's so-called liberals want. And we should be clear about what we *want* and need as a nation. We should be very clear. What are we going to do about our economy? What are we going to do about Afghanistan? How do we get out of the Middle East without killing another 6,000 Americans in a war that can't be won? And so I think it's the *issues* that matter most. And if Andrew, with his bright mind, comes up with good ideas and is able to implement them, then, of course, he ought to be considered for a higher place. I think it should depend upon what he *produces*. That's the way we should be judging our politicians.

I think his answers should be *plain* and very *simple*. We need *jobs*; our economy is weak. And this is the way you make jobs: you do this with our infrastructure. I am looking for a lot of *simple*, *clear*, commonsense ideas that will produce jobs.

Our biggest population is the middle class. People who work for a living because they have to, not because some psychiatrist tells them it's a good way to fill the grim interval between birth and eternity. And they *need* jobs. They need a good health-care plan. Is the plan that was passed [the Affordable Care Act] a good one? Well, that's going to be up for grabs. But everything should be *clear*. Everything should be common sense. Everything should be *plain*. And that's the way we should govern from here on in. Forget the ideology.

wo: Governor, you want *simple* answers. But they say it's the label Barack Obama can't shake, that he's an "elitist," that he's like a college professor. You, with your words and your passion, demolished a shining city on a hill. Is Barack ever going to get it?

MC: Barack Obama is probably one of the brightest presidents, in terms of sheer intelligence. An IQ test would show he is one of the brightest we've ever had. There are other presidents who have been thought of as highly intellectual and intelligent. He's also probably the best orator we've ever had as a president. And for most of his life, he was able to succeed using those two gifts. Being a senator, you use your intelligence in *deriving* positions and you use your eloquence in *describing* them. That's all he needed. And a lot of money!

And so he came into the presidency relying on those two great gifts, his high intelligence and his eloquence. But sometimes you need more than eloquence. I was the one who said you campaign in poetry, but you govern in prose. You campaign in a lot of flowery and perhaps flamboyant rhetoric, but when it comes time to function as a president, then you do it in prose. Hard, plain, *clear* language that works. Then your communications have to be purely pragmatic, not designed to stir the soul and move people. It has to be designed to *educate* people. And that's what Obama has to start doing now, going beyond the gifts he has. Is there a time and a place to use his *intelligence*? Yes, every day. But to use his *eloquence*? There is a special time and place for that. But starting today: talk to me *plainly*: I'm a guy who didn't graduate college, I'm a hardworking guy with four kids and I'm in trouble because I can't pay the tuition for any of them and because I'm worried about my health care. Talk to me. But talk to me in a language I understand. That's what he is going to have to do, starting *today*.

WO: Governor, you've got me confused for a moment—which is my usual lot. But how can you not use your eloquence to explain things? I mean *your* simple, plain eloquence. Why can't *simple* be eloquent?

MC: Well, did you ever describe somebody's attire as elegant?

WO: I have.

MC: What's the difference between elegant and nice?

WO: Sometimes less is more.

MC: Just think about that, O'Shaughnessy. When you have an answer to *that* question, I'll give you an answer to *your* question.

WO: Oh my God, I think I'm over my head trying to mix it up with you. Anyway, I think I'll pull back from Washington and just *ask* you: Did the governor-elect call his father today to check in?

MC: You are not going to believe this, Bill. We have extraordinary work habits. We work all the time. I don't know what time it was when I left the hotel last night. It had to be midnight or one o'clock, and Andrew was there after me. Well, at about four o'clock this morning I got up, and the *New York Times* had been delivered. I get it usually at about 4:15 A.M. together with a copy of the *Wall Street Journal*, the *Daily News*, and the *New York Post*. And I went in to my office in the apartment—I had made coffee already—after only a couple of hours sleep, and the phone rang and it was Andrew. Maybe it was five. Incidentally, he scheduled a meeting for ten o'clock this morning for the whole staff. So I feel sorry for the guys who were partying because they had to show up at ten this morning. And he said to me, "How were the papers? Everything all right in the papers? What did they say? Who won? Who lost? What's big? What should I be looking for?" And I said, "Too early to say. The papers are too early. They're too early on the comptroller race. They're too early on a lot of things, so you should have somebody just gather information for the rest of the day and then maybe by tonight, we'll have a clear picture of everything. But what you have to do now, Andrew, is, as you

know, get to work. Finish up your agenda at the attorney
general's office, at the same time you prepare for the toughest
job you ever had. And probably the toughest job *any* governor
ever had, starting on January 1, 2011."

wo: What did Andrew say?

mc: "Call you later!"

wo: One *final* question: He walked across the stage last night at the
Sheraton in Manhattan and kissed his father, and he whispered
something; what did he say?

mc: He said, "Don't tell them what I'm whispering to you!"

wo: Do you remember? Will you tell me?

mc: Yeah, I do remember, but I'm going to keep it that way.

wo: Thank you, sir. Congratulations. We've talked in moments of
great elation and also during moments of sadness. This is one of
the *good* days.

mc: Have I been clear, Brother Bill?

wo: *Very.*

mc: Then I've been successful. Thank you.

wo: Great stuff. As always.

THE MORNING AFTER:
THE 2012 PRESIDENTIAL ELECTION

We've broadcast many interviews with Governor Mario Cuomo that
have also appeared in my four previous books for Fordham University Press. On the morning after Barack Obama was elected to a second term (which surprised the hell out of my Republican friends!),
we again summoned Mr. Cuomo's wisdom. Then in his eightieth year,
the governor retained a keen interest in the great issues of the day. In
this delightful—and insightful—phone conversation on November 7,

2012, the man the *Boston Globe* calls "the great philosopher-statesman of the American nation" had some sage advice for the president as he was about to begin his second term. And as usual, it was accompanied as well by Mario Cuomo's great wit and charm. Once again I didn't lay a glove on him, and I couldn't even get him to talk about his son and heir, Andrew. Or did he? Mario also offered clues on why he didn't run.

WILLIAM O'SHAUGHNESSY: On this, the morning after the national election of 2012, we repair now to the counsel and wisdom of an individual who almost ran for that job of president of the United States of America: Governor Mario Matthew Cuomo. Governor, were you surprised Barack won?

MARIO CUOMO: Was I surprised? No. I expected he would win, and I was convinced it would be a relatively close race. And it was both those things. He did win. And it was a very close race. I'm not sure it was his best campaign. Notwithstanding, a billion dollars were spent. They didn't get their money's worth. I didn't think there were enough debates. The first one was a knock-out in the first round by [Mitt] Romney, and then there were a couple of other debates which didn't do much to enlighten the American audience. No, I'm not surprised. I'm pleased at the results, and I'm pleased at how the Republicans have responded so far. Let me not say it that broadly—I'm referring to Republicans in the House, who have said very clearly to the president that they wish to deal with him in a collaborative exercise that will produce the kind of policies both sides know we need. It's a very good start, and I hope they keep at it until they get it done.

WO: Mario Cuomo, what about the second term? Your friend Bill Clinton had two terms.

MC: Yes. I hope what happens here is what happened in the
Clinton years. Clinton's first four years were a near-tragedy. He
made a feint at the question of health care and how to get
people the health care they need at a reasonable cost that won't
bankrupt the country. He tried and then had to back off after
various interested parties attacked the approach he was taking.
And so he got that setback and some other failures, which had
people saying we made a mistake electing Bill Clinton. I did not
think so, and I was delighted to see I was right in the second half
of his eight-year term. In the second four-year term, I'll tell you
what happened and why it happened.

What Clinton wound up getting for the people of the United
States of America was 22 million new jobs, an upwardly moving
middle class, an upwardly moving *upper* class. More people
achieved tremendous wealth than ever before in the history of
the country. Balanced budgets. Sharp decline in the number of
poor people. A strengthening of the middle class. All of these
things in the second term. And finally, a projected surplus at the
end of the eight years of trillions of dollars.

WO: Can Obama do the same thing?

MC: One big word is all you need, Bill. And it's called *collaboration*.
The difference between the first four years and the second four
years is that Clinton did not have a collaborative atmosphere
with the Republicans. In the second four years he did, and he
went to all the Republican leaders and he did what he had to do
to create sufficient confidence by the Republicans so they could
work together. And when they worked together, that magic word
collaboration gave us all those successes.

WO: Governor Cuomo, great wordsmith that you are—orator and
careful linguist—what's the difference between *collaboration*
and *compromise*? Is there a difference?

MC: Not really, nuances perhaps. *Collaboration* and *compromise* are other ways of saying "common sense." My mother and father were not given the gift of an education. Not even a grammar school education. But they could make deals. And they had to make deals every day. Because they had very scant resources to live on. They had to be constantly dealing with other people, trading their services for this or that. They learned how to collaborate. Clinton learned how to collaborate. If the Republicans are collaborative, they will have earned our respect and gratitude, notwithstanding they tried to take the presidency from Obama.

WO: Governor, as you get into the Republicans, notice I try to change the subject.

MC: Yes. I don't blame you, O'Shaughnessy.

WO: You hold up Bill Clinton as an example for Barack. Do you realize that if you had done a few things differently, like order that damn plane to take off for New Hampshire [in 1991]—do you realize you might have been holding yourself up?

MC: Let me end this with you right now; maybe we can continue it another time.

WO: I have a few more questions . . .

MC: Well, maybe these two questions I'm going to give *you* will be enough for you. Why would somebody who is considering running for president—maybe Hillary Clinton—decide to consider running for president? This would happen because she's going to obviously leave as secretary of state—get some rest, well-deserved rest. She's done a terrific job. But let's assume she and maybe various governors, from various states, are going to consider running for president.

WO: Anyone we know?

MC: Two questions, Brother Bill, they have to answer. Two questions. More for themselves than for the rest of us. The *first* question is:

"Can I *win*?" Well, that's the question almost all candidates for the presidency will ask. Can I win? And most of the time they will say yes—because, why not? They are probably people who have experience, etc. And yes, they can win. If Bush Jr. can win, if Obama can win, *they* could win. So that is an easy question. But here's the *tough* one. I think if you want to run for president, you have to be able to look into the mirror, and you have to be able to say that person in the mirror is the *best* person available to be president of the United States. If you want to be president, to be morally right, you should convince yourself there is nobody better than you are to run the United States of America. Now, I doubt most candidates ask themselves that question. Because if most candidates asked themselves that question, they would probably have a very difficult time saying, "Yes, I'm the very best person who can run this country." I know I didn't feel that way.

WO: But, sir, with all due respect, a hell of a lot of people who know Mario Cuomo and respect you, they felt you *are* worthy and eminently capable, as you say.

MC: Well, I would have concluded they were wrong, Bill. For my own decision was . . . it's hard to believe that. As a matter of fact, I proved my disbelief that I was the best by supporting John Kerry—not the second Kerry, but the first Kerry who was wounded in action and who I gave money to while I was governor. And when I was asked about it, I said, "Yes, I think he's the best person on the scene for his ability to make a good president."

WO: Governor, you mention Hillary Clinton. Are you saying she should look in the mirror? Or are you giving her permission to run?

MC: No, I just used her name because everyone is using her name. I have no idea whether she wants to run. I have a good idea about her abilities. And I think she's terrific. And she's proven it over and over again. And she made the most convincing case as secretary of state.

WO: Sir, do you have any idea who else might be thinking like this, looking in the mirror?

MC: I have no idea. How about you? You're a smart guy, you're good-looking. Do you see yourself as the best person available?

WO: I'm too young for you. I'm seventy-four. Governor, you said your parents—Immaculata and Andrea Cuomo—had very few gifts. They had the gift of Mario Cuomo, who has been called the great philosopher-statesman of the American nation. We're very grateful to you for sharing Mario Cuomo with us on the morning after a presidential election. Once again, you didn't let me take you where I wanted you to go.

MC: Well, let me say something about that last comment of yours, Bill. They—my parents—didn't think of me as a "gift." And if they did think of me as a gift, why the hell did they keep hitting me on the derriere when I did something wrong?

WO: Weren't you a perfect youngster? Even when you were clandestinely and stealthily playing baseball on four different teams using four different names when you're only supposed to be on one at a time? They didn't catch you.

MC: No, thank goodness they didn't know a lot about me playing as "Lava Libretti." And the umpire over in the New Jersey sandlot league said to me, "Mario, where did you get that name 'Lava'?" I said, "Lava—always *hot!*" I was also known for a time as Oiram Omouc. Exotic, right? That's my name backward.

WO: And didn't you use other names? Connie Cutts? How about Matt Dente? And don't forget the immortal Glendy LaDuke, your most famous *nom de plume*, save A. J. Parkinson. But he didn't play ball, he merely opined.

MC: Dente—yes, indeed, I used Dente. That's also true, O'Shaughnessy. And who can forget the immortal Glendy LaDuke?

WO: You see, I did a little research on your blazing career in the sandlot league in Queens, if not as a candidate for the presidency.

MC: Now you're really getting dangerous and threatening, Brother Bill. So I'm really going to hang up!

WO: Thank you, sir. I still wish you'd just have owned up to the damn name "Mr. President." . . .

ANDY O'ROURKE

I've written often about Andrew P. O'Rourke, the colorful and estimable Republican who served as Westchester County executive and wrote swashbuckling novels.

In a long, distinguished public career he also served as a New York State Supreme Court Justice and an admiral in the New York State Naval Militia (who knew we had a naval militia?).

When the GOP persuaded the popular and good-natured O'Rourke to run for governor against Mario Cuomo in 1986, he famously toured the state with a cardboard cutout of the governor, which he "debated" in town after town. But Andy O'Rourke also used his considerable influence to assist Andrew Cuomo launch his highly praised transitional Housing for the Homeless (HELP) projects. (O'Rourke and Andrew met and bonded at a luncheon at 21 hosted by Yours Truly.) Mario never forgot Andy O'Rourke's encouragement of and kindness to his son. And when the beloved Westchester politician lay dying in Calvary Hospital in the Bronx a few years ago, Mario called his old adversary for a long farewell talk. We spoke about Mr. O'Rourke on the radio on January 4, 2013, when he left us the day before.

Incidentally, Mario echoed on other occasions the sentiments expressed in this interview: "We must get the American public to look past the glitter, beyond the showmanship, to the reality, the hard substance of things. And we'll do it not so much with speeches that will bring people to their feet as with speeches that bring people to their senses." It's almost as if he foresaw the 2016 presidential campaign.

WILLIAM O'SHAUGHNESSY: Governor Cuomo, an old opponent of yours has gone to another—and, we're sure, a better—world. Andy O'Rourke ran against you for governor.

MARIO CUOMO: Bill, it's very difficult to talk about Andy without sounding like you've made an effort to cover him as some kind of heroic figure. I really do think he is—was, and always will be, in my memory—a heroic figure, because he was such a powerful coming together of good things. His intelligence, his vision, his sense of humor, his sense of fairness made all the political labels meaningless. Liberals are supposed to be Democrats, and businesspeople are supposed to be Republicans . . . all of that. Once you meet and see what he is and see his goodness and his charm and see his intelligence, you say, who needs categories, political categories? Just get the best human beings you can to serve you as public servants. He was a wonderful public servant because he was a wonderful human being. He's a great loss to Flora, his wife, and to his children.

WO: Governor Cuomo, do you remember when he was running for governor against you and he had that cardboard cutout of Mario Cuomo?

MC: Talk about a sense of humor. Early in the campaign between Andy and me we had always gotten together. But we had a small "disagreement" for a time, which required on my end that I not debate until the very last moment, and he, bright man that he was, thought of a way to deal with that. He had a cardboard cutout made of me, and it was a very good image of me—except it was considerably thinner than I was because it was just cardboard. And he debated the cardboard figure. Now I didn't know that until—and I happened to be in Westchester on the first day he used it—the reporters came to me and said, "Do you know Andy O'Rourke debated a cardboard figure of you?" And I said, yes, I knew. I told them he's done it more than once and so far the cardboard figure won *two* out of *three*!

WO: But wasn't it because you were something like 1,000 points ahead and said, I don't have to debate this guy?

MC: No, it wasn't that at all, O'Shaughnessy. He said something about Andrew [Cuomo] I didn't like. And I decided to punish him, but he punished me by debating the cardboard figure. But then I put the cardboard figure on my side by saying it won two out of three!

WO: Governor Cuomo, Andy O'Rourke was a Republican. Mario Cuomo, as the world knows, is a Democrat. How did you two get together?

MC: Those are not real distinctions, Bill. And they shouldn't be. Frankly, I think one of the greatest errors made by our Founding Fathers was ignoring George Washington when he said *two* things. First, you should never allow a single person to declare war. And so you should never start a war because the president of the United States asked for it. That's a ridiculous thing because the one person shouldn't be in a position where a bad judgment could be horrible for us. And he also said another thing. He said we should not have political parties. Because as soon as you commit yourself to leftists or rightists, to this kind of person or that kind of person, you choose up sides and you pit them against one another.

He said there should be no parties. And we didn't listen to that. And I think since he said that, we have had something like 176 parties. And the parties do exactly what he projected they would. They would take a position contrary to the other side, because that's the way it is served up to us, our politics. And it's foolish. First of all, we don't stay true to the labels, because there was a lot about Andy O'Rourke that wasn't classical Republican. And there was a lot about Mario Cuomo that wasn't classical Democrat. They are silly labels. And who says so? George Washington. Too bad we didn't listen.

WO: Andy O'Rourke helped your son build housing for the homeless here in Westchester when he was county executive. Do you remember those days? They both got ganged up on by the NIMBYs.

MC: Yes. Almost every time he did something notable, it was praiseworthy. What was a Republican in Westchester doing helping Andrew build housing for poor Democrats who were mainly the kind of people who lived in those humble homes he was building? But Andy O'Rourke, bright and intelligent person that he was, looked up over the labels constantly. If something was good, he recognized it as good, and he found something to do with it for our betterment. And that's what he did with my Andrew and the housing projects. It got him no votes. Got him the irritation of a lot of Republicans in your area. He would smile at that, make a joke, and move on looking for another good thing to do.

WO: Governor, finally, I wonder if there is a lesson. Obama and Romney—clearly they hated each other. But O'Rourke and Cuomo ended up as friends. Any lessons there? Or has it gotten meaner? Nastier?

MC: Essentially you have to go back to George Washington again. Washington made it very clear in simple language. If you create parties, you are declaring that these two groups are different from one another and they should contend with one another. And you will not find your best answers by letting them fight with one another, lie about one another. And that's what we've been doing ever since the people ignored him when they wrote the Constitution.

WO: Governor Cuomo, I hear it in your voice. We've lost Andy O'Rourke here in Westchester. Opponent that he may have been, I think you kind of liked the guy.

MC: I liked him a whole lot. I admired him. And I should. Andrew—my Andrew—I'm sure will have nice things to say about him. Andrew O'Rourke and Andrew Cuomo. Andrew Cuomo in the last poll got at least as many votes as a Republican as he did as a Democrat. It's because Andrew Cuomo has been acting like Andrew O'Rourke at his best. And I hope he keeps doing that.

WO: Politics is a nasty business that only occasionally gets an Andy O'Rourke . . . and a Mario Cuomo.

MC: O'Rourke was good, Bill. O'Rourke was really good. Mario Cuomo is not bad. But I tell you, that cardboard cutout was a winner!

WO: You never forget, Mario. Thank you, sir.

POPE BENEDICT . . . THE CATHOLIC CHURCH
. . . HIS OWN LIFE . . . ED KOCH . . . MARIANO
RIVERA . . . AND IN THIS INSIGHTFUL
CONVERSATION HE ALMOST PREDICTS
POPE FRANCIS

It would be wonderful if we could all get one more shot at it . . . to be given the opportunity to go back and do it over.

—Mario Cuomo, February 11, 2013

WILLIAM O'SHAUGHNESSY: No pope has given up the miter or keys to the kingdom in 600 years. Governor, you're a great student of things theological and a son of the Roman Church. What do you think about the pope's walking away and hanging it up?

MARIO CUOMO: What the pope did, it appears to me, was a practical, selfless, intelligent decision. He is a man who has worked very hard for a long time. He's now concluded he doesn't have enough strength to do the job of being the most important person in the Catholic Church—at least when it comes to the Curia that make the decisions about how we should deal with our religion and how we should keep it strong and how we can improve it. It takes a lot of strength.

He doesn't have that strength anymore. He did, it seems to me, the right thing. If you can't do the job, you have to step aside. Anything else would have been selfish and damaging.

WO: Governor, your friend of so many years Jimmy Breslin once wrote a book called *The Church That Forgot Christ*. And he went to great lengths to say there's a hierarchy running a church that may not resemble what Jesus intended. How do you feel about that stuff?

MC: Well, that "stuff" is a huge amount of religious law that guides those of us that are Catholic in the way we should live, and it's a very difficult thing to try to sum it up in any tidy, neat, and convenient way. This probably is not well understood by people like me and other Catholics. We have to keep in mind that the Church, although it has adopted a rule of infallibility—which means we can't make a mistake if we're talking about our religion; we're not capable of making a mistake—that has been put to one side. That simply is not the working measure of the people who are making the rules. Infallibility was adopted at a time when the Church was already not well supported because it had proven itself vulnerable in a number of ways. To try to deal with that weakness, they suggested that when the pope chooses, because *he* believes it's a matter of very high importance, to make a doctrine, to make a ruling, he does it with infallibility. It means he can't possibly be wrong.

Well, that struck a lot of people as not intelligent and not reasonable, and, in fact, it has never been exercised specifically—except, I think, with respect to the Virgin Mary and the question of whether or not she was assumed into heaven when she passed away. And that's the only issue on which infallibility has been promoted by the pope and the Church that makes the rules. Now, that's a very important thing because it means the Church *is* fallible. It means the Church can make a mistake.

WO: Are you saying the Church made a mistake with the Blessed Mother?

MC: No, I'm saying that it *can* make mistakes and it *has* made mistakes. And that's important because it's corrected a lot of mistakes. And if it can correct a lot of mistakes, that suggests that maybe more corrections are possible. At one time, you could not take any money for lending money to somebody—the interest bankers live with and a lot of other people that lend money. It was a sin to charge somebody for the use of money.

WO: What was that sin called?

MC: Usury, and it was a *major* sin. It was regarded as a very significant sin. And, of course, it's no longer the law of the Church. And there are other things the Church has changed its mind on. There's a great book by an Irish Catholic judge on the Church's policy. And how over the years the Church has accepted and even promoted the reality that it is capable of making mistakes. Usury is one of those issues. They made a big mistake—the Church—when they said it was a sin to charge interest. And certainly a whole lot of people are happy because there are a lot of people in this world who earn a lot of money for lending money, and they didn't want to hear the Church saying it's a sin to charge interest.

WO: Governor, you've written lovingly and also critically—if gently—about the Church. You're not going to like it when I remind you of this, but when you were elected governor of New York three times by tremendous margins, a friend of yours said, "I think Mario really wants to be a cardinal." Forgive me; that really happened.

MC: No, no, that didn't happen, O'Shaughnessy. I could guess who it is that said that. But I'm not going to give you the name for fear that I'm shooting at the wrong target. No . . .

WO: Did you ever think about being a priest?

MC: No. Let's stay with the governorship. I felt capable of being a competent governor before I decided to run. I had a lot of experience as a lay Catholic, and that was useful in terms of being an active Catholic. I had a lot of experience doing that. And in terms of governing, I had four years as secretary of state in which I learned a whole lot about our government and traveled all over the state. And then I had four years working with Hugh Carey as the lieutenant governor, who would take his place if he [had] to step away. I was well armed for the job. I was a lawyer before that, and so I had the confidence I would be competent. I never dreamed I would be more than that, and when people started talking about me as a president, I could not say about myself what I could say about myself when I chose to attempt to be a governor. And that is I know I'm *competent* to do this. I did not have that same feeling about the presidency.

wo: But, Mario Cuomo, excuse me, you've always been drawn relentlessly and consistently to the great cosmic and spiritual issues of the day. Somebody once said famously, "This guy is too good to be worried about how many Bob's Big Boys you should put on the Thruway." You've worked the territory that should be worked by cardinals and bishops on spiritual and moral issues. You know you have. You spoke famously on abortion. And you've tried to make some sense of it all. You sure you didn't go into the wrong business?

mc: No, not at all. If you're suggesting I should have become a priest, I've already confessed I wasn't good enough to be a president. I'm just as sure—or surer—that I'm not good enough to be a priest. Certainly not after I met Matilda!

wo: I'm not asking you to dump Matilda.

mc: The Church is a wonderful thing, Bill. The Church, when it stays close to Christ and what Christ said and what Christ believed and what Christ sought to teach all the rest of us—when the Church does that, it's wonderful. Really wonderful. It can make the world better. And let's stay with the Church and what it represents in terms of religious belief. If you look very closely, the Roman Catholic Church is not very far separated from Judaism. The essence of Judaism is those two simple principles that can be captured with two simple words: *Tikkun Olam* and *Tzedakah*. *Tzedakah* is, roughly in Hebrew, "charity": goodness in dealing with other people. And "fairness." That's *Tzedakah*. *Tikkun Olam* is the Hebrew principle that says God made this world but didn't *complete* it. *Your* mission is to continue the work He began. And to correct some of the misdirections we have become guilty of. *Tzedakah* and *Tikkun Olam*. But those two principles are *exactly* what Christ taught. And, as a matter of fact, there's a kind of dramatic evidence of this in the story about Christ on that night coming out of the synagogue and being confronted by people who are not friendly to Him and demanded to know from Him why it was other rabbis were walking out and expressing astonishment at His intelligence and wisdom, *et cetera*. And what is it He said to these people in the synagogue? And He said simply . . .

wo: The Lord?

mc: Yes. This is Christ talking simply to the people in the synagogue, the rabbis particularly. He said, "Look, this is the Whole Law. Love one another as you love yourself." That's *Tikkun Olam* and the *Tzedakah* principle put together. "Love one another as you love yourself for the love of Me for I am Truth." And what he was saying is "I am God, and you should rest on that principle, and that principle calls upon you to be good to one another. To love one another." Well, if those two principles are the essence of Christ, then what distinguishes them from the Jews? Well, the Hebrews said exactly the *same* thing! One of the great rabbis said, "Love one another as you would love yourself, for the love of God, because that's what God wants you to do. And everything else is commentary." I love that! Loving one another is all you need to do to be right with the religion, whether it's Judaism *or* Christianity. And if we could get that clearer in our minds, we wouldn't have spent all those years trying to blame every Jew for having killed Christ and for being the *massachristis*—this was condemned in the Second Vatican Council. The *massacristy* was a kind of slur on Jewish people to say they are the killers of Christ. In fact, they are *not* the killers of Christ. They didn't do the killing. But more than that, even as a matter of religious principle, they weren't the killers of Christ.

You know, you have all of that going for you. We will continue to refine, to study, and to discuss the relationship between the Christian principles and the Hebrew principles and get even closer together. When that happens, then the great issue of modern religion becomes, what do the rest of the world's religions say about a *new* religion, that is, the New Christianity and the Old Judaism now making up the New Religion. Will they be frightened by it? Will they be attracted by it? There are more people out there that believe in the Qur'an than there are Jews and Christians. So, it's an exciting world we're living in if you judge it just by its religions. The kind of pope we need is the kind of pope who will say, "It's time to look back on our history and to see we have failed in our mission because we simply have ignored opportunities." Wouldn't it be wonderful if women, whom we are so eager to make equal to men in all ways that are practical—wouldn't it be something if all the women who wanted to be priests could be priests? And all the women who want to be able to conduct the Mass, could? Then all the women would be the equal of all the men. How much stronger would that make us as a Christian nation?

wo: Governor, would you want to go to Confession to a woman? It's hard enough telling a guy your sins!

mc: I'll take your word for it, Bill.

wo: At least for me.

mc: OK, let's leave it there, O'Shaughnessy.

wo: Governor, you're a politician. That's what you are. A governor, a politician.

mc: I'm a lawyer. That's what I am: a lawyer.

wo: A lawyer. But governors and politicians and lawyers are not supposed to talk about things like this. About *Tikkun Olam* and *Tzedakah*. Soulful, religious, deep issues.

mc: Why not?

wo: See, you prove my point. You've always been drawn to this stuff. So again I ask you . . .

mc: It's not "stuff." It's the rules by which you lead your life.

wo: One of our callers is nominating *you* for pope, and Mariano Rivera [the great Yankees relief pitcher] for vice pope. Will you serve if elected?

mc: No, but I tell you, I would love to see how he throws that one pitch. I mean, it's just one pitch this guy has—the cutter. And I hope he hasn't lost it to this year while he was sitting it out.

wo: The *Boston Globe* called you the great philosopher-statesman of the American nation. Did you ever get the feeling you'd like to get in there and save your Church?

mc: No, no. I'm too weak to do a lot of the things I'd love to be able to do. It would be wonderful if we could all get one more shot at it, at one point be given the opportunity to go back and do it over. Imagine how much better you could do it. And that's the way we should feel about the Church now. We should feel

the Church is invited to have a new day. A new era of the
Church. If you could find the right person to lead it, then
wonderful things can happen to our religion and to the world
affected by that religion.

WO: Governor, speaking of a final shot, you gave an exceptional
interview with *New York* magazine about sometimes a friend,
sometimes not so much a friend, Ed Koch. Would you like one
final comment on the man?

MC: Final word on Ed Koch? I'll give you one final word. I wrote
something; can I read it to you, Bill?

WO: We'd love to hear it, sir.

MC: "Everyone who has ever sat in the magnificence of Temple
Emmanuel cannot be unmoved by the dazzling and soaring
beauty that surrounds them. Some of our great city's greatest
citizens have chosen it as the platform for their last goodbyes, as
did Ed Koch on Monday, February 4, 2013. I knew Ed Koch for
most of the quarter of a century that we both became involved in
politics. During those years we had our ups and downs, but no
politician I know ever equaled Koch's mastery of the media. All
of it—television, radio, newspapers, public appearances. It made
him, perhaps, the best-known political leader in New York City's
history. That was made clearer by the unprecedented media
coverage his passing received. He deserved to be well known. Ed
devoted his life to two great loves: the world of politics and his
family. He spent his entire adult life in public service as a soldier,
mayor, congressman, writer of books and columns. In the end he
was more than a uniquely honored mayor. He was an institution
that became an ineradicable part of our city's history, like the
Statue of Liberty and the great bridges. New Yorkers will never
stop answering his question, which was 'How Am I Doing?' And

they'll answer it with their reply. 'You did good, Ed. You did good!'"

WO: Governor, I couldn't talk you into running for pope, but you've given us some great gifts, as you always do. I'm glad you're a friend of this radio station, sir. Thank you.

MC: Thank you for having me once again, Brother Bill.

9

Early Commentaries about Mario

We've broadcast many editorials and commentaries about Mario on WVOX. This was the very first one, on June 22, 1982. I called it "Reality with a Red Rose."

In 1982 the race for governor of New York was wide open. Hugh Carey was not seeking reelection, and Mario M. Cuomo, the articulate, graceful lieutenant governor, decided to make the run, as did Edward I. Koch, who had beaten Cuomo five years earlier to become mayor of New York City. This set up a bruising primary battle within the Democratic Party.

But first came the state convention in June of 1982, at which the party regulars and the Democratic establishment regulars backed Koch. But Cuomo won enough votes to force that historic primary.

Our thoughts the first week of summer are upstate in Syracuse, where Mario Cuomo fights for his political life and for the soul of the Democratic Party. In this task, he will come up against Edward Irving Koch, who is the mayor of New York. The bosses and elders of the Democratic Party are almost certain to designate Koch to run for governor. He is colorful, a media event, a winner as they see it, and he is quick, diverting, and funny.

Koch is also cutting and cruel. He plays to the worst instincts of people with his pandering and vengeance in the matter of killing sanctioned by the state known as the death penalty.

In other times, delegates to this state convention would bring forth Franklin Roosevelt or Herbert Lehman or Averell Harriman or Alfred Emanuel Smith. But it is 1982, and the Democratic Party is just as confused and lost as the rest of us. And so it will choose Koch as the "official" designee, because David Garth, the media manipulator and political wizard, assures them Koch is a stronger media event. His Honor Mayor Koch will raise millions from his realtor friends in New York. Not as much as he saved them. But they will not forget what he has done *for* them or what he can still do *to* them even if he should lose the race for governor.

We're for the other man, Mario Matthew Cuomo, the lieutenant governor. He speaks in paragraphs while Koch speaks in headlines. He makes sense while Koch makes jokes. He makes us think, while Koch makes news. He talks of love and reconciliation, while Koch talks of vengeance and punishment.

Koch is the best horse David Garth has ever had. But William Haddad, the Cuomo campaign director, faces the same problem we have now in trying to tell you about Cuomo the mediator, the conciliator, who is like nothing we've ever seen in the body politic.

It is almost impossible to package this fine, bright man, the philosopher whose name is laden with too many vowels. But as we've been telling you, Cuomo has been in Westchester a lot in recent months, and we detect the old stirrings again among the party faithful here. Grandmotherly Miriam Jackson is moving around our home heath again, under her sunbonnet, and using Yiddish phrases to tell people about this son of Italian immigrant parents who would be governor. And Samuel George Fredman, the famous matrimonial lawyer, who is himself a decent man in a murky calling, accused Cuomo of being a "mensch." "A 'mensch'?" said Cuomo, "how nice; that's the way you *lose!*"

Mario Cuomo stood there at the Mulino restaurant in White Plains the other night in a baggy, rumpled suit with a rose on his lapel and a lawyer's vest. His watch looks like a Timex deluxe. As he began to speak to the Westchester Democrats, the orchestra leader reached over and tried to smooth the jacket pocket on Cuomo's blue suit. The only style the man has is in his mind and on his face. Even Fredman, who is a master politician, is stumped. "Cuomo is a real, decent man. I want people to know him for what he is," Fredman said.

Later, Cuomo appeared at a party for Dick Ottinger. And Gary Hart, the senator from Colorado who wants to be president of the United States, stood waiting while Cuomo spoke. Although Hart has been around a lot, you could see him warm to Cuomo.

It happens everywhere whenever someone stops to actually *listen* to the man. It happened again at a dinner for four hundred people who had come to honor the Reverend Calvin Sampson, pastor of Shiloh Baptist Church in New Rochelle. Jesse Jackson, the preacher, was the guest speaker, and Ossie Davis, a marvelous human being and neighbor of this radio broadcasting station, was to introduce Jesse Jackson. Jackson and Davis are as strong in front of a crowd as any two men in America. And then a tired Cuomo approached the microphone to talk to these four hundred people who had come to be inspired, but not to hear a political speech. And up on the dais, Jesse Jackson whispered to Ossie Davis, "This Cuomo is no lightweight."

We predict Koch and his Realtor friends will find this out soon enough. The smart-money guys, the movers and shakers at the bar of 21, tell you Koch will win. Their main slam against Cuomo is that "he won't deal; you can't *do business* with Mario." But can you say anything better about a politician in this day and age?

"This is a hard business," Cuomo the politician told us. "It's easier when you have something to believe in," Cuomo the philosopher reminded us. In this day of media events, practically every politician is something less in person than he appears to be on television. Reality, as they say, is a downer. But then along comes Cuomo with a red rose on his lapel, who is stronger, one on one, than his image on television.

All his fellow Democrats have to do is *listen*. Or they could just go ahead and let Garth pick the next governor. But word is getting around about this Cuomo. The old stirrings are there, in the Democratic Party, and in the land.

Here is another commentary, "Cuomo and the Moonbeams," from September 20, 1982, that was widely circulated all across the state and quoted in several newspapers and political journals all across the nation.

On Sunday afternoon, Henry Kissinger, the rich Republican author and commentator and friend and counselor of Nelson Rockefeller, stood in the elegant living room of Peter Flanagan's country house in Purchase, telling marvelous, witty stories. Mario Cuomo of Queens was in Bill Haddad's disorganized office in New York, writing a last-minute appeal to registered voters of another political party, those Democrats who could make him their nominee for governor of New York.

Other candidates in this strange political season hire paid flacks, like David Garth and Howard Rubenstein, to string words together for them. The eager candidates then push these words through manufactured smiles. But Cuomo would handle and record his own appeal for the radio. The words on the tape would be coming out of his own mind.

But not even Cuomo the candidate knows how to capture Cuomo the man in thirty seconds. And so yesterday, the words came across the paper off his pen—tight, precise, factual, and dull. One hundred neat little words aimed at convincing you that Ed Koch is a good, colorful mayor who would be a terrible governor.

On his feet talking to poor people, blacks, Hispanics, or a man out of work, Cuomo is as good as we have in this country today. He reaches those people as precisely as Henry Kissinger zeroes in on the rarefied wavelength of Peter Flanagan's rich, conservative, country-squire neighbors here in Westchester. "There is a place for believers," Cuomo says. It is as thrilling as anything the Madison Avenue crowd could push together for this final week. "The Democratic Party is a party of hope. Koch preaches fear and speaks of death, while I speak of *life!*"

I asked Pete Hamill, the street-smart writer of the poor and of the city, if Cuomo was really as good as we have heard. "He's better," said Hamill, "but I'm afraid they can't package this particular politician in thirty seconds. The trouble with the son of a bitch is he really *believes.*"

I don't know what Mario Cuomo has decided to say in his final appeal to the Democrats of New York state. He may go with the dull litany he read aloud yesterday while Bill Haddad stood over him with a stopwatch, counting off the precious seconds, up to thirty. I hope he will just look up from the paper and lean into the microphone and say he has done what he could to help this party find its soul and now it's up to you. "There *is* a place for believers," he should tell them. "There *is* hope!"

A lot of people are rooting for Cuomo. Sam Fredman, the former chief of the Democratic Party in Westchester, who is now chairman of the Westchester Jewish Congress, heard the Italian from Queens defending Israel the other night. Fredman said, "I only wish I, as a Jew, could do as well."

However, the *Daily News*, which would have you believe it is the paper of the people of New York, is against him. The *New York Times*, the best paper in the world, is for Koch too. And so is William Paley's flagship television station, WCBS-TV. Each of these instruments of communication is run by people who do a lot of business in New York City, and an angry Mayor Koch could be somewhat dangerous to their corporate health. It has to do with property taxes and abatements and printing plants and labor unions; also with Phyllis and Robert Wagner and Frank Sinatra and Harry Helmsley and Lou Rudin and Steve Ross and Jimmy Robinson of Amex.

Hugh Leo Carey in his thousand-dollar suits is for Koch, sort of. I say this because Carey is of my tribe. I know him and I like him, and he didn't look too good as he stood up with Koch on the TV last week.

It is probably futile to broadcast this kind of piece the Monday before the great primary. Anyway, I don't believe in miracles anymore. And yet . . . and yet, this Italian from Queens nags at me. He is what politicians were before they wore thousand-dollar suits. He is what the party of our fathers used to be. But, forget it. The big Realtors in New York and Hugh Carey and the *Times* and WCBS-TV are never wrong. Koch will probably clobber Cuomo and his moonbeam crowd of liberals.

It is 1982, and the Democrats wear thousand-dollar suits just like those Republicans having drinks and fawning over Henry

America's greatest orator! Mario appeared often over the years at the New York State Broadcasters' high councils like this one back in the 1970s at the fabled old Otesaga Hotel in Cooperstown. (Don Pollard)

"Look, a Republican—no socks!" In this marvelous scene at Grossinger's in the Catskills, Mario couldn't resist pointing out that I was a "sockless wonder"! (Whitney Media Archives)

Leaning in to the mike to make a point. The governor appeared on WVOX and WVIP many times, during which the conversations went in directions both temporal and spiritual. (Whitney Media Archives)

After a delightful lunch (one of several) with legendary *New York Post* columnist (and "Page Six" founder) Neal Travis, who observed, "Look at those damn moguls watching us ... they'd never believe we were talking about our bloody *souls*!"

Maestro Sirio Maccioni, ringmaster of Le Cirque, fed Presidents Reagan, Nixon, and Bush. Also many kings and potentates ... including Frank Sinatra and Jack Kennedy. But Mario was a special favorite. "Sirio *does* look like John Wayne!" said the governor when they first met. (Wendy Moger-Bross)

Greeting folks on Madison Avenue. "Just remember, *I'm* the governor!" (Don Pollard)

The governor and Matilda commissioned a painting of a white-haired friend for a birthday celebration of some significance (7-0)! (Whitney Media Archives)

No free lunch! The governor at the prestigious Dutch Treat luncheon club. "I wanted to just do a Q&A session. But O'Shaughnessy said, 'No—you have to pay for your lunch with a full speech!'"

Airborne over upstate New York during Mario's first campaign for governor in 1982. (Or is it Kevin Spacey, who, I've always said, should play Mario Cuomo in the movie version of a remarkable life.) (Don Pollard)

(*Left to right*) The author; Matilda Cuomo; Ambassador Ogden Rogers Reid, a great First Amendment champion and our first U.S. ambassador to the infant state of Israel. He was also publisher of the *Herald Tribune* and a congressman; and MMC. (Wendy Moger-Bross)

The governor loved to tell pals about the time President Reagan mistook him for Lee Iacocca. Here he poses with a cardboard cutout dummy of the president at 55th Street and Fifth Avenue in Manhattan.

"Now I've *really* made it!" Workers at the General Mills plant in Buffalo put the governor's mug on the iconic Wheaties box during a visit in 1990. (Don Pollard)

MMC, deep in thought. He was always looking toward the light. (Don Pollard)

Kissinger up at Peter Flanagan's house in Purchase. But the question lingers; is there a place for believers?

———————————————

Cuomo beat Koch in that hard-fought primary, which set up a bruising race against millionaire Lewis Lehrman in the general election. Cuomo won that one too . . . and was on his way to becoming a national figure.

I wrote this next piece, "An Implausible New Year's Day," while going back down the Thruway to Westchester after a few drinks at Windham Mountain with former Governor Hugh Carey and his pal Kevin McGrath on the day Mario became governor, January 1, 1983.

It was beautiful and bright, that first day of 1983, out of season for winter. Even upstate New York threw off its dullness and gray pallor. When you saw Bella Abzug smiling and coloring her cheeks with extra rouge at the New Baltimore service area on the Thruway, you knew something special would happen this day farther on up the Hudson Valley.

This, then, is how I spent that New Year's Day, and what I saw and heard. It started with Bella Abzug in a Thruway service area south of Albany. And it ended with Hugh Leo Carey, the former governor, drinking a Molson's in a Windham ski lodge and saying he is glad he is not governor anymore.

Everything else that happened that day belonged to Mario Matthew Cuomo. The day was his, having been earned across eight years and thousands of nights and hundreds of lonely rides up and down the Thruway, with his butt against a small, flat, hard board to relieve the relentless pain in his back.

I have always been pretty straight with you and those seated around your breakfast table. But for almost a year now, as the listeners of these broadcasts know, it has been increasingly difficult for me to be entirely objective about a certain politician from Queens whose name ends in a vowel and who is a member of a political tribe quite different from my own. He is not a Republican.

So, up front: I *like* Mario Cuomo. I like his style. I like the stuff he is pushing off from his bright, fine mind and from his heart. I am nuts about his wife, who is a sheer, pure, natural force. And I like his family, too. I like almost everything about this attractive and appealing man, who is a politician the way the men of my father's time imagined them to be. I like his music. Thus, any comments I might make on the radio about what happened in the capital city of our state when this man became governor ought to be greatly suspect. In point of fact, we were there on Saturday only because he prevailed in what he himself has called "an implausible pursuit." Which means Cuomo was rejected by his own and rose from the rebuke of the elders of the Democratic Party, which he distinguished for so long. He won against their official designee, Edward I. Koch, the enormously popular mayor of New York, and then he went out and beat a man who spent $15 million to defeat him. You cannot spend more money to buy an election in the state of New York, and Lewis Lehrman may even sue his ad agency for not purchasing more time on the airwaves in the final week. As Cuomo said, his victory was implausible. But it happened.

And now in Albany, this day, there were American Indians and Mayor Koch and Engie Carey, who is married to Hugh, and flags and an orchestra and a chorus with young, black faces, and pomp and ceremony, and Al DelBello, the lieutenant governor. There were, however, no Realtors from New York. The big bankers and moneymen of the state and the powerbrokers and fat cat lawyers were elsewhere—so were all the people at the bar at 21 who had written off this man who became governor of the only state in the nation that really matters.

Hugh Carey was there Saturday in the Empire State Plaza, which he had graciously—and characteristically—renamed for Nelson Rockefeller. And Carey, in only a few hours, would be in the lodge at the base of Windham Mountain telling them why he is glad he is not governor anymore. No one believed him.

But earlier that afternoon, as he waited for the new governor, you had to remember that if Carey did nothing else, he kept this state from becoming New Jersey or Texas or Virginia, which are places in this country where they kill human beings with lethal injections as part of their tidy, most efficient, and functional capital punishment programs.

As this day belonged to the man from Queens, an aide to the new governor, Tonio Burgos, gently and kindly helped Carey and his wife depart from the state capitol building before the crush. To the sound of cannon fire outside and flanked by state troopers, Cuomo came at last to become governor of New York. He first appeared in the far corner, in the far reaches of the great hall, and he moved through the crowd and down the aisle with the easy grace of the natural athlete that he is. And as the applause rose, he stopped and found a child with disabilities and a woman in a wheelchair, ignoring all the elders and powerbrokers grasping for his hand.

As he began his talk to the people of the state, many of us who have seen him on a flatbed truck in the Garment District or on lonely street corners were concerned that he might be distracted by the sophisticated electronic TelePrompTer or just overwhelmed by the moment and by the sweep and architecture of the building that bears Rockefeller's name. And it did take him a while to get rhythm into his words and sentences in front of these three thousand people. Those who love the man knew he has sounded better out on the streets, and some in the audience began to despair when he seemed to be relying on [those] damn TelePrompTers to either side of him. He went on like this, without music and without poetry to his opening remarks.

And then . . . then Mario Cuomo became Mario Cuomo. It happened about five minutes into the speech: "I want to talk about the *soul* of the administration." And then everything this man is exploded all over the room. "I would rather have laws written by Rabbi Hillel or by the good Pope John Paul II than by Darwin. I would rather live in a state that has chipped into the marble face of its capitol these memorable words of the great Rabbi: 'If I am not for myself, who is for me? And if I am for myself alone, what am I?'" He then continued with "I am the child of immigrants" and went on to speak of his parents, going back sixty years, to tell how his mother, Immaculata, arrived at Ellis Island to join her husband, Andrea, who had come before her.

"Remember who we are and where we came from and what we have been taught." To some, it was philosophy; to him, it was a battle plan, a blueprint for a government.

"And no family that favored its strong children or failed to help its vulnerable ones would be worthy of the name. And no state or nation that chooses to ignore its troubled regions and people, while watching others thrive, can call itself justified," Cuomo said.

As he talked like this about the poor and the weak in our society, hard-nosed political veterans sat with glistening eyes. Bill Haddad, his campaign manager, who has been with Jack and Bobby Kennedy, fought back tears. Samuel Fredman, the famous Jewish leader and matrimonial lawyer, who is a good man in a murky profession, gripped the hand of his wife, Mims. Even Andrew Cuomo, Mario Cuomo's son and heir, who is supposed to be such a big, tough guy, clenched his teeth and bit his lip as he watched his father talk about the "Family of New York."

And then Cuomo pulled himself again from the TelePrompTer for one last thought, which came up from his gut and out of his heart. And no one in Albany on that first day of the New Year will ever forget what he said: "I ask of all of you, whatever you think of me as an individual, to help me keep the moving and awesome oath I just swore before you and before God. Pray that I might be the state's good servant and God's too."

That would have been enough for the history books and for the front page of the *New York Times* or the archives of the capital. But Cuomo had to add this: "And Pop, wherever you are—and I think I know—for all the *ceremonia* and the big house and the pomp and circumstance, please don't let me forget."

In the stilted beginning of this first inaugural address, Cuomo had directed himself to President Reagan and the syndicated columnists. But in the end, as he spoke from his heart, it was for Andrea Cuomo, the Italian laborer who became a greengrocer in South Jamaica and who had a son who is now our governor. At that moment Mario Cuomo became the most compelling political figure in the nation today.

When he finished, Cuomo stood with his aching back in the receiving line, next to Matilda Raffa and their children, for three hours. I left Albany to go down to Windham Mountain to have a drink with Carey and Kevin Barry McGrath. But that night, and all the way back to Westchester with my own sons, I thought of the greengrocer's son. The way he talked about the homeless and the infirm and the destitute kept coming back to me.

There is no one in this country quite like Cuomo, and on New Year's Day of 1983, he became the governor of New York. Implausible or not.

––––––––––––––––––

Mario loved to repair to his home office and sit at his desk behind boarded-up windows on the second floor of the Executive Mansion on Eagle Street, where he could write. But he wasn't crazy about the business of publishing and promoting the product of his bright, fine mind once his brilliant genius was printed and bound.

On April 18, 1984, we covered the announcement of one of the governor's books, *The Diaries of Mario M. Cuomo*, at the headquarters of Random House in New York City. Predictably, it was, at Mario's insistence, held on a Saturday so as not to interfere with his official duties "at the people's business."

There was to be a press conference to introduce a new book. The author was not even there yet and already there was talk of "family" in the air—about parents and children and generations.

It was a Saturday morning with a spring rain falling on Manhattan. Robert Bernstein, the tall, elegant chairman of Random House, waited for one of his authors in the big paneled conference room high in a glass building on the East Side. Bennett Cerf used to run this place. Now he looks down from a large oil painting with that marvelous whimsical squint we remember from television.

It is Bernstein's turf now, and the chairman of this great publishing house, the grandson of Litvak Jews, talked about his grandfather, who, it seems, was quite a brave man in Lithuania during the time of the Nazis. The talk then turned to his newest

Random House author, who has written of a father named
Andrea, a laborer who became a greengrocer. He had a son who
became the governor of New York, just like Franklin Roosevelt
and Nelson Rockefeller. That son, Mario Matthew Cuomo, has
now written a book.

So, as the reporters and cameramen adjusted their minicams
and microphones in the bright, hot lights, Bernstein moved
among them. Croissants and muffins and clear, strong coffee
were on a sideboard, all of it being so plentiful and completely
free that the reporters ate a lot from the Random House larder as
Bernstein talked up the new book. Because the politicians they
usually cover for a living throw a box of doughnuts on the desk,
the reporters were receptive. The publisher has done this little
spread for the likes of Gore Vidal, E. L. Doctorow, Norman
Mailer, Truman Capote, and James Michener. This time, he
waited for Andrea Cuomo's son. "Do you think this book will
sell?" asked Bernstein. "He's quite a marvelous man, isn't he?"
He was also late this busy Saturday morning, stuck in traffic at
one of the East River crossings the Queens people know all too
well. And then, at about 10:30, his heralds began to appear:
Andrew, his son and heir; Fabian Palomino, the one he calls
"Professor," who goes way back with him; Tim Russert, the
shrewd, street-smart counselor to the governor; and Harvey
Cohen, a deputy commissioner. They lived part of this book with
him, and it was right for them to be here. And then Mario Cuomo
came into the room and sat again before the lights and the
cameras as the questions began. The New York reporters probed
and poked for an angle and a tidy headline to please their editors
and tantalize readers and viewers.

The Diaries of Mario M. Cuomo: The Campaign for Governor—
like the man who wrote it, the book is difficult to define, hard to

categorize. It is, at once, a political book, a travel book, a mystery book, a religious book, a history book. I can't label it. But this I assure you: *Diaries* is a haunting, powerful, disturbing, demanding, and, ultimately, joyful book.

Mayor Koch has recently produced his own book—a marvelous, glib, slick, entertaining piece of work, a quick read. Cuomo's book is anything but. As you go through *Diaries*, you will find lots of famous political names strewn about. It's heady and fascinating to read the governor's observations about all the movers and shakers in the political world. But you won't find any glibness or, indeed, any meanness of spirit in Cuomo's retelling of his setbacks and his triumphs. His betrayal at the hands of former Democratic chairman Dominic Baranello is one of the most touching examples of Cuomo's generosity of spirit, as he worries about Baranello's health on the very day he was deserted by the political warlord. *Diaries* is a political book, all right. But the thought occurs that it is also a travelogue, even a mystery story. It is the journey of one man's soul over a two-year period. And his search for Mario Cuomo is much more compelling than his pursuit of the governorship. You sit with Cuomo in the lonely hours of the night, and you greet the cold light of early dawn as he struggles to put some meaning to the implausible and tumultuous events that culminated in his upset victories over Koch and Lewis Lehrman.

The recollections about his late father are haunting and almost lyrical as, again and again, the governor returns to his familiar theme—family—and his admonition, "Don't let us forget who we are and where we've come from," echoes through the pages. Some entries are absolutely devastating, as Cuomo confronts death, or, what Teilhard de Chardin, his favorite philosopher, called the "diminishment" we all suffer as we get older. The reader will also find five of the governor's speeches, including his brilliant and soaring inaugural address delivered in Albany on January 1, 1983.

As you read Cuomo's book, you keep remembering something Ken Auletta of the *Daily News* said: "He's awesome . . . he's so damn bright, it's scary . . . sometimes you have to get away from him." There are passages in the book that are so insightful and sensitive they almost make you want to flee. But when you've finished, you're glad you stayed the course. Awesome or not, everything this man is, is in this book.

Politicians are not supposed to write or even think like this. Cuomo will discourage a lot of writers—and even a few broadcasters—from ever going near a typewriter or a yellow legal pad once they discover what this graceful son of a greengrocer has done to the language. This book, which Cuomo says he wrote only for himself and was never meant to be published, has almost preempted the arena of the written word around here. Maybe some of the New York writers and Albany political correspondents will want to try baseball now that Cuomo is working their side of town.

I think you will enjoy this book and the penetrating insights, which flow so effortlessly and candidly from the governor's fine, intelligent mind and generous heart. It may not sell as well as the Koch book, but this I know. *The Diaries of Mario M. Cuomo* will be read and treasured long after other recent books are forgotten.

After the press conferences in New York on Saturday, the chairman of Random House was trying to think of a place to take the new author to dinner, someplace where they could celebrate the publication of a new book. The publisher was gently advised not to take this author to a grand place like the 21 Club, Le

Cirque, the Four Seasons, or Mortimer's. Bernstein said: "Very well, then, I think we'll celebrate with a fine dinner at Le Perigord. The chef will do anything for me there."

Out on East 50th Street, in the rain, Cuomo stood and talked with his son Andrew and Palomino in order to unwind and disengage himself from this business of selling books. He took a deep breath and appeared to hyperventilate. And then Captain Joseph Anastasi, of the state police, put him in an unmarked car, which moved out through the rain in the direction of the East River, toward Queens and home. Cuomo the writer was again Mario Cuomo the governor. And still the son of Andrea Cuomo. Now all he has to do is get through a dinner at Le Perigord.

I'm going to buy his book for my family and friends. And then I think I'll read it again—for myself—when I'm alone, late at night, before the dawn, when the Bible and the Tums don't work.

10

Letters to a Friend

Over the years I worked both sides of the street on the question of whether Mario's considerable talents were best utilized in Albany or on the national—and world—scene in Washington.

In this 1988 missive I was trying to nudge him into a national race.

> Personal & Confidential
>
> April 11, 1988
>
> Mario:
>
> I'm writing this note early in the morning as I make my way down from the country on Route 17. The seven o'clock CBS Radio Network news via WINR in Binghamton has just mentioned the *Times* story that you're "edging closer" to a Shermanesque statement.
>
> I've been thinking about this whole damn dilemma, and I had just about decided to do another most brilliant O'Shaughnessy Editorial of the Air when I get to the station. But I think I'll opt instead for this note to a friend I care a great deal about. So, here goes:
>
> As your friend, I'm torn between wanting what's truly *best for you* and also trying to figure out who the hell can lead this marvelous country, which has been so good to me and mine.

I've tried, as you know, to refrain from giving you the benefit of my meager genius and wisdom on this topic for several reasons. For one thing, I know you're getting a hell of a lot of counsel, not only from the power brokers, but also from those friends who, although they greatly respect and admire you, would not at all mind having an acquaintance at 1600 Pennsylvania Avenue.

Another reason I've declined to offer my views is because you are, as always, brighter, wiser, and more sensitive than the rest of us. Indeed, I'm reminded of that rich fellow [Jack] Horenstein telling me at Maria's wedding how your judgment was always superior to the counsel of his Park Avenue law firms. And I've also been thinking about [Jack] Newfield's piece in the [*Village*] *Voice* last week in which he attributes your defeat in the New York City mayoral primary some years ago to your own *instinctive* feeling that you weren't "ready" and that the timing "just wasn't right."

I guess this brings me to the main thought I want to share. No one could admire MMC any more than I do. But for all your smarts and capacity for hard work, I am emboldened to tell you—straight out—that you are, with all your faults, *better than you think you are.* Good God, I almost cringe from *that* observation because it sounds so much like something H. E. John J. O'Connor once uttered—about all of us.

No one can ever truly know what's in another's heart of hearts. But I think I know the governor well enough to be sure of the *goodness* and, yes, the sweetness you bring to everything you do. In other words, I'm *sure* of that relentless instinct that resides in you to "do the right thing." I also admire your fidelity and commitment to the people of New York, and I can only respect your desire to stay at your post and fulfill the considerable trust you've been given here in our own state. I've said a thousand times over to everyone and all who would listen that you are "operating on a level far beyond every other contemporary politician," and your becoming desire to "stay the course" in Albany bears testimony to just how unique and special you really are.

Now comes the "However." I love this country and I am persuaded—nay, I'm sure—that no other Democrat—or Republican—could even begin to bring your sensitivity and intellect to the presidency. You were quite correct when, in a recent conversation, you told me that people are looking for a "moral leader," and I can well understand your reluctance to take on that awesome responsibility. But I also want to remind you that while you *are* imperfect and capable of occasional human failings, the governor of New York has become, whether *you* like it or not, that great moral figure. In other words, Mario Cuomo may not be good enough for Mario Cuomo, but he's *more* than good enough for the rest of us. So I think it's time you got off that kick.

"People are looking for noble ideas," you once told me at two in the morning while sitting in that suite in Anaheim as your tired eyes looked out in the distance over Disneyland, "and they're not getting them in the pronouncements of those candidates."

There is no question the same judgment, patience, and diplomacy that served you so well in Forest Hills, Corona, and Albany would enable you to almost instantly master international and national problems, rivalries, and disputes, but I see you bringing a lot more than negotiating and diplomatic skills to the task. I see you bringing Mario Cuomo to the job, with all that good stuff inside him, with that sensitive heart and with that *sweetness*. And strength.

Newfield told me last week that Jesse Jackson has to be the one to invite you to come in, and I'm sure Frucher, Andrew, Garth, Burgos, Zambelli, Fabian, Marino, Kirwan et al. are bombarding you with their own game plans. But as I once suggested in an editorial: you do some of your best work *alone*. So I think this goes beyond them and beyond [Michael] Dukakis and Jackson and [George H.W.] Bush and Paul Kirk and Willie Brown, and beyond delegates and superdelegates.

I don't know where I'm going with this rambling note. I think I merely want to make the point that you *are* imperfect. You *are* flawed. And, of course, you are, *at all times*, "a failed baseball player with too many vowels in his name."

I'd like to see you go for this. There! I said it! Or at least not shut the damn door. I'm convinced Dukakis can't win—even that poor, tortured bastard Nixon says he's a "word processor," while you're a "poet." The scenario wherein we allow the Republicans to proceed to further polarize and fuck up the country for the next four years, thus causing the nation to summon you in 1992 to clean up the mess, is cynical and terrible to contemplate. But it's on a lot of people's lips.

This letter may be too late. And as Pete Hamill wrote in a similar plea to Bobby [Kennedy] in 1968: "I don't want to sound like someone telling a friend he should mount the white horse; or destroy his career."

Or his conscience.

But who the hell else could ever inspire such disparate types as Malcolm Forbes, General Al Gray of the Marine Corps, Newfield, [Richard] Ottinger, Nancy Keefe, Lou Boccardi, Bruce

Babbitt, Ken Auletta, Abe Rosenthal, Bob Strauss, Tom Mullen, Andrew O'Rourke (who, despite the thrashing you gave him is now telling people he'll endorse *you*), not to mention the Irish Counsel General O'Caillaigh! Plus those millions of people whose names you don't even know. But *they know*.

Like you once said: they *know*. Like it or not, you have the capacity to go inside people, to a place where politicians rarely reach—and most don't belong.

As I conclude this brilliant advice, I'm struck with the feeling that perhaps it's unfair, if not impertinent, to try to push you out there toward all the hazards and rigors of a national race when I am so reluctant to step up to all the dilemmas in my own life.

And yet the feeling lingers that you would probably be the greatest president since Franklin Roosevelt.

All I want you to be . . . is Mario Cuomo.

Yours,

B.B.

P.S. Nancy Keefe just called to tell me I'm crazy. But you already knew that!

As I reflect on our friendship of thirty-eight years, it seems I was always bombarding him with unsolicited advice. Here's yet another note to someone much brighter:

Personal & Confidential

March 12, 1990

Governor:

Another "what I *really* meant *was* . . ." note, after our conversation Monday morning.

Or . . . call them more scattered and impertinent thoughts on a day when Roger Stone, Fred Dicker et al. score some hits . . .

Rather than worry about these guys, I would love to see that loving, generous failed baseball player sitting this morning behind the plywood-boarded-up window on the second floor at 138 Eagle Street focus more on the hurting, confused, disillusioned folks who are, each day, the beneficiaries of the compassionate government you control—when it works right:

The state trooper racing across the Tappan Zee [Bridge] to slow down an erratic driver before he kills a family coming back from a skiing vacation.

A clerk in the motor vehicle office in Yonkers helping an Hispanic woman fill out difficult forms.

An assistant D.A. in the Eastchester court loaning $5 to a defendant for bus fare home.

Hank Dullea taking time from state operations to do a kindness for a man [Andrew O'Rourke] who stumped the state with a cardboard dummy of you.

Encouraging young twenty-five-year-old Nelson Rockefeller Jr.—a kid who has wealth, a famous name, but no father.

A student at SUNY New Paltz who got up early this morning to work on a term paper who can't forget he was rejected by Dartmouth and couldn't afford it anyway.

Tom Mullen driving two and a half hours to a remote town in Delaware County to help a German butcher market his sausage statewide.

A youth worker in the Bronx who, on his own time, pulls a kid out of a bad situation.

The toll taker at Harriman who smiles and says, "Thank you" as she retrieves two quarters with chapped, freezing hands.

All the wrongs that will be righted today in all the courtrooms across the state by patient, compassionate judges.

The AIDS patient whose pain will be eased by the money you
    directed to Cardinal O'Connor.

The tree your ENCON ranger will save this day in the
    Adirondacks.

The bridge your DOT crew will strengthen in Batavia, and all
    the families who will cross it in years to come.

The social service program(s) that stayed in the budget
    because the governor looked straight at Dall Forsythe and
    insisted, "Don't touch that one . . . it *stays.*"

Sam Fredman sitting in his courtroom, sweating under his
    black robes, trying to settle a nasty, draining, long-running
    battle between a husband and a wife.

Nita Lowey on the floor of the House, trying to remember all
    the lessons you taught her.

Kathy Behrens—and all the other ombudsmen—untangling
    red tape for people. They wouldn't exist unless a former
    secretary of state had thought of the idea.

The cabinetmaker in Cayuta who hired five more joiners with
    the $40,000 economic development loan.

Andrew puffing on Parliaments, trying to do an end run past
    Ed Brady and going out on weekends to check his housing
    for the homeless H.E.L.P. sites.

Matilda visiting a daycare center and hugging a child, or
    taking endless tours of senior citizens around the mansion
    to show them where Roosevelt slept. (We watched a tape of
    Dan DiNicola's program up in Waverly last weekend and
    someone said, "My God, she's *real.*" I, however, thought she
    took *inordinate* pleasure in telling the story about your
    getting beaned!)

And I've told you this one before: Mario Cuomo standing on
    Fifth Avenue outside the Metropolitan Museum and giving

a high school kid and his girlfriend the same attention he gave the Premier of Quebec inside.

I don't know where I'm going with all this, Mario, except maybe to suggest that, for *all* your gifts as an advocate, you really haven't sold the *spirit* of your administration.

And you don't sell it, if you'll allow me, with the editorial boards of *Time* or *Gannett,* or with Evans and Novak, or at sidewalk press conferences outside the White House. You sell it, I think, by just *being* Mario Cuomo. By just *doing.*

The hell with [Joe] Bruno, [Rudy] Giuliani, and the guy in Buffalo who takes shots at Andrew.

Ralph Marino and political "strategy" don't matter. I love feeding you bulletins on [Wayne] Barrett and Guiliani and Roy Goodman. But they don't matter either. *Who* the governor *is* matters.

Every thinking person in this republic knows you would make a superb president. Everyone except you and that damn Nancy Keefe woman at Gannett Westchester, who loves you. As I do.

But *for now*, I guess I would have you concentrate on that lovely, deserving entity known as New York state, which has been entrusted to your care and keeping.

I love Keefe's line about you "chasing ideas." But you can do that later. Pursue instead that vision of a caring, loving New York state that you described so well in your first inaugural.

And if you do: all those people who disagree with you on Shoreham, or Staten Island, or capital punishment, or taxes, or McGivern will count for nothing.

Don't freeze out [Fred] Dicker or fret Bruno or outflank O'Connor. Just *be* Mario Cuomo.

And just remember all the lovely stuff which comes out of your generous heart.

And that which proceeds from the government you run so well, some of which I've mentioned in this note.

Show them not how *bright* you are, but how *good* you are. Show them Cuomo.

Thus I guess I would probably have you ground the damn chopper and pull the plug on your phone and instead take a walk around the Mall in Elmira—or have the $6.95 fish fry, *including* salad bar, at Shepard Hills Country Club on Friday night.

Or just take Fabian and Broughton to Barnaby's for a burger and a *negroni*. I'm off to sell some advertising.

It's much easier to pick on you.

Yours,

Brother Bill

P.S. In all of this, as always, I'm not at all sure I'm right.

P.P.S. [Vincent] Tese has recently done an extravagant brochure outlining all you've done for *business*. How about a recitation of all you've done for the *weak* and the *poor* whose champion you've always been? Or, perhaps, what you've done for the merely *ordinary*, struggling as they/we are?

The following missive was dispatched right after the statewide election of 1990, which the governor won handily with 53 percent of the vote against Republican economist Pierre Rinfret. But an unexpectedly strong challenge by Conservative Herb London caused the election to be somewhat closer than expected.

November 8, 1990

MMC:

Maybe I'm a day late with this, but as I sat at my kitchen table early this morning looking at the *Times*'s picture of you out walking alone yesterday, the thought occurred that I wish I could have whispered in your tired ear:

Maybe, like Sam Roberts suggested, you took a few shots in this election—your armor is dented and your lance slightly bent. But as far as I can see, they never touched your good and generous heart.

I know you're getting lots of advice from your staff and political counselors while you are going through this period of "gathering," on which I am reluctant to intrude.

Some must be urging a Bradleyesque mea culpa: "I heard your anger, I heard your frustration, etc. . . . I got the message."

And the temptation thus is that you now be only Mario the Competent, tight-fisted Manager.

My plea, as always, is that you only be Mario Cuomo. Nancy Keefe, the conscience of Gannett, whose goodness bedeviled us all, and I had a lemon squeeze this morning, during which we agreed that the *Family* idea is, ultimately, the only thing that recommends Cuomo. "In tough times, families pull together."

You were quite correct in your observation that the opponents of the governor (and, indeed, the bond issue) sought to *divide* and put one against the other. That's the complete opposite of everything you stand for and everything you are.

You *are* the champion of the weak and the homeless and the untitled and the confused and the hurting, because they have no other.

So, as you now consider a course for your third term, I guess I would have you go back to basics and forget any "practical" advice or tactics or strategy.

To that end, I would love to see the governor revisit those upstate towns and confront those women in the P & C market on the south side of Elmira or go to the Korean grocery store in Queens.

And it's not just to the streets I would direct you. How, I wonder, does one explain to *my* Nancy's wealthy father that *he* goes down unless you help these minorities to help themselves!

This *is* a mean, nasty time. People *are* confused and searching. And, as much as you want to flee from the damn "moral leader" designation, there is no one else to make any sense of this chaos and sense of hopelessness. It goes beyond the policies of Bush and Reagan and my Republicans, or the greed of the fat cat establishment or the entrenched unions. It goes beyond politics and labels.

I'm *not* suggesting you do a Florio, who may be capable of some bravery but is unable to *explain* his tactics as part of a compassionate, enlightened *philosophy* of governance.

And I think I would again urge you to consider getting Rinfret, London, Wein, Marino, Barrett, Long, Goodman, Winner, Bruno et al. to table at the mansion to ask their help in all this. You will recall not one of them, during the campaign, ever once suggested a *specific* cut in spending. (I would also get Malcolm and Anderson and Carey and even Koch and let them contribute ideas.) You and I both know they will probably bring only rhetoric, but the idea of MMC *reaching out*, even to his enemies and detractors, is something to consider. Let them call their press conferences after the session. Let Pierre Rinfret trumpet that he is, at last, an advisor to Mario Cuomo.

And go to every one of those counties you lost to *present yourself* and *listen* and preach and try to turn some of those hardened hearts with that basic, simple message of love and sharing.

[249]

And, yes, reach out even to those poor, hurting bastards who denied you and your family a moment of victory at the Sheraton. Tell them what you're doing to save their lives and ease their pain—and then draw the line, if you must, on spending. But remember too your comment that they're also trying to save their souls. And give them the compassion and understanding of which only you are capable.

Enough from me. Enough! As you can see, I guess I've enlisted in Keefe's campaign to deny you the presidency.

Now that you've read all *my* ramblings and as you dust yourself off after a night that was less than great, I add only one more suggestion: that you read pages 332–334 of *The Diaries*. Friday, October 22, 1982, has it all.

And the last three lines on page 10 of *Lincoln on Democracy*.

As always, I end with the hope that you will forgive the presumption and boldness of someone who only loves you.

Yours,

Bill

The following haunting and lovely piece was written by Mario's granddaughter Samantha O'Donoghue as he took his final breath.

Samantha spoke for so many in his family—and also for all those whom Mario always called "the family of New York."

Dear Grandpa,

As I look back and think about *everything* that has happened, you come to my mind often. If you were not physically with me, you still found a way to be with me mentally. Your voice always spoke loudly, and it never went through one ear and out the other. It and you were always vivid memories in my head. Whenever I had a tough time with something or did not know what to do, I always thought of you and asked myself what you would do. An answer would always come to me. You had such a good sense of humor . . . some of the best times of my life were with you. You had so many inspiring values and were a hero to me in so many ways. You will always be remembered by so many people besides me, because you have touched so many hearts, more than you will ever know. You have touched mine too. I could go on forever telling you how great you were, but that really would not serve much of a purpose, because I don't really need to tell you that. Everyone just *knows*, and I hope *you* know too. I love you more than you will ever know, and I will miss you more than you will ever know. We all will. The last time I saw you (today) I knew you were going to die, either today, tomorrow, the next day, or in a week. I knew you didn't have a month though. So I said goodbye to you today but I didn't think my goodbye was good enough. I was not the only one who felt that way. There really isn't a goodbye that is fully sufficient . . . considering how good a man you were . . . not just a man, but a human being. You once wrote a book called *More than Words*. I will always remember you for so many attributes and reasons. I therefore think my goodbye did not have to be perfect . . . through words at least. Actions speak louder than words. Your legacy was too good for words, but it is never too good for actions. It is our actions that really show how grateful we are for you and what you have done for us. You did not deserve to suffer like you did these past months. I am so glad your last breath was peaceful because that is what you deserved. Every breath you took was worth it and changed the world for the better. Every word you ever spoke was golden, and every action you took was meaningful. God has a purpose for everyone . . . no person is put here by accident. Your story is so inspiring, especially to me, and I will always remember you when I want to give up. It is a story everyone should learn from. A poor, simple Italian boy who was raised in the back of a grocery store grew up to become the phenomenal governor who touched so many hearts. You were not just a governor. There isn't just one way to describe you. You were the governor, but also a friend, a gift, a legend, an uncle, a father-in-law, a father, a grandfather (MY grandfather) and the list just keeps going. You have helped so many people follow their dreams and your legacy will always be in the hearts of so many . . . including mine. I wish you could see how many people are sad and what they are saying, but I think you already knew that. You held on for us. You were always modest, but you always thanked God and told me to thank God for who I am and for who helped me to get there. I'm so glad you were one of them, and one of the greatest gifts you could have ever given me was love, but not just any love. You gave me my mother, a gift alone, who also misses you so much, and the fact I got to be with you and know you for the time I did is one of the greatest gifts I ever received. I love you to the Moon and back, and five hundred more times. I love you more than you will ever know, and I'm proud to call myself your granddaughter. Any girl would die to have you as their grandfather for so many reasons. God needed another angel, but not just any angel. He needed you, Grandpa, to help Him, to stand by His side and remain faithful to Him. I know that I have a guardian angel now, and I could not have asked for a better one. You aren't just any angel . . . you're MY special angel. I love you, Grandpa, forever . . . even more than that. Lots of people try to change the world for the good, or maybe for the worse. You said you were going to try, and you didn't just do that . . . you didn't just succeed. You DID change the world . . . you didn't just touch the family's hearts, and not only the hearts of the state, but the hearts of the nation. People say we lost a giant, and we did. After you are gone, it feels as if the world became half-empty. The whole nation mourns your loss, and we should. Rest in peace.

Samantha

———————————————

Here is a recent note from the legendary ninety-year-young Broadway and Hollywood columnist Liz Smith.

August 6, 2015

Dear Bill:

One thing about Mario and Matilda Cuomo: He always was down to earth and candid with me and liked to "brag" on her good works. I think his favorite thing when he appeared with her at the Landmarks Conservancy was to tease her about how "faithful" he always was to her—"and nobody should doubt it for a minute" because she was "a *jealous* Sicilian wife."

I never knew if this was just a joke, but it was fun because she was so ladylike and un-temperamental.

I saw them together at lunch only months before he died. Their faces would light up when they saw someone they approved of. It occurred to me they were still very much in love, though time had taken its toll.

I think we lost a great potential president and first lady.

Can't wait for your book.

Love, Liz

II

Andrew's Eulogy

Over the years Mario did many wonderful eulogies for departed friends: Among them were lovely tributes to Bill Modell and for Modell's son Michael. He also spoke movingly and lovingly of his old Queens friend John Aiello and the columnist Jack Newfield. His remarks for his mother, Immaculata, which I've included earlier in its entirety, is a classic. He also had gracious and graceful words for Ed Koch, Malcolm Wilson, Andy O'Rourke, and Ted Kennedy that were carried on our radio stations.

But the most stunning and riveting eulogy during my time was delivered last year not *by* Mario, but by his son and heir Andrew Mark Cuomo, who did himself—and his father—proud. Although Mario famously said on many occasions that he wanted no eulogies, Andrew's tribute to his father was absolutely spectacular. It takes nothing away from Andrew—or from Mario—to observe that MMC himself could not have done better, perhaps not even as well. Andrew's lips and heart and passion put Mario Cuomo right in front of every sad admirer of his late father there assembled in that huge, beautiful Jesuit church on January 6, 2015. Here is Andrew's perfect tribute to his father:

First let me begin by thanking the pastor and priests at St. Ignatius Loyola for their courtesy, hospitality, and this beautiful ceremony, especially Father Alex Witt and all the co-celebrants, on behalf of the Cuomo family and fourteen grandchildren—by which we defied all odds. Thirteen girls! And the boy was born just before Christmas to my brother, Christopher. My brother, Christopher, and Cristina named the boy Mario because some people will do anything to earn the praise of their father. There is no jealousy on my part, however.

We want to thank Columbia-Presbyterian [Hospital] for their really fantastic care of my father during these difficult months. Dr. Engel and Dr. Maurer were extraordinary. The health aides who took care of my father at home: Steve Crockett, Dan O'Conner, Tom, Fran, Sharon. For twenty-four hours a day, they were really magnificent and made his life much more pleasant and also looked out for the family. We thank his partners at Willkie, Farr & Gallagher. He practiced law for twenty years after public service, and he really enjoyed it. It was a beautiful partnership.

To his team. No administration, no government works without a team. And my father really had a fantastic team. They worked twenty-four hours a day, seven days a week, because that's the only way they knew how to work. Mary Tragale and Mary Porcelli, Michael DelGiudice, Jerry Crotty, Drew Zambelli, Tonio Burgos, John Howard, John Maggiore, Mary Ann Crotty, and my father's third "son," whom I sometimes think he loved the most, Joe Percoco. They did an extraordinary job with his funeral, and we want to thank them.

I want to thank President Clinton for being here, and Senator Clinton. They both meant so much to my father for so long and we are all so proud, not only that you're here, but that you're New Yorkers. President Obama sent his remarks. Vice President Biden was here last night. Senator [Kirsten] Gillibrand is here. Attorney

General Eric Holder; U.S. Attorney Loretta Lynch, who soon we hope will be attorney general of the United States. Mayor Bill de Blasio, whom my father and I were with the other day. Mayor [Michael R.] Bloomberg, whom my father had tremendous respect for; Mayor [David N.] Dinkins, who served with my father when the city and the state were in a very difficult time.

And the literally thousands of New Yorkers who showed up yesterday to pay tribute to my father at the wake—it was an amazing outpouring of support. Thousands of people standing outside in the cold. My father hasn't been in public service in twenty years. And he had gotten very quiet after public service. But people remembered to show up twenty years later. People from all walks of life, all across the state, whom he touched.

One day when I was at HUD I was talking to my father on the phone. He had given a big speech that day, and I called to ask how it went: did he do it from notes, did he do it on cards, did he do it off-the-cuff? He said it was a very important speech so he wrote it out and read every word. He went on to explain his theory that you can't possibly deliver a speech extemporaneously that is as well done as a written speech. He then invoked Winston Churchill as a proponent of the reading-word-for-word theory of speech making.

Now you must understand the rules of engagement in debate with Mario Cuomo. Invoking an historical figure as a source—in this context—was more of a metaphor than a literal interpretation. It really meant Winston Churchill could have said, or should have said, or would have said, that reading was best. But my father's invoking the gravitas of Churchill meant he was truly serious about this point.

I explained I was uncomfortable reading a speech word for word because I needed to see the audience's reaction and adjust accordingly. He summarily dismissed my point and said that was all unnecessary. And he said who cares about what the audience wants to hear. It's not about what they want to hear, it's about what you need to say.

And that, my friends, was the essence of Mario Cuomo.

He was not interested in pleasing the audience: not in a speech, not in life. He believed what he believed, and the reaction of the audience or the powers that be or the popularity of his belief was irrelevant to him.

Mario Cuomo was at peace with who he was and how he saw the world. This gave him great strength and made him anything but a typical politician.

But then again, he wasn't really a politician at all. Mario Cuomo's politics were more a personal belief system than a traditional theory. It was who he was. Not what he did. In his early life, my father was never interested in politics. In general, he disrespected politicians and the political system. He never studied politics or joined a political club. He never campaigned for anyone, and his early life, until his late thirties, was all about becoming a lawyer and practicing law. Once in practice, he became quickly bored with the typical corporate practice. My father was a humanist. He had strong feelings of right and wrong based on his religion, philosophy, and life experiences. He was very concerned with how people were treated, and that was the arena that drew him in. The bridge from law to politics arrived for him when he took on the representation of the homeowners in Corona, Queens, whose homes were being condemned by the city to build a ball field. They were poor, working families and couldn't possibly fight City Hall. Poor, working-family ethnics. He took on their cause to right the injustice he saw. Central to understanding Mario Cuomo is that Mario Cuomo was from Queens.

For those not from New York: Queens is an "outer" borough, like Brooklyn, the Bronx, Staten Island. Interestingly, there is no borough referred to as the "inner borough," only outer boroughs: and that's probably the point. There are insiders and outsiders, and one defines the other. There are those from the other side of the tracks; there are those from the other side of town. An outer borough is where the working families lived: the tradesmen, the civil servants, the poor. Mario Cuomo was the son of Italian immigrants who were part of the unwashed masses, who came with great dreams but also with great needs. Who struggled but ultimately succeeded due to the support they received in this great state of New York.

Mario Cuomo's birthmark from the outer borough was deep, and he wore it with pride. He had a natural connection with the outsider looking in, the person fighting for inclusion, the underdog, the minority, the disenfranchised, the poor. He was always the son of an immigrant. He was always an outsider, and that was his edge.

His early days in politics were not awe-inspiring. He had an early aborted run for mayor in 1973. In 1974 he lost the Democratic primary [for lieutenant governor] to Mary Anne Krupsak. He ran for mayor in 1977, losing to Ed Koch. In 1978 he was elected lieutenant governor to Governor [Hugh L.] Carey.

While it is different now, the job of lieutenant governor was not all that taxing. Governor David Paterson said it best when describing his role as lieutenant governor. David said he would wake up, call the governor, and if the governor answered the phone, he would hang up and go back to sleep.

My father was living in the Hotel Wellington in Albany at the time, and I started law school there, and we were roommates. The typical schedule was my father was in Albany Monday, Monday night, Tuesday, Tuesday night, and would leave on Wednesday during session. Our third roommate was Fabian Palomino, my father's lifelong, dear friend, whom he clerked with in the Court of Appeals. Fabian was from mixed origins. He called himself a "Heinz 57," part Italian, part Native American, part African American, part anything else. He was truly a unique and powerful man, and we would have dinner together on the nights they were in town.

My mother would send up care packages with my father on Monday, and all we had to do was warm up the prepared meals. My father insisted we sample every wine made in the state of New York, and we were soon connoisseurs of New York's best wines. Fabian, who was a portly fellow, wore a shirt with no sleeves, stretched over his belly tighter than a drumskin. He wore boxer shorts with dark dress socks over the calf. I assumed he had chronically cold calf muscles. My father, who was modest and always formal in attire, was perpetually frustrated with Fabian's dress. And he would say to Fabian, "Why can't you dress for dinner, Fabian?" And Fabian would say, "Out of respect for you, I have." He would say, "I wore my fancy boxers out of respect for you. I respect that you are the lieutenant governor and one heart attack away from having a real job." And then Fabian would laugh, and the laugh would make his belly shake, and my father, not loving being mocked, would smile, but slowly.

After dinner they would turn on the TV, and we would sit on the couch and watch television. We would watch a ballgame or the news, but it didn't really matter. The function of the TV was just to introduce a topic they could debate. And they could debate anything. An item on the news or a soap commercial, it didn't really matter. They debated to debate. They just loved it, and they were great at it. Eventually, the debate invariably turned to politics and government, and I could see my father refining and honing his own personal philosophy.

In 1982 my father ran against Ed Koch for governor. It was the impossible race that couldn't be won, but my father was ready and believed he was better suited to be governor than Ed Koch. The pollsters, with their charts demonstrating the impossibility of his pursuit, were unpersuasive. If my father thought he was fighting the right fight, it didn't matter whether we were going to win or lose. It was "the right thing to do." And there is one rule to live by, which is you always *do the right thing*.

Mario Cuomo did not fit neatly into any political category. He believed government had an affirmative obligation to help the excluded join the mainstream. He believed it was the country's founding premise and that more inclusion made the country a stronger country. Better education, better health care, economic opportunity, and mobility helped the new immigrants progress and made the community stronger. Not to invest in the progress of others was a disservice to the whole. He believed in compassion for the sick and the needy. This was also the essence of Christianity and Jesus's teachings. But there were no giveaways. Responsibility and hard work were expected from all. He was not a spendthrift and came from a culture of fiscal responsibility. He was an executive and needed to balance a budget. He cut taxes and the workforce. When he took office the top tax rate in New York was 14 percent. When he left office twelve years later, it was 7 percent. The state workforce twelve years later was smaller than when he took office.

Mario Cuomo, intellectually, was all about subtlety and nuance. He was called The Great Liberal. He resisted the label. His philosophy defied a label, especially an undefined and nebulous one. My father called himself a "progressive pragmatist." Progressive values, but a pragmatic approach. He believed he needed to separate the two components, the goals and the means. His goal was progressive, but his means were pragmatic. I told him it was too complicated to communicate and no one would understand what he was saying. Frankly, I still don't understand what he was saying. But he said he didn't care and wouldn't be reduced by the shortcomings of others, including mine. My father was skeptical of people and organizations that profited from government, to whom government was a business, rather than an avocation. And he always focused on the goal of government rather than the means—the product, not the process—to help the people, the student, the parent, the citizens.

The truth is he didn't love the day-to-day management of government; the tedium and absurdity of the bureaucracy [were] mind-numbing for him. Nor did he appreciate the political back-and-forth with the posturing legislature. As governor, he was criticized by the right. As the icon of the left, he was criticized by the zealots on the left because his lofty rhetoric couldn't match the reality of his government programs.

At his core he was a philosopher and he was a poet, an advocate, and a crusader. Mario Cuomo was the keynote speaker for our better angels. He was there to make the case, to argue and convince, and in that purist mindset he could be a ferocious opponent and powerful ally.

And he was beautiful.

A speech never started with the words—it was about the principle, the idea and the passion, the righteousness, the injustice—and then came the words, arranged like fine pearls, each chosen for its individual beauty but also placed perfectly, fitting just so with the one that came before and the one that followed so there was a seamless flow, in logic and emotion, leading one ultimately to the inevitable conclusion—his conclusion—which was the point of the speech in the first place.

He was a religious man, and his relationship with the Church was important and complicated. His famous and influential speech at Notre Dame was done more for himself, to explain how he separated his personal views from his professional responsibilities. The public official fulfilling a constitutional responsibility was different but consistent with laymen following Christ's teachings. He believed Jesus's teachings could be reduced to one word. And the word was *love*. And *love* means acceptance, compassion, and support to help people. To do good. And that's what he wanted government to be. A force for good. His love was not a passive love, but an active love. Not tough love, but a strong love. The good fight was a fight for love, and it was a fight he was ready to wage.

In many ways my father's view on the Church was ahead of his time.

He was excited about our new Pope Francis and his enlightened perspective on Catholicism with an emphasis on inclusion and understanding. My father thought Pope Francis would agree that Jesus himself was probably from an outer borough.

My father loved Teilhard de Chardin, a French Jesuit who modeled service and a dedication to sustainable community as a way of life.

My father was a Lincoln scholar attracted by Lincoln's example of government as the pursuit of the great principles.

He also appreciated that Lincoln was the triumph of substance over style and that his life exemplified the relative isolation of people in power.

We were a working-class family and proud of it. No fancy trips, no country clubs for us. He was the workingman's governor and remained loyal to the old neighborhood values always.

His grandchildren, my children, will speak of Grandpa's sweetness. My father always had a "sweetness," but it grew over the years, much as a fine wine turns into a brandy.

I, however, remember his younger years, and *sweetness* is not the first word that comes to mind. Make no mistake, Mario Cuomo was a tenacious, competitive, incredibly strong man. He was impatient with the bureaucracy, unrelenting in the face of bigotry, uncompromising in remedying injustice. And he was really, really tough. It would have been malpractice not to be. These battles were for real consequences and made a difference to real people. And he was also competitive by nature. Whether in a campaign, fighting the legislature, or on a basketball court, you opposed him at your own risk and peril. I have the scars to prove it.

The basketball court remained the one place he could allow himself to be his fully aggressive self. Governors, you see, are supposed to comport themselves with dignity and decorum. The basketball court was his liberation. We had epic battles. He hated few things as much as a timid opponent on the court because you cheated him of a real contest.

We played in the State Police gym in Albany. He liked to play one-on-one because it was the purest form of competition. He was a solid 240 pounds and fast for a big man.

He would make faces at you, taunt you, talk constantly in a distracting and maddening banter designed to unnerve you. He would hit you in places the human body did not have anatomical defenses. The issue of calling fouls plagued us. We tried using state troopers as referees, but they were afraid of angering my father. With one wrong call they would wind up on a weigh station somewhere up on the Northway. We tried letting the trooper be anonymous so there was no fear of retaliation.

After I left Albany, the basketball competition became more institutionalized. My father started a basketball league with a number of teams. They had professional referees, and any disputes were settled by the commissioner. And my father served as the commissioner, and also captain of one of the teams. At the end of the season there would be draft selections depending on the results. Some people accused my father of hiring state employees only for their basketball talents. He denied it. Well, at least let's say it didn't happen often. Basketball was my father's outlet, and it was always in good humor and always with good sportsmanship.

My father also loved to battle the press. They were like the opposing counsel in a courtroom. He thought if they could judge his actions and communicate that to the public then he had the right to challenge their facts and judgment. He was unmoved by his staff's passionate arguments that this was counterproductive. You don't fight with people who buy ink by the barrel, as the old saying goes. My father was undeterred. The press was too important to tolerate sloppiness or misinterpretation. The public deserved the truth, and the press did not have the right to distort it, certainly not with impunity. He railed against ivory tower pundits and reporters with an agenda. He had no problem calling a reporter at 7 A.M. to give them a critique of their article. Most often, it was fair to say the critique was not overly positive. I have evolved, and I would never call a reporter at 7 A.M. I wait until at least 9 A.M. But he also admired journalism done well, and he respected Jimmy Breslin, Pete Hamill, Jack Newfield, Murray Kempton and Mike Lupica, Mary McGrory, Marcia Kramer, all stars in the constellation of lives well lived.

He was humbled to be in public service and had disdain for those who demeaned it, with scandals or corruption, or cheap public relation stunts. It was a position of trust and deserved to be honored. Mario Cuomo served twelve years as governor with integrity. You can disagree with Mario Cuomo over those twelve years, but he never dishonored the state and he never dishonored his position.

In his private life he was exactly as he appeared in public life. He had a sixty-year love affair with his wife, Matilda. Not a storybook romance—no late-night kissing in the park, at least as far as we knew—but a real life partnership built on a foundation of mutual respect and tolerance. Commitment to Mario Cuomo was sacrosanct.

His children were everything to him. Although I may look the oldest, Margaret is actually the oldest and a source of great pride. He beamed when he said, "My daughter is a doctor." Maria, his artistic, altruistic delight. With Maria, he had the purest loving relationship. Madeline made him proud as a great mother and a tenacious attorney. Chris, talented, facile and funny, could always make him laugh.

He loved his daughters-in-law, Sandy and Cristina, and his sons-in-law, with whom he had a special relationship: Kenneth, Howard, and Brian. They enjoyed a true father–son relationship with him. It was mutual, and they were adored.

He had a small group of friends: Jimmy Breslin, Vincent Tese, Fabian Palomino, Mike DelGiudice, Sandy Frucher, and Joe Percoco were his intimate world.

Over the years the press would love to give their dime-store psychoanalysis of our "complex" father and son relationship. It was all a lot of hooey. It is this simple: I was devoted to my father, from the time I was fifteen, joining him in every crusade. My dad was my hero, my best friend, my confidante, my mentor. We spoke almost every day, and his wisdom grew as I grew older. When it works, having a working partnership with your father adds an entirely new dimension to the father–son relationship. And for us, it worked. Politics is not an easy business. It shouldn't be. But we carried the same banner. I helped him become a success, and he helped me become a success, and we enjoyed deeply each other's victories, and we suffered the pain of each other's losses. My only regret is that I didn't return from Washington to help in his 1994 race. Whether or not I could have helped, I should have been there. It was the right thing to do, and I didn't do it.

I loved winning the governorship more for him than for myself. It was redemption for my father. Cuomo was elected governor—the first name was not all that relevant. It was a gift to have him with us this past election night. The doctors didn't want him to go, but I insisted, bringing him on the stage for one more fist pump. Holding up his hand, I felt his energy surge; his face brightened and his eyes shined as he gave us that great, satisfied smile one more time. He walked off the stage and said, "Wow, what a crowd that was!" It was the best medicine I could provide for Mario Cuomo that night.

He loved being governor and thought he could do four terms, and he valued that over anything else—even the Supreme Court. Why didn't he run for president? people ask. Because he didn't want to—he was where he thought God wanted him to be.

He was a man of principle—of honor, of duty, of service—and that defined his life. He had simple tastes: no expensive cars, no planes, no fancy homes. A weekend meal with family. Watching a baseball or basketball game with my father's running commentary, reading a good book, and just talking—but really talking—there was no small talk or superficiality with Mario Cuomo.

My father never lost his interest in public affairs. We would talk at 5 A.M., and he would have read all the papers and was ready to tell me everything I did wrong the day before. We would talk about the problems and how to find a way through the maze.

He was recently very troubled by the Washington "mess," as he would call it. He was concerned about the city. My father's 1984 convention speech was called "The Tale of Two Cities," and he was adamant about pointing out inequities and divisions in our society. But the goal was always to unify, never to divide. And the current factions in New York City were very disconcerting to him. He governed during [the] Howard Beach and Bensonhurst [racial incidents] and knew racial and class divisions are the New York City fault lines.

They say your father never leaves you. If you listen carefully, you will hear his voice. I believe that's true. But one doesn't need to listen that carefully or be his son to know what Mario Cuomo would say today: that it's time for this city to come together; it's time to stop the negative energy and keep moving forward. The positive course is to learn the lessons from past tragedies, to identify the necessary reforms, to improve our justice system, better safety for police officers, and to move this city forward.

And that's just what we will do, Dad. I promise you.

For Mario Cuomo, the purpose of life was clear: to help those in need and leave the world a better place (Mathew 25); *Tikkun Olam*, to heal the divide; *Tzedakah*, to do justice. It's that simple and yet that profound. It's that easy, and yet that hard. By any measure, Mario Cuomo's voice inspired generations; his government initiatives helped millions live better lives. He left the world better than he found it. He was a leading opponent of the death penalty and proud of appointing the first African American to the Court of Appeals, of his Liberty Scholarship Programs, his pioneering child health insurance program, his leadership in AIDS treatment research.

New York is a better state thanks to Mario Cuomo.

The last few days as he was slipping I said to him, to give him something to look forward to, that he needed to stay strong for the inaugural because I wanted him to hold the Bible. And he asked, in a semiconscious state, "Which Bible?" Which only Mario Cuomo would ask. And I said the St. James Bible. He said the St. James Bible would be good for this purpose. I didn't follow up. A few weeks later he said he was too weak to hold the Bible, but he would be there. I stopped at his apartment, went to his bed, and said, "Dad, the inauguration is today. You want to come? You can hold the Bible, or you don't have to hold the Bible." There was no response. I said, "Well, let me know because there is a second event in Buffalo, and if you change your mind you can come to Buffalo." During that afternoon, my sister played the inaugural speech for him. He knew the Buffalo event was at 4:00. My father passed away at 5:15.

He was here. He waited. And then he quietly slipped out of the event and went home. Just as he always did. Because his job was done.

We believe the spirit lives, and I believe my father is not gone and that his spirit is with us—in Amanda's song, Michaela's charisma, Tess's dance, Christopher's laugh, and in every good deed I do.

I believe my father's spirit lives in the hope of a young boy sitting in a failing school who can't yet speak the language. His spirit lives in a young girl, pregnant and alone and in trouble. It lives in South Jamaica and the South Bronx. His spirit lives in those outsiders still living in the shadow of opportunity and striving to join the family of New York.

And Pop, you were right once again, and I was wrong: Tell Winston Churchill I now agree, I read every line, Pop, word for word, because it's not about what they want to hear. It's about what I wanted to say. And I said it, Pop.

Tell Officer Ramos and Officer Liu we miss them already, tell Fabian and Jack Newfield, Grandma and Grandpa, and Uncle Frank we love them.

I will listen for your voice. You taught us well. You inspired us. We know what we have to do, and we will do it. We will make this state a better state, and we will do it together.

On that, you have my word, as your son.

I love you, Pop, and always will.

I deeply regret that, especially in recent years, I never had quite the same relationship with Andrew I was privileged to enjoy with Mario, but as I read—and savor—these beautiful words constructed and delivered by his son and heir, one can only observe that the great Mr. Churchill would have given them his enthusiastic and hearty approval. And Mario himself would have certainly loved it. Praying over your departed father is a damn difficult assignment. You get to do it only once. And you'd better get it right. Andrew did it brilliantly and powerfully and with stunning effect. In Andrew's best moments he resembles his magnificent father.

Not all the citizens of New York could have heard Andrew's magnificent eulogy that sad morning, but as a stunning reminder of Mario's importance to the state of New York, that evening of his funeral, the Empire State Building reached into the night sky of midtown Manhattan bathed in blue and gold in his honor.

As I set my pen aside and wind down these reminiscences of a remarkable man, my mind drifts back over the thirty-eight years I was privileged to know Mario Matthew Cuomo. It is now winter in the Litchfield hills of western Connecticut and in Westchester where I work. On the television and our own community radio stations, WVOX and WVIP, the talk is of the early presidential primaries of 2016 and a most colorful and disparate cast of characters vying for the blessing and imprimatur of the American voters.

We are enveloped by the nasty dialogue about who will follow President Obama. The discourse is heavily laden with bombast, braggadocio, and meanness. And as I watch this sad tableau unfold, I can't help but think once again of the extraordinary individual we've been discussing in this memoir. And I wonder, I really wonder, how Mario Cuomo would fare in this mean political season. Could you see Mario standing there under the lights on a stage at one of these made-for-television cattle shows as the announcer intones, "We'll be right back . . . after this word from Cialis"?

I've watched most of the presidential "debates" and listened to thousands of words spoken by the all-too-eager aspirants. And not *one* of the candidates—not one!—has uttered anything of meaning or beauty. And so to paraphrase Mario's oft-used plaintive cry about the great DiMaggio, I can only ask, "Where have you gone, Mario Cuomo? Our nation turns its lonely eyes to you . . . ."

On second thought, maybe those of us who loved the man should be glad Mario never had to endure the degradation, vulgarity, and phoniness of a contemporary presidential campaign, circa 2016.

But . . . but couldn't you just hear him out there now . . . if only, if only for a little while?

Come to think of it, maybe Mario *is* still around to make us "better, stronger—even sweeter." That very thought occurred to me as I heard his son and heir Andrew take to a lectern recently to speak about marriage equality, immigrant policies, and diversity in America:

I want to talk about good American values. This country was founded on the premise of accepting people from all over the world. Different people, different cultures, different races, difference ethnicities—an amalgamation of them all. That's the American value. It never said people who are different are bad. The founding motto of this nation is *E pluribus unum*—"out of many, one." We invite them, they will come, and we will forge one community.

We are not threatened by diversity. We are celebrating it. We are not born of exclusion; we are born of the exact opposite—we are born of inclusion. We are black, we are white, we are Asian, we are Latino, we are gay, we are straight, we are transgender, we are rich, we are poor, and we invite all in and we say we will forge one community all together. That's what America really is all about.

And we only had two rules when we founded this nation: acceptance of all by all; discrimination of none by none. And our experiment of diversity rested on one basic premise, and that basic premise comes down to one word: equality. That whoever you are and wherever you come from, we treat everyone the same. That's the rule: to take the diverse population we have attracted and forge one society, one community. We're all equal. We don't judge, we accept, and we are all equal.

Equality is not really about a specific goal or destination. It is about a constant process of improvement. Martin Luther King used to talk about "the arc of the moral universe bends toward justice." He didn't mean that it bends naturally. He meant you can bend it toward justice, but it takes an effort. I am not so sure that society, left to its own devices, bends the arc toward justice; it takes effort, it takes strength, it takes advocates.

I believe the inherent role of government is to fight for equality and for justice. That's the number one role, and that's what we've brought to New York state. That's why marriage equality was so important.

When you said only "civil unions" for gay people, you said *their* love is not equal to *your* love. Their relationship is not equal to your relationship. Their child is different than your child. You demeaned the relationship. You invalidated the love, and you set up two different classes. And that's why we fought so hard for marriage equality, and that's why we got it done here in New York. And when it happens in New York, it radiates all across the country. When it happens in New York, every politician, the next day, gets the question "What would *you* do about marriage equality?" And "What would *you* do, Mr. President, about marriage equality?"

The fight will go on, and it will only end when we reach a more perfect union. And a wholly equal society, which is probably a goal that is unobtainable, but the struggle will always go on.

Because—with all the arrogance of a New Yorker—New York is not just another state. New York is a special state. And New York always has been. By birth, it was born special. We are the laboratory of the American experiment in democracy. That

Statue of Liberty stands in *our* harbor. The words of Emma Lazarus are on *our* doorstep. We are the place that said to the world, "Come here, we welcome you. Poor, huddled masses, come here, we welcome you." And we have done that since we were founded. And we have made it a great success. You want a model of diversity? You want a model of acceptance? You want a model that has rejected bigotry and taken people from all over the world, with one simple promise of opportunity and dignity and equality for all? That's New York! Eighteen million people from everywhere. But we are one at the end of the day. We are one community, and we are there, one for another!

So don't tell us diversity doesn't work. Don't try to pit us against each other. Don't try to threaten us with differences. We know it because we live it. And we live it in close proximity, altogether, and it has been a joyous celebration. That's why so many of the great fighters for equality have come from New York: Eleanor Roosevelt, FDR, Stonewall, and . . . Mario Cuomo: people who knew in their DNA that we are all different and we are all immigrants, except for the Native Americans. And we all came to the same place for the same promise and the same rights. That banner New York will carry for the rest of our lives.

So I'll give Mario Cuomo's son the last sweet word.
Or is it Mario himself who speaks as this mean, nasty winter fades and yields yet again to springtime . . . ?

March 2016
Westchester, New York

APPENDIX: COLLECTED NOTES FROM "PROFESSOR" A. J. PARKINSON

Mario spoke often of a mysterious desk drawer that was a repository for the wise and pithy sayings of the legendary "A. J. Parkinson," his favorite philosopher. "Doctor" Parkinson, of course, was, in reality, a *nom de plume* for a "failed baseball player with too many vowels in his name," which is the affectionate appellation I conjured up for him many years ago.

A few years ago, his daughter Maria Cuomo Cole put together a little booklet with some of A.J.'s musings. Here are a couple of highlights: I can see and hear the governor in every phrase and word. Mario used these same words in the Christmas cards he and Matilda sent out over the years.

"LOVE"

No word is more discussed, written about, thought about or misunderstood.

Everyone seeks it, and when it's found, it makes everything else seem no longer worth seeking.

It costs nothing to give and it can't be bought.

It's best when graciously received and then passed on.

It brings with it warm smiles, deep contentment—sometimes tears of joy—and even a sense of justification.

Wise men analyze it; poets romanticize it, but no one improves upon it.

Our word for it is "love."

Some of us believe it was personified nearly two thousand years ago in a manger, in a stable, far from here.

Others see it embodied in other symbols and other events.

Almost all of us celebrate festivals to it at this time of year. In doing so we are reminded how good a whole year could be—if only we were wiser.

[UNTITLED]

There are those who pass like ships in the night
Who met for a moment then sail out of sight
With never a backward glance of regret:
Those we know briefly then quietly forget
Then there are those who sail together
through quiet waters and stormy weather
Helping each other through joy and through strife
and they are the kind who give meaning to life.

———————

During most of those thirty-seven years we exchanged gifts at Christmas—some humorous and others of great significance. One year he surprised me with a radio designed to resemble a jukebox. It still works. Over the years I have been the recipient of many lovely Waterford crystal bowls from Ireland and a carved wooden Sinatra-style fedora. And then there was a very rare collector's volume on the mighty Hudson River from "Mario, Matilda, Maria and Kenneth" which I treasure among all the books in my personal library as I also do the portrait they commissioned from a photograph of Yours Truly.

The governor also sent me a handsome set of cufflinks and an engraved belt buckle from Tiffany. But my favorite gift had to be the four "Mario Cuomo Signature" miniature baseball bats run up by the Hillerich and Bradsby company, manufacturers of the iconic Louisville Sluggers, which were signed by Mario's *noms de plume* from the sandlot days: "Matt Dente" . . . "Connie Cutts" . . . "Lava 'Always Hot' Libretti" . . . and the immortal "Glendy LaDuke."

Another "gift" I treasure is my "official" Mario Cuomo Butt Board, the small, almost square, polished plank with the official state seal, a version of which went almost everywhere with the governor to relieve the almost constant pain in his aching back.

For my part, I am afraid I wasn't nearly as creative as, year after year, I would dispatch a rare antique or contemporary real ink signature pen that I hoped he might use for some historic occasion. But he always seemed more comfortable with his trusty Sharpie or Artline 210. And from time to time I would jokingly get on the governor for his taste in ties and send him a cravat by Hermes or Charvet, none of which I ever saw on him.

Through it all he was a most generous friend, to be sure. But I still treasure most the great gift of his friendship and presence in my life.

And as I put--30--to this memoir I am left only with the wish that I could have given *him* . . . just one more podium.

And one more . . . spring.

AFTERWORD

One of Mario Cuomo's favorite venues was the venerable Dutch Treat Club, a prestigious New York institution whose membership includes illustrators, actors, authors, Broadway producers, editors, cabaret singers, broadcasters, journalists, and even a former U.S. president (Gerald Ford). For several years, Mario opened the Dutch Treat's fall season as featured speaker at the 108-year-old club's kick-off luncheon usually held at the National Arts Club in Gramercy Park. Over the years he and the luminous nonagenarian Liz Smith vied for the all-time attendance record. (Both drew standing-room-only crowds.)

In May 2014 the Dutch Treat Club honored one of its favorite speakers with a prestigious Gold Medal for Lifetime Achievement in the Arts. After Mario accepted the honor, the governor's family decided he wasn't up to receiving the award in person. In the toughest "booking" of my life, I went in his stead. Here are my own poor remarks given that May night at the Harvard Club:

> Fellow Dutch Treaters, I have never felt less worthy in my life. We all make our living with *words*. That's certainly true for the brilliant Mark Russell and for a legendary lyricist like Sheldon Harnick. And *words* are equally essential to the brilliance of Mark Nadler and Anita Gillette and Alan Schmuckler. As for me, I'm afraid they usually emerge inartfully, awkwardly, and imprecisely.

So I feel most inadequate indeed to the task of presuming merely to thank you for your marvelous gesture in bestowing your prestigious Gold Medal on Mario Matthew Cuomo, from whom *words* cascade with such grace and beauty and precision and power on all the great issues of the day.

The governor, who has graced our influential podium to kick off several seasons, deeply and dearly wishes he could join you. And recently, in a voice laden with emotion and regret, asked me to assure you of that. He *loves* the Dutch Treat Club, and he loves especially the "give and take" of the question-and-answer sessions that always followed his formal presentations. Every time he appeared I would get a call: "Can't we just do Q and A? They're so damn bright!" But Donnelly and Fox always insisted he pay for his lunch with a major address!

And speaking of which, I hope you'll allow me just a personal observation while we're on the subject: I don't think we've encountered—any of us—nicer individuals than our two leaders, John Donnelly and Ray Fox!

Dutch Treat has a lot of luminous and vivid characters, many here assembled at the Harvard Club tonight.

Now I won't intrude for very long on your evening. You've struck your Gold Medal for the governor with the lovely—and accurate—phrase "Lifetime Achievement in the Arts."

I'll tell you who would have loved this night: Kitty Carlisle Hart, who for many of her ninety-six years headed the New York State Council on the Arts. Mrs. Hart *loved* Mario Cuomo. For one thing, he never failed to reappoint her or denied a request for funding! Maybe that's why she called him "Governor Darling!"

Come to think of it, I think she called Nelson Rockefeller and Hugh Carey the same thing. But Mario was her absolute *favorite*!

When he heard of your generosity and the Arts Gold Medal, the governor dispatched an immediate e-mail touched with his marvelous wit: "I don't *dance*; I don't *sing*; what do you want of me, O'Shaughnessy?" I've thought about this and what we "want" from him even in his eighty-second year. Especially in his eighty-second year.

We want him only to continue to be Mario Cuomo, to instruct us, to enrich the public discourse all about and around us, to enlighten us, to *inspire* us. And, to use his own favorite word, to make our world "sweeter" than it is.

You have chosen well. He's a great man. And, like I said at the beginning, I'm not worthy to loose the strap of his sandal. He is surely one of the very greatest of our time, who has had a lot written and said about him—as when the *Boston Globe* called him "the great philosopher-statesman of the American nation." So a lot of recognition in his already long life; a lot of encomiums for this extraordinary man are appropriate and well deserved.

And now, by your generous hand, one more: he now has a Dutch Treat Gold Medal, thanks to you.

Of course Mario took great pride in the accomplishments of his own children. He would be proud of them to this day. A recent example: After Lady Gaga had performed the haunting and beautiful song "'Til It Happens to You" at the 2016 Academy Awards earlier this year, Chris Cuomo was telling all his CNN colleagues and Facebook friends that the song was "from my sister Maria Cuomo Cole's documentary *The Hunting Ground*, about sexual assault on campus." Chris reminded his followers that Maria also "runs one of the nation's largest homeless operations in the country . . . and makes socially conscious documentaries on the side."

And then the youngest of Mario's progeny observed on Facebook: "When I say I never had to look outside my family for role models . . . people rightly assume I'm referring to Pop. And, of course I am. But not just Pop. My family is filled with people who guide my personal and professional behavior. No one does more than Maria. Oh, and she has three amazing daughters and a husband [Kenneth Cole]—and all are trying to make the world a better place in their own ways."

The apple doesn't fall . . .

Still, on more than one occasion I asked Mario, "Did you ever think about becoming Father Cuomo, a priest?"

> I became Grandfather Cuomo instead. My grandchildren make it very easy. No matter how many elections I lost, strikeouts I suffered when I played baseball, and bad moments I endured, I contributed to the birth of eleven new beautiful creatures, grand*daughters*, and before them, five others who produced the eleven.
>
> It's a good feeling. I know you have grand*sons*, O'Shaughnessy. When we decide to have grand*sons*, we are going to have twelve!

Mario's departure leaves in Matilda's care and keeping three daughters—Margaret, Maria, and Madeline—and two sons—Andrew and Christopher—as well as fourteen grandchildren: Emily, Amanda, and Katharine Cole; Samantha, Kristine, and Tess O'Donoghue; Cara, Michaela, and Mariah Cuomo; Christina Perpignano; Mariana Maier; and Bella, Carolina Regina, *and* that one grandson, Mario Cuomo.

Those thirteen granddaughters, it should be noted, all arrived in this world well *before* the grandson, Mario. And in the weeks preceding young Mario's natal day, his grandfather was telling friends: "Something's up. Chris has been on the phone to his sisters, inquiring if there are any 'good girls' names that haven't already been taken.' He's trying to throw us off the track, I'm sure of it. I think it could be a *boy* this time!"

It was. And his name is Mario Cuomo.

His grandfather also leaves behind his three sons-in-law, who adored him: Brian O'Donoghue, a handsome fireman who, at Mario's urging, became a successful lawyer; Howard Maier, a wealthy telemarketer and entrepreneur; and the estimable Kenneth Cole, the internationally known designer, merchant prince, philanthropist— and a lovely guy—with whom Mario had breakfast most mornings in recent years. Mario also took special delight in his daughter-in-law Christina Greeven Cuomo, a well-known editor and publisher of upscale magazines, wife of CNN's Chris Cuomo (and mother of Mario); and Sandra Lee, companion, friend, and very significant other of Andrew. She has become a lifestyle multimedia phenom and is as smart as she is attractive.

Mario has got to be looking kindly and with great enthusiasm on the enlightened papacy and ministry of Jorge Mario Bergoglio— although his "candidate" during the conclave, let the record show, was Cardinal Timothy Michael Dolan. When a friend suggested they put together a "ticket" with Mario for pope and Mariano Rivera, the great Yankees relief pitcher, for "vice pope," Cuomo promptly killed the idea. But he did say, "I *would* take Mariano on the 'ticket' *if* he would show me just once how to hold the ball for [Mariano's famous killer pitch] the cutter!" But the "Cuomo–Rivera" ticket went nowhere when the power brokers of the Curia gathered to elect the spectacular Jesuit from Argentina who took the name Francis.

Mario's friends suggested over the years that he would have made a wonderful *priest*. His glib but probably true answer was, "Well, I did think of it, for a few brief, fleeting minutes—until I met Matilda Raffa that day in the cafeteria at St. John's." Still, one of his favorite quotations was from the Jesuit priest Teilhard de Chardin: "By means of all created things, without exception, the Divine assails us, penetrates us and molds us. We imagine it as distant and inaccessible, whereas, in fact, we live steeped in its burning layers." Indeed, he did just that.

His life was a gift, as his son and heir Andrew reminded all those assembled in the big, beautiful Jesuit church on Park Avenue in New York City on that sad but ultimately joyful day in early January where, just a few weeks earlier, the swells from the fashion world had prayed over Oscar de la Renta. De la Renta, the Dominican fashion icon, it should be noted, was praised for the elegance of his eye, whereas Mario M. Cuomo was eulogized for the elegance of his soul. Or, as Hillary Clinton remarked at the end of 2015, the first year without his brilliance and powers of articulation among us, "Mario was not just a great man, he was a good man." Perfect.

At the funeral Vice President Joe Biden said Mario was "a man of great intelligence and a moral force who shamed the nation into doing things we should have been doing all along." The vice president, with a catch in his throat, then added, "I've been in politics in this country since I was a twenty-nine-year-old kid, and the minute I saw Mario Cuomo, I knew he was better than I was."

Such was Mario's impact on his time among us that as of the end of February 2015, more than 10,000 personal notes, letters handwritten and typed, Mass cards, and sympathy and condolence cards were dispatched from all over the world to members of the Cuomo family. *Not* including the thousands of heartfelt e-mails and social media tributes delivered via the Internet. If, indeed, the measure of a man or woman is related to the lives he or she may have touched, these tens of thousands of expressions of love and admiration show that Mario Cuomo was certainly a man without peer!

As long as a man's name is spoken, he is not dead. . . .

I bless the day we met.

AUTHOR'S NOTE

This book, which I've undertaken as only a "memoir of a friendship," is not at all intended as a formal biography of Mario M. Cuomo. Others of much greater gifts will in years to come produce more complete and much more learned biographies of the great man who so enriched our lives and elevated the public discourse during our lifetimes.

I have not the scholarship or the skill to attempt a formal biography. In this personal memoir I've tried to let the governor speak for himself in selected excerpts from his soaring speeches, candid radio interviews, notes, musings, commentaries, and correspondence.

There is so much more to the man awaiting scholars, historians, and even theologians who will one day discover anew Mario Cuomo's towering genius—and relentless goodness—as more of his work is discovered.

The greatest and most exhaustive confirmation of Mario's skill and handling of the dazzling array of issues that daily confront a sitting governor can be found in the New York State Archives and in his personal files, which now reside in the care and keeping of his daughter Maria Cuomo Cole and her husband, the designer-philanthropist Kenneth Cole. She is herself working on a tribute to her father.

I would also direct those interested in learning more about the governor's keen knowledge of and great skill in handling the minutiae of governance and his rigorous mastery and attention to the everyday details of running New York state's $970 billion economy to the bright, dedicated associates who served with him in state government for those heady and productive twelve years, from the first day of 1983 to the last day of 1994.

Information and specific examples of the governor's considerable skills at statecraft can be found in the collective—and individual—recollections of Michael DelGiudice, Steven Cohen, William Eimicke, William Mulrow, Drew Zambelli, Jerry Crotty, Al Gordon, David Wright, Tonio Burgos, John Marino, Ellen Conovitz, Stan Lundine, Bob Morgado, Martin Begun, Michael Dowling, Martha Eddison, Stephen Schlesinger, Robert Milano, Mary Porcelli, Pam Broughton, Mary Tragale, Judge Joseph Bellacosa, Bishop Howard Hubbard, Meyer "Sandy" Frucher, Jason P.W. Halperin, Larry Kurlander, Jennifer Cunningham, Dennis Rivera, Jim Cunningham, Dan Klores, Andrew Stengel, Ken Sunshine, Joe Mahoney, Ken Lovett, Vincent Albanese, Martha Borgeson, Pat Caddell, Dan Lynch, Joel Benenson, Hank Sheinkopf, Paul Grondahl, Steve Villano, Luciano Siracusano, Peter Quinn, Kathy Behrens, Leonard Riggio, Joseph Mattone, Dr. Nick D'Arienzo, Marc Humbert, Judge Sam Fredman, Floss Frucher, Vincent Tese, Todd Howe, Lincoln scholar Harold Holzer, Royce Mulholland, John Iacchio, Joseph Percoco, and Joe Spinelli. Researchers should also refer to the papers and archives of the late Tim Russert, Fabian Palomino, Governor Hugh Leo Carey, Geraldine Ferraro, David Garth, Rabbi Israel Mowshowitz, Howard Samuels, David Burke, Judge Judith Kaye, Thomas Constantine, and Joseph Anastasi.

Another great source for reflection on the governor would be that cadre of Albany political-watchers, which includes the brilliant and cerebral observer Fred Dicker, who as state editor of the *New York Post* is dean of the Albany press corps. He also broadcasts daily on WGDJ and WVOX. That cadre also includes the stunningly bright Dr. Alan Chartock, who publishes the *Legislative Gazette*; he also heads a network of public radio stations throughout the Northeast and broadcasts on WAMC and WVOX. Other keen Mario Cuomo observers include the cerebral and erudite Professor Gerald Benjamin and his daughter Liz Benjamin of Time Warner Cable; the WCBS-TV veteran reporter Marcia Kramer; the New Jersey professor, journalist, and author Terry Golway; and the great Wayne Barrett, formerly of the *Village Voice*. *The New Yorker*'s Ken Auletta is a great student of Mario Cuomo as well.

And who, indeed, knows more—then *and* now—about the levers of government than Governor Andrew Mark Cuomo, who was, in every season, Mario's confidant and most trusted advisor.

A great deal of valuable information that may one day be useful to journalists and historians of far greater gifts than I possess resides in the archives of Whitney Radio here in Westchester: Actually, more than eight file drawers filled with correspondence, interviews, notes, pictures, and Cuomo memorabilia await the review and inspection of future scholars, for which permission is hereby granted. Some of these radio conversations, as broadcast over WVOX, are included within the covers of this book, illustrating not only the brilliance and goodness of the man but also his magnificent sense of humor. We also have a complete bound set of Mario Cuomo's *Public Papers*, which were given to us by New York State Assemblyman Gary Pretlow.

Finally, there is also much to be learned—and savored—from the incomparable Matilda Raffa Cuomo, whom Mario once called "the single most effective instrument of our success." Nobody knew Mario like Matilda, who once told me, in some frustration, "He spends and handles the state's money like it was his own. He's very frugal, and very careful."

So there will be other—and better—books about Mario M. Cuomo, and maybe someday they'll even make a movie about his life, the people he inspired, and the lessons he taught us. Incidentally, I've got the perfect guy to play the governor: Kevin Spacey. Perfect. Just perfect.

One of my previous books for Fordham University Press was titled *It All Comes Back to Me Now*. In the pages of this new book, I have really relied only on my own poor memory. So I hope these deeply personal flashes of *déjà vu* will do justice to the memory of a great man.

Thomas Fogarty, a wise man from Pelham, New York, once told me, "Two hundred years from today no one will ever know you existed." I expect that's true of thee and me. But as I've opined elsewhere in this memoir, I'm absolutely persuaded that Mario's graceful powers of articulation and his relentless goodness will stand the test of time.

I'm sure of it.

ACKNOWLEDGMENTS

This has not been an easy book to write.

By profession, I'm a community broadcaster, and my day job has afforded me a career spanning fifty-eight years. I've also stood in great cathedrals and in country churches and given a lot of eulogies for all kinds of friends and acquaintances, politicians, business associates, in-laws (and out-laws!).

And with the indulgence of the generous inhabitants of the New York area, I've also sat the before microphones in our Westchester radio studios reciting tributes and encomiums to the departed—some famous and others merely wonderfully colorful "townie" characters in our home heath.

But this book is not at all intended as a eulogy. As I suggest elsewhere in these pages, I would have no objection if it might be categorized only as a heartfelt missive or even as a love letter to a unique and special friend. By any name, it was first envisioned as a stand-alone chapter in my fifth anthology for Fordham, the great Jesuit university press in the City of New York.

The scholarly and erudite—and altogether forgiving and generous—editors of my previous collections for Fordham at first suggested we again insert "An Obligatory Mario Cuomo Section in Every O'Shaughnessy Book" in my next anthology.

But with Mario's passing on January 1, 2015, my wise and prescient editors opted instead for the expanded book you now hold. Like I said, it didn't come easy, as I had a difficult time, which lingers still, putting Mario Cuomo in the past tense.

My gratitude to the elders of Fordham University Press again thus knows no bounds.

Fordham has an enviable national reputation for bold, timely, and relevant scholarship. And much of the credit for Fordham's estimable rep goes unequivocally and directly to Director Fred Nachbaur and his brilliant associates, including the stunningly bright Eric Newman, managing editor, who is a literary maestro, and Fred's assistant, Will Cerbone. I also thank Jennifer Rushing-Schurr, who provided the indexes on some of my earlier books for Fordham as well as for this one.

This book—and all of Fordham's recent issues, you should know— also owes a great deal to the dazzling creativity of Ann-Christine Racette, their multitalented production chief and designer. These dedicated folks—all of them—do their magic in a nondescript three-story building that sits cheek-by-jowl next to Fordham's magnificent Rose Hill Campus in the Bronx. Other stellar denizens of the Press include Kate O'Brien-Nicholson, who justifiably waves Fordham's banner higher than the standard of any other university press these days, and Margaret Noonan, the "Mother Glue" of this extraordinary publishing enterprise. In 1999 when I came calling down from Westchester with great trepidation bearing the manuscript for my first anthology, *Airwaves*, a collection of interviews, commentaries, and profiles of the great and the good as well as profiles of the townies and characters in the Golden Apple, Margaret was the first to welcome me.

This book also owes so much to Anthony Chiffolo, a dear man of many talents who himself once served as managing editor at Fordham. Anthony is a multimedia phenom. He's a brilliant photographer. He writes *prayer* books. And he gently and generously forgives my clumsiness with the English language (although he did once remind me that he "edited a *pope*" and that I might be well advised not to mess with him). Anthony's enthusiasm—and that of Fred Nachbaur—was essential to this "labor of love."

I was first introduced to Fordham University Press when I came across a book of speeches by the legendary federal judge William Hughes Mulligan. This great Jesuit university was led at the time by the renowned Father Joseph O'Hare, S.J., and it now resides in the enlightened care and keeping of Father Joseph McShane, S.J., a great American educator who has built Fordham into a national treasure. I only hope my literary efforts have not tarnished or diminished their reputation.

And, closer to home, once again I also must thank the incomparable Cindy Hall Gallagher of Whitney Media, my dear friend, amanuensis, and confidante for forty years, without whom my life would resemble a seven-car pile-up. It should tell you something that when my friends—Mario Cuomo most prominently included— ring up our Westchester radio stations, they usually ask for *Cindy*, and most are quite disappointed when I pick up the phone.

My professional life as a community broadcaster, without which portfolio I would never have met Mario Cuomo, relies heavily on the dedication, creativity, and brilliance of several colleagues. The influential contributions of Kevin Scott Elliott are everywhere apparent in my life. His genius, loyalty, and personal devotion are great gifts that I treasure. Kevin is not alone in terms of devotion. Don Stevens, our senior vice president and chief of staff, is essential to the success of these, the last two independent community stations in the New York area. Speaking of which, WVOX and WVIP are very fortunate to enjoy the talent and wisdom of Judy Fremont, president of our Stations Division and about a two-handicap golfer. She's also a woman of culture and the theater. Why she hangs around with me, I'll never know. All my efforts—including this book—rely as well on Maggie Cervantes Hernandez, who is a star in the office *and* on the air.

One absolutely essential reason our local radio stations have survived and prevailed despite all the social and technological challenges swirling around our profession is my son David Tucker O'Shaughnessy, now our president. He's a rising star in our profession. And I am a proud—and grateful—father. David's mother, Ann Wharton Thayer; his brother, Matthew O'Shaughnessy; and his sister, Kate Warton O'Shaughnessy—who serve as directors—will confirm David's standing and stature in our lives. And David himself will also second my admiration for Gregg Pavelle, Richard Littlejohn, Irma Becerra, Ahmet Alloqi, Bob Partridge, and Ralph Kragle.

And two more: Judge Jeffrey Bernbach and his estimable wife, Karen, have been fierce advocates and defenders of these stations— and yours truly—for many years. Judge Bernbach is a gifted public servant who served in the administrations of both Mario and Andrew Cuomo. But he's always found time to watch over me and mine.

And for reasons they must know, everything I do—on the air or in print—is with the forbearance and encouragement of Michael Assaf, Alan Rosenberg, Charlie Kafferman, James O'Shea, Erwin Krasnow, and my *compadre* Gregorio Alvarez. Those who know this eminently decent—and loving—gentle Dominican man will agree that many of the lovely qualities I found in Mario Cuomo also exist in great abundance in Gregorio. I am capable of no greater praise.

The handsome cover of this book was designed by Rich Hendel of Chapel Hill, North Carolina. And the cover *photo* as well as most of the magnificent and exclusive photos in this volume are by Don Pollard, who has served both Mario and Andrew as the Cuomo family's "chief photographer" for decades. A great guy as well as a marvelous photographer, Don is married to the estimable *New York Times* reporter Lisa Foderaro.

When Mario finally succumbed to the long, debilitating illness I describe in these pages, listeners—hundreds of them, in fact—who knew of my great affection and admiration for the governor called the station to inquire when (and if) we were going to do an on-air tribute to the great man. I actually started and discarded several pieces as not good enough, not worthy of him. As I said, talking—or writing—about Mario in the past tense didn't come easy. In fact, if you must know, it was painful.

And then when the word got around that I was finally attempting a book on Mario Cuomo, we received several calls from mainstream and quite well-known publishing houses expressing considerable interest. Each inquiry was met with, "If I can summon up the resolve to do this, I'll stick with *my* present publisher, *Fordham*, the first to encourage me and provide a forum and platform for my poor, erratic literary endeavors. Go Rams!"

INDEX